the SALAD book

the SALAD book

Over 200 delicious salad ideas for hot and cold lunches, suppers, picnics, family meals
and entertaining, all shown step-by-step and with 800 fabulous photographs

Editor: Steven Wheeler

LORENZ BOOKS

This edition is published by Lorenz Books, an imprint of Anness Publishing Ltd, Blaby Road, Wigston, Leicestershire LE18 4SE; info@anness.com

www.lorenzbooks.com; www.annesspublishing.com

If you like the images in this book and would like to investigate using them for publishing, promotions or advertising, please visit our website www.practicalpictures.com for more information.

© Anness Publishing Ltd 2012

All rights reserved. No part of this publication may be reproduced, stored in a retrieval system, or transmitted in any way or by any means, electronic, mechanical, photocopying, recording or otherwise, without the prior written permission of the copyright holder.

Publisher: Joanna Lorenz
Senior Editor: Joanne Rippin
Designer: Bill Mason
Illustrator: Anna Koska
Editorial reader: Richard McGinlay
Production controller: Ann Childers

NOTES

Bracketed terms are intended for American readers.
For all recipes, quantities are given in both metric and imperial measures and, where appropriate, in standard cups and spoons. Follow one set of measures, but not a mixture, because they are not interchangeable.
Standard spoon and cup measures are level. 1 tsp = 5ml, 1 tbsp = 15ml, 1 cup = 250ml/8fl oz.
Australian standard tablespoons are 20ml. Australian readers should use 3 tsp in place of 1 tbsp for measuring small quantities.
American pints are 16fl oz/2 cups. American readers should use 20fl oz/2.5 cups in place of 1 pint when measuring liquids.
Electric oven temperatures in this book are for conventional ovens. When using a fan oven, the temperature will probably need to be reduced by about 10–20°C/20–40°F. Since ovens vary, you should check with your manufacturer's instruction book for guidance.
The nutritional analysis given for each recipe is calculated per portion (i.e. serving or item), unless otherwise stated. If the recipe gives a range, such as Serves 4–6, then the nutritional analysis will be for the smaller portion size, i.e. 6 servings. The analysis does not include optional ingredients, such as salt added to taste.
Medium (US large) eggs are used unless otherwise stated.

PUBLISHER'S NOTE

Although the advice and information in this book are believed to be accurate and true at the time of going to press, neither the authors nor the publisher can accept any legal responsibility or liability for any errors or omissions that may have been made nor for any inaccuracies nor for any loss, harm or injury that comes about from following instructions or advice in this book.

Contents

Introduction
6

Light & Side Salads
28

Cooked Side Salads
74

Main Course Salads
124

Special Occasion Salads
184

Fruit Salads
220

Index
254

INTRODUCTION

Introduction

A well-made salad is almost lyrical in its combination of fresh tastes, textures and colours. This book looks at a large variety of salad themes and shows that there is far more to salads than meets the eye.

Seasonal changes are important and provide a useful lead when you are searching for inspiration. The finest salads begin with one or two ingredients that may catch the attention. If you come across a butter-rich pear, partner it with a handful of toasted pecan nuts and a few leaves of young spinach and combine with a blue cheese dressing. If a freshly boiled crab takes your fancy, consider the rich flavours of avocado, coriander (cilantro) leaves and lime. Some new potatoes and young lettuce leaves will make it a salad to remember.

Most salads fit into the summer season and are inspired by an abundance of freshness and colour. Summer salads are wonderful if eaten out of doors. In autumn and winter we move inside to enjoy the warm flavours of wild mushrooms, duck breast and chicken livers. The richness of these ingredients combines well with hearty leaves of oakleaf lettuce, escarole and chicory. Spring sees the arrival of young vegetables and tender salad leaves: corn salad, spinach and rocket (arugula). These delicate flavours marry best with grilled (broiled) fish, eggs, ham and chicken. In fact, simplicity is the key to a successful salad: where two or more ingredients combine, their flavours should blend well together but should also still be identifiable.

Whether you want a snack or a full meal, a side dish or celebratory feast, this book has a salad for every occasion. There are cooked and uncooked salads using a vast range of vegetables, pasta, rice, fish, meat, poultry and fruit, all of them mouth-wateringly tasty.

May your salads bring good health and happiness to your table!

Salad Vegetables

The salad vegetable is any type of vegetable that earns its keep in a salad by virtue of freshness and flavour. Vegetables for a salad can be raw or lightly cooked. If cooked, they are best served at room temperature to bring out their full flavour. Here is a selection of the most commonly used salad vegetables.

Avocado pear
This has a smooth, buttery flesh when ripe and is an asset to many salads, of which Guacamole is perhaps the best known. Avocados can also be served on their own as an appetizer, with a vinaigrette dressing or a spoonful of lemon mayonnaise, or even just a squeeze of lemon juice and salt.

Carrots
These should be young, slender and sweet to taste. Either cooked or raw, they bring flavour and colour to a salad.

Celery
A useful salad vegetable, celery is grown year round for its robust, earthy flavour. The crisp stems should be neither stringy nor tough. Celery partners well with cooked ham, apple and walnut in Waldorf Salad and is also used as a crudité.

Courgettes (zucchini)
These can be bitter to taste and are usually cooked before being combined with other young vegetables. Smooth in texture when cooked, they blend well with tomatoes, aubergines (eggplants), (bell) peppers and onions. Use baby courgettes for a sweeter flavour if you want to serve raw ones as a crudité.

Cucumbers
A common salad ingredient that turns up, invited or not, in salad bowls everywhere. The quality of this vegetable is best appreciated in strongly-flavoured salads.

Fennel
The bulb (or Florence) variety has a strong, aniseed flavour and looks like a squat head of celery. Because the flavour can be dominant, it may be blanched in boiling water for 6 minutes before use in a salad.

Garlic
Strong to taste, garlic is essential to the robust cooking of South America, Asia and the Mediterranean. Garlic should be used carefully as it can mask other flavours, but it is a vital part of salad preparation. To impart a very gentle hint of garlic rub round the inside of your salad bowl with a cut clove. Another way to moderate the strength of fresh garlic is to store a few crushed cloves in a bottle of olive oil, and use the oil sparingly in dressings.

Green beans
The varieties are too numerous to mention here, but they all have their merits as salad vegetables. To appreciate the sweet flavour of young tender green beans, cook them for 6 minutes and then refresh immediately in cold running water so that the crispness and colour are retained. An essential ingredient of Salade Niçoise, green beans are an ideal crudité and also partner well with a spicy tomato sauce.

Mushrooms
These provide a rich tone to many salads and are eaten both raw and cooked. The oyster mushroom, which grows wild but is also cultivated, has a fine flavour and texture. Button (white) mushrooms are widely available and are often used raw, thinly sliced, in a mixed salad. Chestnut mushrooms are similar to white mushrooms but have slightly more flavour.

Onions
Several varieties are suited to salads. The strongest is the small, brown onion, which should be chopped finely and used sparingly. Less strong is the large, white Spanish (Bermuda) onion, which has a sweeter, milder flavour and may be used coarsely chopped.

Potatoes
A staple carbohydrate ingredient to add bulk to a salad or provide a main element.

Spring onions (scallions)
These have a milder flavour than the common onion and give a gentle bite to many popular salads.

Baby corn
Baby corn cobs can be eaten whole, lightly cooked or raw, and should be served warm or at room temperature.

Tomatoes
Technically a fruit rather than a vegetable, tomatoes are valued for their flavour and colour. Dwarf varieties usually ripen more quickly than large ones and have a better flavour.

Salad Fruit

The contents of the fruit bowl offer endless possibilities for sweet and savoury salads.

Apples
This versatile fruit offers a unique flavour to both sweet and savoury salads.

Apricots
Use apricots raw, dried or lightly poached.

Bananas
These bring a special richness to fruit salads, although their flavour can often interfere with more delicate fruit.

Blackberries
With a very short season, wild blackberries have more flavour than cultivated ones.

Blueberries
These tight-skinned berries combine well with the sharpness of fresh oranges.

Cherries
Cherries should be firm and glossy and are a deliciously colourful ingredient in many kinds of fruit salad.

Cranberries
Too sharp to eat raw but very good for cooking.

Dates
Fresh dates are sweet and juicy, dried ones have a more intense flavour. Both kinds work well in fresh fruit salads.

Figs
Green or purple skinned fruit, with sweet, pinkish-red flesh. Eat whole or peeled.

Gooseberries
Dessert types can be eaten raw but cooking varieties are more widely available.

Grapefruit
These can have yellow, green or pink flesh; the pink-fleshed or ruby varieties are the sweetest.

Grapes
Large Muscat varieties, whose season runs from late summer to autumn, are the most coveted and also the most expensive.

Kiwi fruit
Available all the year round.

Kumquats
Tiny relatives of the orange and can be eaten raw or cooked.

Lemons and limes
Both these indispensable citrus fruits are used for adding flavour, and to prevent fruit turning brown.

Lychees
A small fruit with a hard pink skin and sweet, juicy flesh.

Mangoes
Tropical fruit with an exotic flavour and golden-orange flesh that is wonderful in sweet or savoury salads.

Melons
These grow in abundance from mid to late summer and provide a resource of freshness and flavour. Melon is at its most delicious served icy cold.

Nectarines
A relative of the peach with a smoother skin.

Oranges
At their best during winter, they can be segmented and added to sweet and savoury salads.

Papaya
These fruits of the tropics have a distinctive, sweet flavour. When ripe they are yellow–green.

Peaches
Choose white peaches for the sweetest flavour, and yellow for a more aromatic taste.

Pears
Perfect for savoury salads, and with blue cheese and pecan nuts.

Physalis
Small, fragrant, pleasantly tart orange berries, wrapped in a paper cape.

Pineapples
Ripe pineapples resist firm pressure in the hand and have a sweet smell.

Plums
There are many dessert and cooking varieties.

Raspberries
Much-coveted soft fruits that partner well with ripe mango, passion fruit and strawberries.

Rhubarb
Technically a vegetable, too tart to eat raw.

Star fruit (carambola)
When sliced, this makes a pretty shape perfect for garnishes.

Strawberries
A popular summer fruit, especially served with cream.

Lettuces and Leaves

One particular aspect of lettuce that sets it apart from any other vegetable is that you can only buy it in one form – fresh.

Lettuce has been cultivated for thousands of years. In Egyptian times it was sacred to the fertility god Min. It was then considered a powerful aphrodisiac, yet for the Greeks and the Romans it was thought to have quite the opposite effect, making one sleepy and generally soporific. Chemists today confirm that lettuce contains a hypnotic similar to opium, and in herbal remedies lettuce is recommended for insomniacs.

There are hundreds of different varieties of lettuce. Today, an increasing choice is available in the shops so that the salad bowl can become a wealth of colour, taste and texture with no other ingredient than a selection of leaves.

Round (butterhead)

These are the classic round lettuces. They have a pale heart and floppy, loosely packed leaves. They have a pleasant flavour as long as they are fresh. Choose the lettuce with the best heart by picking it up at the bottom and gently squeezing to check there is a firm centre.

Lollo Rosso

Lollo rosso and lollo biondo – similar in shape but a paler green without any purple edges – are both non-hearting lettuces. Although they do not have a lot of flavour they look superb and are often used to form a nest of leaves on which to place the rest of a salad.

Cos

The cos lettuce would have been known in antiquity. It has two names, cos, derived from the Greek island where it was found; and romaine, the name used by the French. Cos is considered to have the best flavour and is the correct lettuce for use in Caesar Salad.

Escarole

Escarole is one of the more robust lettuces in terms of flavour and texture. Like the frisée, escarole has a distinct bitter flavour. Served with other leaves and a well-flavoured dressing, escarole and endive (US chicory) will give your salad a pleasant "bite".

Oak Leaf Lettuce

Oak leaf lettuce, together with lollo rosso and lollo biondo, is another member of the loosehead lettuce group. Oak leaf lettuce has a very gentle flavour. It is a very decorative leaf and makes a beautiful addition to any salad, and a lovely garnish.

Little Gem (Bibb)
These look like something between a baby cos and a tightly-furled round. They have firm hearts and a distinct flavour. Their tight centres mean that they can be sliced whole and the quarters used for carrying slivers of smoked fish or anchovy as a simple appetizer.

Chinese Leaves (Chinese Cabbage)
This has pale green, crinkly leaves with long, wide, white ribs. Its shape is a little like a very fat head of celery, which gives rise to another of its names, celery cabbage. It is crunchy, and since it is available all year round, it makes a useful winter salad component.

Radicchio
This is a variety developed from wild chicory. It looks like a lettuce with deep wine-red leaves and cream ribs and owes its splendid foliage to careful shading from the light. If it is grown in the dark the leaves are marbled pink. Its bitter flavour contrasts well with green salads.

Lamb's Lettuce
Lamb's lettuce or corn salad is a popular winter leaf that does not actually belong to the lettuce family, but is terrific in salads. Called mache in France, lamb's lettuce has small, attractive, dark green leaves and grows in pretty little sprigs. Its flavour is mild and nutty.

Watercress
Watercress is perhaps the most robustly flavoured of all the salad ingredients and a handful of watercress is all you need to perk up a dull salad. It has a distinctive "raw" flavour, peppery and slightly pungent, and this, together with its shiny leaves, make it a popular garnish.

Rocket (arugula)
Rocket has a wonderful peppery flavour and is excellent in a mixed green salad. It was eaten by the Greeks and Romans as an aphrodisiac. Since it has such a striking flavour a little goes a long way; just a few leaves will transform a green salad and liven up a sandwich.

Herbs

For as long as salads have drawn on the qualities of fresh produce, sweet herbs have played an important part in providing individual character and flavour. When herbs are used in a salad, they should be as full of life as the salad leaves they accompany. Dried herbs are no substitute for fresh ones and should be kept for cooked dishes such as casseroles. Salad herbs are distinguished by their ability to release flavour without lengthy cooking.

Most salad herbs belong finely chopped in salad dressings and marinades, while the robust flavours of rosemary, thyme and fennel branches can be used on the barbecue to impart a smoky herb flavour. Ideally salad herbs should be picked just before use, but if you cannot use them immediately keep them in water to retain their freshness. Parsley, mint and coriander (cilantro) will keep for up to a week in this way if also covered with a plastic bag and placed in the refrigerator.

Above: Clockwise from top left; thyme, coriander (cilantro), parsley, chives, lavender, rose, mint and basil.

Basil

Remarkable for its fresh, pungent flavour unlike that of any other herb, basil is widely used in Mediterranean salads, especially Italian recipes. Basil leaves are tender and delicate and should be gently torn or snipped with scissors, rather than chopped with a knife.

Chives

Chives belong to the onion family and have a mild onion flavour. The slender, green stems and soft mauve flowers are both edible. Chives are an indispensable flavouring for potato salads.

Coriander (cilantro)

The chopped leaves of this pungent, distinctively flavoured herb are popular in Middle Eastern and Eastern salads.

Lavender

This soothingly fragrant herb is edible and may be used in both sweet and savoury salads as it combines well with thyme, garlic, honey and orange.

Mint

This much-loved herb is widely used in Greek and Middle Eastern salads, such as Tzatziki and Tabbouleh. It is also a popular addition to fruit salads. Garden mint is the most common variety; others include spearmint and the round-leafed apple mint.

Parsley

Flat and curly leaf parsley are both used for their fresh, green flavour. Flat leaf parsley is said to have a stronger taste. Freshly chopped parsley is used by the handful in salads and dressings.

Rose

Although it is not technically a herb, the sweet-scented rose can be used to flavour fresh fruit salads. It combines well with blackberries and raspberries.

Thyme

An asset to salads featuring rich, earthy flavours, this herb has a penetrating flavour.

Spices

Spices are the aromatic seasonings found in the seed, bark, fruit and sometimes flowers of certain plants and trees. Spices are highly valued for their warm, inviting flavours, and thankfully their price is relatively low. The flavour of a spice is contained in the volatile oils of the seed, bark or fruit; so, like herbs, spices should be used as fresh as possible. Whole spices keep better than ground ones, which tend to lose their freshness in 3–4 months.

Not all spices are suitable for salad making, although many allow us to explore the flavours of other cultures. The recipes in this book use curry spices in moderation so as not to spoil the delicate salad flavours.

Caraway
These savoury-sweet-tasting seeds are widely used in German and Austrian cooking and feature strongly in many Jewish dishes. The small ribbed seeds are similar in appearance and taste to cumin. The flavour combines especially well with German mustard in a dressing for frankfurter salad.

Cayenne pepper
Also known as chilli powder, this is the dried and finely ground fruit of the hot chilli pepper. It is an important seasoning in South American cooking and is often used when seasoning fish and shellfish. Cayenne pepper can be blended with paprika if it is too hot and should be used with care.

Celery salt
A combination of ground celery seed and salt, this is used for seasoning vegetables, especially carrots.

Cumin seeds
Often associated with Aisan and North African cookery, cumin can be bought ground or as small, slender seeds. It combines well with coriander seeds.

Curry paste
Prepared curry paste consists of a blend of Indian spices preserved in oil. It may be added to dressings, and is particularly useful in this respect for showing off the sweet qualities of fish and shellfish.

Paprika
This spice is made from a variety of sweet red pepper. It is mild in flavour, and adds colour.

Pepper
Undoubtedly the most popular spice used in the West, pepper features in the cooking of

Above: Flavoursome additions to salads include (clockwise from top left) celery salt, caraway seeds, curry paste, saffron strands, peppercorns and cayenne pepper.

almost every nation. Peppercorns can be white, black, green or red and should always be freshly milled rather than bought already ground.

Saffron
The world's most expensive spice, made from the dried stigma of a crocus, real saffron has a tobacco-rich smell and gives a sweet yellow tint to liquids used for cooking. It can be used in creamy dressings and brings out the richness of fish and shellfish dishes. There are many powdered imitations which provide colour without the flavour of the real thing.

Oils, Vinegars and Flavourings

OILS

Oil is the main ingredient of most dressings and provides an important richness to salads. Neutral oils, such as sunflower, safflower or groundnut (peanut), are ideally used as a background for stronger oils. Sesame, walnut and hazelnut oils are the strongest and should be used sparingly. Olive oil is prized for its clarity of flavour and clean richness. The most significant producers of olive oil are Italy, France, Spain and Greece. These and other countries produce two main grades of olive oil: estate-grown extra virgin olive oil; and semi-fine olive oil, which is of a good, basic standard.

Olive oils

French olive oils are subtly flavoured and provide a well-balanced lightness to dressings.

Greek olive oils are typically strong in character. They are often green with a thick texture and are unsuitable for use when making mayonnaise.

Italian olive oils are noted for their vigorous Mediterranean flavours. Tuscan oils are noted for their well-rounded, spicy flavour. Sicilian oils tend to be lighter in texture, although they are often stronger in flavour.

Spanish olive oils are typically fruity and often have a nutty quality with a slight bitterness.

Nut oils

Hazelnut and walnut oils are valued for their strong, nutty flavour. Tasting richly of the nuts from which they are pressed, both are usually blended with neutral oils for salad dressings.

Seed oils

Groundnut (peanut) oil and sunflower oil are valued for their clean, neutral flavour.

SALAD FLAVOURINGS

Capers

These are the pickled flower buds of a bush native to the Mediterranean. Their strong, sharp flavour is well suited to richly flavoured salads.

Lemon and lime juice

The juice of lemons and limes is used to impart a clean acidity to oil dressings. They should be used in moderation.

Mustard

Mustard has a tendency to bring out the flavour of other ingredients. It acts as an emulsifier in dressings and allows oil and vinegar to merge for a short perod of time. The most popular mustards for use in salads are French, German, English and wholegrain.

Above: Top left to right; Italian virgin olive oil, Spanish olive oil, Italian olive oil, safflower oil, hazelnut oil, walnut oil, groundnut (peanut) oil, French olive oil, Italian olive oil, white wine vinegar. Left to right bottom; lemon, olives, limes, capers and mustard.

Olives

Black and green olives usually belong in salads with a Mediterranean flavour. Black olives are generally sweeter than green ones.

VINEGARS

White wine vinegar

This should be used in moderation to balance the richness of an oil. A good-quality white wine vinegar will serve most purposes.

Balsamic vinegar

Sweeter than other vinegars, only a few drops of balsamic vinegar are necessary to enhance a salad or dressing. It is also a good substitute for lemon juice.

Making Herbed Oils and Vinegars

Many herbed oils and vinegars are available commercially, but you can very easily make your own. Pour the oil or vinegar into a sterilized jar and add your flavouring. Allow to steep for 2 weeks, then strain and decant into an attractive bottle which has also been sterilized properly. Add a seal and an identifying label. Flavoured vinegars should be used within 3 months, and flavoured herbs within 10 days. Fresh herbs should be clean and completely dry before you use them.

TARRAGON VINEGAR

Steep tarragon in cider vinegar, then decant. Insert 2 or 3 long sprigs of tarragon into the bottle.

ROSEMARY VINEGAR

Steep a sprig of fresh rosemary in red wine vinegar, then decant. Pour into a sterilized, dry bottle and add a few long stems of rosemary as decoration.

LEMON AND LIME VINEGAR

Steep strips of lemon and lime rind in white wine vinegar, then decant. Pour into a sterilized, clean bottle and add fresh strips of rind for colour and decoration.

RASPBERRY VINEGAR

Pour vinegar into a saucepan with 15ml/1 tbsp pickling spices and heat gently for 5 minutes. Pour the hot mixture over the raspberries in a bowl and then add 2 sprigs of lemon thyme. Cover and leave the mixture to infuse for two days in a cool, dark place. Strain the liquid and pour the flavoured vinegar into a sterilized bottle and seal.

DILL AND LEMON OIL

Steep a handful of fresh dill and a large strip of lemon rind in virgin olive oil, then decant. Use for salads containing fish or shellfish.

MEDITERRANEAN HERB OIL

Steep rosemary, thyme and marjoram in virgin olive oil, then decant.

BASIL AND CHILLI OIL

Steep basil and 3 chillies in virgin olive oil, then decant. Add to tomato and mozzarella salads.

WARNING

There is some evidence that oils containing fresh herbs and spices can grow harmful moulds, especially once the bottle has been opened and the contents are not fully covered by the oil. To protect against this, it is recommended that the herbs and spices are removed once their flavour has passed into the oil.

Left: Beautiful and delicious, herbal vinegars make exquisite gifts. From left: Tarragon vinegar, Rosemary vinegar, Raspberry vinegar and Lemon and Lime vinegar.

Vegetable Preparation

SHREDDING CABBAGE

Cabbage features in many salad recipes such as coleslaw and this method for shredding can be used for white, green or red varieties.

1 Use a large knife to cut the cabbage into quarters.

2 Cut the hard core from each quarter and discard; this part is not really edible when raw.

3 Slice each quarter to form fine shreds. Shredded cabbage will keep for several hours in the refrigerator but do not dress it until you are ready to serve.

CHOPPING AN ONION

Chopped onions are used in many recipes and, whether they are finely or roughly chopped, the method is the same; just vary the gap between cuts to give different sized pieces.

1 Cut off the stalk end of the onion and cut in half through the root, leaving the root intact. Remove the skin and place the halved onion, cut-side down, on the board. Make lengthways vertical cuts into the onion, taking care not to cut right through to the root.

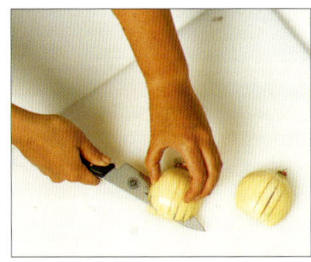

2 Carefully make two or three horizontal cuts from the stalk end through to the root, but without cutting all the way through the root.

3 Turn the onion on to its side. Cut the onion across from the stalk end to the root to dice it finely. The onion will fall away in small squares. Cut further apart for larger squares.

PREPARING GARLIC

Don't worry if you don't have a garlic press: try this method, which gives wonderful, juicy results.

1 Break off the clove of garlic, place the flat side of a large knife on top and strike with your fist. Remove all the papery outer skin. Begin by finely chopping the clove.

2 Sprinkle over a little table salt and, using the flat side of a large knife blade, work the salt into the garlic, until the clove softens and releases its juices. Use the garlic pulp as required.

PREPARING CHILLIES

Chillies add a distinct flavour, but remove the fiery-hot seeds.

1 Always protect your hands, as chillies can irritate the skin; wear rubber gloves and never rub your eyes after handling chillies. Halve the chilli lengthways and remove and discard the seeds.

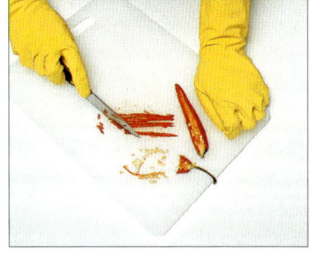

2 Slice the chilli, then finely chop it and use as required. Immediately wash the knife and board thoroughly in hot, soapy water. Always wash your hands very well after preparing chillies, especially if you didn't wear gloves.

PEELING TOMATOES

If you have the time, peel tomatoes before adding them to sauces or purées. This avoids rolled-up, tough pieces of tomato skin that don't soften during cooking.

1 Make a cross in each tomato with a sharp knife and place in a bowl.

2 Pour over enough boiling water to cover and leave to stand for 30 seconds. The skins should start to come away. Slightly unripe tomatoes may take a little longer.

3 Drain the tomatoes and peel the skin away with a sharp knife. Don't leave the tomatoes in the boiling water for too long.

CHOPPING HERBS

Chop herbs just before you use them.

1 Remove the leaves and place on a clean, dry board. Use a large, sharp cook's knife.

2 Chop the herbs, as finely or as coarsely as required, by holding the tip of the blade on the board and rocking the handle up and down.

CUTTING JULIENNE STRIPS

Small julienne strips of vegetables make an attractive salad ingredient or garnish. Use this technique for carrots, cucumber and celery.

1 Peel the vegetable and use a large knife to cut it into 5cm/ 2in lengths. Cut a thin sliver from one side of the first piece so that it sits flat on the board.

2 Cut each piece into thin slices lengthwise. Stack the slices of vegetable and then cut through them again to make fine strips.

PREPARING SPRING ONIONS

Spring onions (scallions) make a crisp and tasty addition to salads. They are rather fiddly to prepare, but the flavour is worth it.

1 Trim off the root of the spring onion with a sharp knife. Peel away any damaged or tough leaves.

2 For an intense flavour and an attractive green colour cut the dark green part into matchsticks.

3 For a milder flavour just use the white part of the spring onion. Discard the root and slice the white part thinly on a slight diagonal. Use the green part in another dish.

Fruit Preparation

CITRUS FRUIT

1. To peel, cut a slice from the top and from the base. Set the fruit base down on a work surface.

2. Cut off the peel lengthways in thick strips. Take the coloured rind and all the white pith (which has a bitter taste). Cut following the curve of the fruit.

1. To remove the thin, coloured rind, use a vegetable peeler to shave off the rind in wide strips, taking none of the white pith. Use these strips whole or cut them into fine shreds with a sharp knife.

2. Alternatively, rub the fruit against the fine holes of a metal grater, turning the fruit so that you take just the coloured rind and not the white pith. Or use a special tool, called a citrus zester, to take fine threads of rind. Finely chop the threads for tiny pieces.

1. For slices, cut across the fruit in slices with a serrated knife.

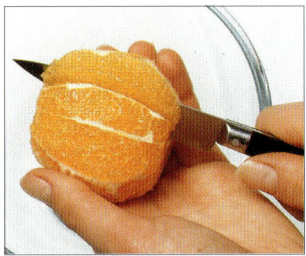

1. For segments, hold the fruit over a bowl to catch the juice. Working from the side of the fruit to the centre, slide the knife down first one side of a separating membrane and then the other. Continue cutting out segments.

FRESH CURRANTS

1. Pull through the prongs of a fork to remove red, black or white currants from the stalks.

APPLES AND PEARS

1. For whole fruit, use an apple corer to stamp out the whole core from stalk end to base.

1. For halves, use a melon baller to scoop out the core. Cut out the stalk and base with a knife.

2. For rings, remove the core and seeds. Set the fruit on its side and cut across rings, as required.

1. For slices, cut the fruit in half and remove the core and seeds. Set one half, cut side down, and cut it across into neat slices. Repeat with the other half.

FRESH DATES

1. Halve the fruit lengthways and lift out the stone (pit).

PAPAYA AND MELONS

1. Halve the fruit. Scoop out the seeds from the central hollow, then scrape away any fibres. For slices, follow the pear technique.

KIWI FRUIT AND STAR FRUIT (CARAMBOLA)

1. Cut the fruit across into neat slices; discard the ends.

PINEAPPLES

1. To peel the pineapple, set the pineapple on its base, hold it at the top and cut thick slices of skin from top to bottom. Dig out any eyes that remain with the point of the knife.

2. For chunks, halve the peeled fruit lengthways and then cut into quarters. Cut each quarter into spears and cut out the core. Cut each spear into chunks.

3. For rings, cut the peeled fruit across into slices and cut out the core.

KEEPING FRESH COLOUR

If exposed to the air for long, the cut flesh of fruits such as apples, bananas and avocados starts to turn brown. So if cut fruit has to wait before being served, sprinkle the cut surfaces with lemon juice, or immerse hard fruits in water and lemon juice, but do not soak or the fruit may become soggy.

MANGOES

1. Cut lengthways on either side of the stone (pit). Then cut from the two thin ends of the stone.

2. Remove the skin and cut the flesh into slices or cubes.

PEACHES, NECTARINES, APRICOTS AND PLUMS

1. Cut the fruit in half, cutting around the indentation. Twist the halves apart. Lift out the stone (pit), or lever it out with the tip of a knife. Or cut the unpeeled fruit into wedges, removing the stone. Set each wedge peel side down and slide the knife down to peel.

Salad Dressings

Although the ingredients of a salad are important, the secret of a perfect salad is a good dressing. A French dressing made from the very best olive oil and vinegar can rescue even the dullest selection of lettuce leaves, while a homemade mayonnaise is always impressive. If you are a confident and experienced salad dresser you might feel able to add oil and vinegar directly to your salad just before serving, but the safest way of creating a perfect dressing is to prepare it in advance. Home-made dressings can be stored in the refrigerator for up to a week and will improve in flavour. Here is a selection of dressings that should be part of every cook's repertoire.

THOUSAND ISLANDS DRESSING

This creamy dressing is great with green salads and grated carrot, hot potato, pasta and rice salads.

INGREDIENTS

Makes about 120ml/4fl oz/½ cup
60ml/4 tbsp sunflower oil
15ml/1 tbsp orange juice
15ml/1 tbsp lemon juice
10ml/2 tsp grated lemon rind
15ml/1 tbsp finely chopped onion
5ml/1 tsp paprika
5ml/1 tsp Worcestershire sauce
15ml/1 tbsp finely chopped fresh parsley
salt and ground black pepper

Put all the ingredients into a screw-top jar and season to taste. Replace the lid and shake well.

FRENCH DRESSING

French vinaigrette is the most widely used salad dressing.

INGREDIENTS

Makes about 120ml/4fl oz/½ cup
90ml/6 tbsp extra virgin olive oil
15ml/1 tbsp white wine vinegar
5ml/1 tsp French mustard
a pinch of caster (superfine) sugar

1 Place the extra virgin olive oil and white wine vinegar in a clean screw-top jar.

2 Add the mustard and sugar.

3 Replace the lid and shake well.

FRENCH HERB DRESSING

The delicate scents and flavours of fresh herbs combine especially well in a French dressing. Use just one herb or a selection. Toss with a simple green salad and serve with good cheese, fresh bread and wine.

INGREDIENTS

Makes about 120ml/4fl oz/½ cup
60ml/4 tbsp extra virgin olive oil
30ml/2 tbsp groundnut (peanut) or sunflower oil
15ml/1 tbsp lemon juice
60ml/4 tbsp finely chopped fresh herbs (parsley, chives, tarragon and marjoram)
a pinch of caster (superfine) sugar

1 Place the olive oil and groundnut or sunflower oil in a clean screw-top jar.

2 Add the lemon juice, chopped fresh herbs and sugar.

3 Replace the lid and shake well.

Thousand: Energy 1104kcal/4540kJ; Protein 1g; Carbohydrate 5g, of which sugars 3g; Fat 120g, of which saturates 14g; Cholesterol 0mg; Calcium 27mg; Fibre 1g; Sodium 64mg.
French: Energy 827/3403kcal/kJ; Protein 1g; Carbohydrate 2g, of which sugars 2g; Fat 91g, of which saturates 13g; Cholesterol 0mg; Calcium 6mg; Fibre 0g; Sodium 237mg.
Herb: Energy 818kcal/3365kJ; Protein 0g; Carbohydrate 2g, of which sugars 2g; Fat 90g, of which saturates 12g; Cholesterol 0mg; Calcium 25mg; Fibre 0g; Sodium 4mg.

MAYONNAISE

Mayonnaise is a simple emulsion made with egg yolks and oil. For consistent results, ensure that both egg yolks and oil are at room temperature before combining. Home-made mayonnaise is made with raw egg yolks and may therefore be considered unsuitable for young children, pregnant mothers and the elderly.

INGREDIENTS
Makes about 300ml/½ pint/1¼ cups
2 egg yolks
5ml/1 tsp French mustard
150ml/¼ pint/⅔ cup extra virgin olive oil
150ml/¼ pint/⅔ cup groundnut (peanut) or sunflower oil
10ml/2 tsp white wine vinegar
salt and ground black pepper

1 Place the egg yolks and mustard in a food processor and blend smoothly.

2 Add the olive oil a little at a time while the processor is running. When the mixture is thick, add the groundnut or sunflower oil in a slow, steady stream.

3 Add the vinegar and season to taste with salt and pepper.

YOGURT DRESSING

This is a less rich version of a classic mayonnaise and is much easier to make. It can be used as a low-fat substitute. Change the herbs as you wish, or leave them out.

INGREDIENTS
Makes about 210ml/7fl oz/scant 1 cup
150ml/¼ pint/⅔ cup natural (plain) yogurt
30ml/2 tbsp mayonnaise
30ml/2 tbsp milk
15ml/1 tbsp chopped fresh parsley
15ml/1 tbsp chopped fresh chives

Put all the ingredients together in a bowl. Season to taste and mix well.

BLUE CHEESE AND CHIVE DRESSING

Blue cheese dressings have a strong, robust flavour and are well suited to winter salad leaves such as escarole, chicory (Belgian endive) and radicchio.

INGREDIENTS
Makes about 350ml/12 fl oz/1½ cups
75g/3 oz blue cheese (Stilton, Bleu d'Auvergne or Gorgonzola)
150ml/¼ pint/⅔ cup medium-fat natural (plain) yogurt
45ml/3 tbsp olive oil
30ml/2 tbsp lemon juice
15ml/1 tbsp chopped fresh chives
ground black pepper

1 Remove the rind from the cheese and combine with a third of the yogurt in a bowl.

2 Add the remainder of the yogurt, the olive oil and the lemon juice.

3 Stir in the chopped chives and season to taste with ground black pepper.

Mayonnaise: Energy 2828kcal/11631kJ; Protein 6g; Carbohydrate 1g, of which sugars 0g; Fat 311g, of which saturates 55g; Cholesterol 403mg; Calcium 51mg; Fibre 0g; Sodium 166mg.
Yogurt: Energy 347kcal/1442kJ; Protein 10g; Carbohydrate 14g, of which sugars 14g; Fat 28g, of which saturates 7g; Cholesterol 43mg; Calcium 346mg; Fibre 0g; Sodium 269mg.
Cheese: Energy 797kcal/3298kJ; Protein 24g; Carbohydrate 12g, of which sugars 12g; Fat 73g, of which saturates 24g; Cholesterol 84mg; Calcium 492mg; Fibre 0g; Sodium 698mg.

BASIL AND LEMON MAYONNAISE

This luxurious dressing is flavoured with lemon juice and two types of basil. Serve with all kinds of leafy salads, crudités or coleslaws. It is also good with baked potatoes or as a delicious dip for French fries. The dressing will keep in an airtight jar for up to a week in the refrigerator.

INGREDIENTS

Makes about 300ml/½ pint/1¼ cups

2 large (US extra large) egg yolks
15ml/1 tbsp lemon juice
150ml/¼ pint/⅔ cup extra virgin olive oil
150ml/¼ pint/⅔ cup sunflower oil
4 garlic cloves
a handful of fresh green basil
a handful of fresh opal basil
salt and ground black pepper

1 Place the egg yolks and lemon juice in a blender or food processor and mix them briefly until lightly blended.

2 In a jug (cup), stir together both oils. With the machine running, pour in the oil very slowly, a little at a time.

3 Once half of the oil has been added, and the dressing has successfully emulsified, the remaining oil can be incorporated a little more quickly. Continue processing until a thick, creamy mayonnaise has formed, then turn off the machine.

4 Peel and crush the garlic cloves and add to the mayonnaise. Alternatively, place the cloves on a chopping board and sprinkle with salt, then flatten them with the heel of a heavy-bladed knife and chop the flesh. Flatten the garlic again to make a coarse purée. Add to the mayonnaise.

5 Remove the basil stalks and tear both types of leaves into small pieces. Stir into the mayonnaise.

6 Add salt and pepper to taste, then transfer the mayonnaise to a serving dish. Cover and chill until ready to serve.

Energy 484kcal/1992kJ; Protein 1.8g; Carbohydrate 0.4g, of which sugars 0.3g; Fat 52.9g, of which saturates 7.4g; Cholesterol 101mg; Calcium 37mg; Fibre 0.6g; Sodium 9mg.

Instant Dressings and Dips

If you need an instant dressing or dip, try one of these quick and easy recipes. Most of them use store-cupboard (pantry) ingredients.

CREAMY BLACK OLIVE DIP

Stir a little black olive paste into a carton of extra-thick double (heavy) cream until smooth and well blended. Add salt, ground black pepper and a squeeze of lemon juice to taste. Serve chilled.

CRÈME FRAÎCHE DRESSING WITH SPRING ONIONS

Finely chop a bunch of spring onions (scallions) and stir into a carton of crème fraîche. Add a dash of chilli sauce, a squeeze of lime juice, and salt and pepper.

GREEK-STYLE YOGURT AND MUSTARD DIP

Mix a small carton of Greek (US strained plain) yogurt with 5–10ml/1–2 tsp wholegrain mustard. Serve with crudités.

HERB MAYONNAISE

Liven up ready-made French-style mayonnaise with a handful of chopped fresh herbs – try flat leaf parsley, basil, dill or tarragon.

PASSATA AND HORSERADISH DIP

Bring a little tang to a small carton or bottle of passata (bottled strained tomatoes) by adding some horseradish sauce or 5–10ml/1–2 tsp creamed horseradish and salt and pepper to taste. Serve with lightly-cooked vegetables.

PESTO DIP

For a simple, speedy, Italian-style dip, stir 15ml/1 tbsp ready-made red or green pesto into a carton of sour cream. Serve with crisp crudités or wedges of oven-roasted Mediterranean vegetables, such as (bell) peppers, courgettes (zucchini) and onions.

SOFT CHEESE AND CHIVE DIP

Mix a tub of soft cheese with 30–45ml/2–3 tbsp snipped fresh chives and season to taste with salt and black pepper. If the dip is too thick, stir in a little milk to soften it. Use as a dressing for all kinds of salads, especially winter coleslaws.

Above: Top row; creamy black olive dip, creme fraîche dressing with spring onions. Second row; herb mayonnaise, yogurt and sun-dried tomato dip. Third row; greek-style yogurt and mustard dip, soft cheese and chive dip, spiced yogurt dressing. Fourth row; pesto dip, passata and horseradish dip.

SPICED YOGURT DRESSING

Stir a little curry paste and chutney into a carton of yogurt.

SUN-DRIED TOMATO DIP

Stir 15–30ml/1–2 tbsp sun-dried tomato paste into a carton of Greek (US strained plain) yogurt. Season to taste.

Light & Side Salads

~

Crudités

A colourful selection of raw vegetables, or crudités, may be served with drinks or as small salad appetizers. The term "crudités" is used both for small pieces of vegetables served with a tasty dip and for a selection of vegetable salads presented in separate dishes. By choosing contrasting colours, it is possible to make a beautiful presentation of any combination of vegetables, raw or lightly cooked, attractively arranged on a platter or in baskets and served with a tangy dip, such as aïoli (garlic mayonnaise) or tapenade (olive paste). Allow 75–115g/3–4oz of each vegetable per person.

AÏOLI

Put four crushed garlic cloves (or more or less, to taste) in a small bowl with a pinch of salt and crush with the back of a spoon. Add 2 egg yolks and beat for 30 seconds with an electric mixer until creamy. Beat in 250ml/8floz/ 1 cup extra virgin olive oil, by drops, until the mixture thickens. As it begins to thicken, the oil can be added in a thin stream until the mixture is thick. Thin the sauce with a little lemon juice and season to taste. Chill for up to 2 days; bring to room temperature and stir before serving.

TAPENADE

Put 200g/7oz pitted black olives, 6 canned anchovy fillets, 30ml/ 2 tbsp capers, rinsed, 1–2 garlic cloves, 5ml/1 tsp fresh thyme leaves, 15ml/1 tbsp Dijon mustard, the juice of ½ lemon, ground black pepper and, if you like, 15ml/1 tbsp brandy in a food processor fitted with the metal blade. Process for 15–30 seconds until smooth, then scrape down the sides of the bowl. With the machine running, slowly add 60–90ml/4–6 tbsp extra virgin olive oil to make a smooth, firm paste. Store in an airtight container.

RAW VEGETABLE PLATTER

INGREDIENTS

Serves 6–8

2 red and 2 yellow (bell) peppers, seeded and sliced lengthways
225g/8oz fresh baby corn cobs, blanched
1 chicory head (red or white), trimmed and leaves separated
175–225g/6–8oz thin asparagus, trimmed and blanched
1 small bunch radishes with small leaves
175g/6oz cherry tomatoes
12 quails' eggs, boiled for 3 minutes, drained, refreshed and peeled
aïoli or tapenade, to serve

Arrange the prepared vegetables on a serving plate together with the quails' eggs. Cover with a damp dish towel until ready to serve. Serve with aïoli or tapenade for dipping.

TOMATO AND CUCUMBER SALAD

INGREDIENTS

Serves 4–6

1 medium cucumber, peeled and thinly sliced
5–6 ice cubes
30ml/2 tbsp white wine vinegar
90ml/6 tbsp crème fraîche or sour cream
30ml/2 tbsp chopped fresh mint
4 or 5 ripe tomatoes, sliced
salt and ground black pepper

Place the cucumber in a bowl, sprinkle with a little salt and 15ml/ 1 tbsp of the vinegar and toss with the ice cubes. Chill for 1 hour to crisp, then rinse, drain and pat dry. Return to the bowl, add the cream, pepper and mint and stir to mix well. Arrange the tomato slices on a serving plate, sprinkle with the remaining vinegar and spoon the cucumber slices into the centre.

CARROT AND PARSLEY SALAD

INGREDIENTS

Serves 4–6

1 garlic clove, crushed
grated rind and juice of 1 unwaxed orange
30–45ml/2–3 tbsp groundnut (peanut) oil
450g/1lb carrots, cut into very fine julienne strips
30–45ml/2–3 tbsp chopped fresh parsley
salt and ground black pepper

Rub a bowl with the garlic and leave in the bowl. Add the orange rind and juice and salt and pepper. Whisk in the oil until blended, then remove the garlic. Add the carrots and half of the parsley and toss well. Garnish with the remaining parsley.

Aïoli: Energy 2381kcal/9794kJ; Protein 7g; Carbohydrate 2g, of which sugars 0g; Fat 261g, of which saturates 39g; Cholesterol 403mg; Calcium 49mg; Fibre 0g; Sodium 215mg.
Tapenade: Energy 351kcal/1449kJ; Protein 19g; Carbohydrate 3g, of which sugars 2g; Fat 29g, of which saturates 4g; Cholesterol 38mg; Calcium 318mg; Fibre 8g; Sodium 7302mg.
Platter: Energy 72kcal/302kJ; Protein 5g; Carbohydrate 3g, of which sugars 6g; Fat 3g, of which saturates 1g; Cholesterol 169mg; Calcium 39mg; Fibre 2g; Sodium 24mg.
Tomato: Energy 19kcal/81kJ; Protein 1g; Carbohydrate 3g, of which sugars 3g; Fat 0g, of which saturates 0g; Cholesterol 0mg; Calcium 17mg; Fibre 1g; Sodium 9mg.
Carrot: Energy 31kcal/131kJ; Protein 1g; Carbohydrate 7g, of which sugars 7g; Fat 0g, of which saturates 0g; Cholesterol 0mg; Calcium 23mg; Fibre 2g; Sodium 20mg.

Lettuce and Herb Salad

Stores now sell many different types of lettuce leaves all year, so try to use a mixture. Look out for pre-packed bags of mixed baby lettuce leaves.

INGREDIENTS

Serves 4

½ cucumber
mixed lettuce leaves
1 bunch watercress, about 115g/4oz
1 chicory (Belgian endive) head, sliced
45ml/3 tbsp chopped fresh herbs such as parsley, thyme, tarragon, chives, chervil

For the dressing
15ml/1 tbsp white wine vinegar
5ml/1 tsp prepared mustard
75ml/5 tbsp olive oil
salt and ground black pepper

3 Toss the cucumber, lettuce, watercress, chicory and herbs together in a bowl, or arrange in the bowl in layers. Stir the dressing

4 Pour the dressing over the salad and toss lightly to coat the salad vegetables and leaves. Serve immediately.

1 To make the dressing, mix the vinegar and mustard together, then whisk in the oil and seasoning.

2 Peel the cucumber, if liked, then halve it lengthways and scoop out the seeds. Thinly slice the flesh. Tear the lettuce leaves into bitesize pieces.

Energy 185kcal/763kJ; Protein 1g; Carbohydrate 1g, of which sugars 1g; Fat 19g, of which saturates 3g; Cholesterol 0mg; Calcium 67mg; Fibre 2g; Sodium 75mg.

Minted Melon and Grapefruit Cocktail

Melon is always a popular appetizer. Here the flavour is complemented by the refreshing taste of citrus fruit and a simple dressing.

INGREDIENTS

Serves 4

1 small Galia melon, about 1kg/2¼lb
2 pink grapefruit
1 yellow grapefruit
5ml/1 tsp Dijon mustard
5ml/1 tsp raspberry or sherry vinegar
5ml/1 tsp clear honey
15ml/1 tbsp chopped fresh mint
fresh mint sprigs, to garnish

1 Halve the melon and remove the seeds with a teaspoon. With a melon baller, carefully scoop the flesh into balls.

2 With a sharp knife, peel all three grapefruit and cut away all the bitter white pith. Remove the segments by cutting between the membranes, holding the fruit over a bowl to catch any juice.

3 Whisk the mustard, vinegar, honey, chopped mint and grapefruit juice together in a mixing bowl. Add the melon balls and grapefruit segments and mix well. Chill for 30 minutes.

4 Ladle the fruit mixture into four serving dishes, garnish each one with a sprig of fresh mint and serve immediately.

Energy 101kcal/429kJ; Protein 2.3g; Carbohydrate 23.2g, of which sugars 23.2g; Fat 0.5g, of which saturates 0g; Cholesterol 0mg; Calcium 61mg; Fibre 2.6g; Sodium 118mg.

Black and Orange Salad

This dramatically colourful salad, with its spicy dressing, is very unusual. It is a feast for the eyes as well as for the taste buds.

INGREDIENTS

Serves 4

3 oranges
115g/4oz/1 cup pitted black olives
15ml/1 tbsp chopped fresh
    coriander (cilantro)
15ml/1 tbsp chopped fresh parsley

For the dressing
30ml/2 tbsp olive oil
15ml/1 tbsp lemon juice
2.5ml/½ tsp paprika
2.5ml/½ tsp ground cumin

1 With a sharp knife, cut away the peel and pith from the oranges and divide the fruit into segments.

2 Place the oranges in a salad bowl and add the black olives, coriander and parsley.

3 Blend together the olive oil, lemon juice, paprika and cumin. Pour the dressing over the salad and toss gently. Chill for about 30 minutes and serve.

Rocket and Coriander Salad

Rocket leaves have a wonderful, peppery flavour. However, unless you have a plentiful supply of rocket, you may well have to use extra spinach or another green leaf to pad out this salad.

INGREDIENTS

Serves 4

115g/4oz or more rocket (arugula) leaves
115g/4oz young spinach leaves
1 large bunch fresh coriander (cilantro),
    about 25g/1oz
2–3 fresh parsley sprigs

For the dressing
1 garlic clove, crushed
45ml/3 tbsp olive oil
10ml/2 tsp white wine vinegar
a pinch of paprika
cayenne pepper
salt

1 Place the rocket and spinach leaves in a salad bowl. Chop the coriander and parsley and scatter them over the top.

2 In a small jug (cup), blend together the garlic, olive oil, vinegar, paprika, cayenne pepper and salt.

3 Pour the dressing over the salad and serve immediately.

Black: Energy 129kcal/537kJ; Protein 1.8g; Carbohydrate 11.1g, of which sugars 10.6g; Fat 9g, of which saturates 1.3g; Cholesterol 0mg; Calcium 79mg; Fibre 3g; Sodium 654mg.
Rocket: Energy 68kcal/280kJ; Protein 2g; Carbohydrate 1.3g, of which sugars 1.2g; Fat 6.1g, of which saturates 0.9g; Cholesterol 0mg; Calcium 123mg; Fibre 1.8g; Sodium 85mg.

Caesar Salad

There are many stories about the origin of Caesar Salad. The most likely is that it was invented by an Italian, Caesar Cardini, who owned a restaurant in Mexico in the 1920s. Simplicity is the key to the success of this salad.

INGREDIENTS

Serves 4
3 slices day-old bread, 1cm/½in thick
60ml/4 tbsp garlic oil
50g/2oz piece Parmesan cheese
1 cos or romaine lettuce
salt and ground black pepper

For the dressing
2 egg yolks, as fresh as possible
25g/1oz canned anchovy fillets, drained and roughly chopped
2.5ml/½ tsp French mustard
120ml/4fl oz/½ cup olive oil
15ml/1 tbsp white wine vinegar

2 Remove the crusts from the bread with a serrated knife and cut into 2.5cm/1in fingers.

4 Cut thin shavings from the Parmesan cheese with a vegetable peeler.

3 Heat the garlic oil in a large frying-pan, add the pieces of bread and fry until golden. Sprinkle with salt and leave to drain on kitchen paper.

5 Wash the lettuce leaves and spin dry. Toss with the dressing, and scatter with the garlic croûtons and Parmesan cheese shavings. Season and serve.

1 To make the dressing, combine the egg yolks, anchovies, mustard, oil and vinegar in a screw-top jar and shake well.

> ### COOK'S TIP
>
> The classic dressing for Caesar Salad is made with raw egg yolks. Ensure that you use only the freshest eggs, bought from a reputable supplier. Expectant mothers, young children and the elderly are not advised to eat raw egg yolks. You could omit them from the dressing and grate hard-boiled yolks on top of the salad instead.

Energy 261kcal/1083kJ; Protein 9.2g; Carbohydrate 11.5g, of which sugars 1.5g; Fat 20.1g, of which saturates 5g; Cholesterol 60mg; Calcium 190mg; Fibre 1.9g; Sodium 305mg.

Turkish Salad

This classic salad is a wonderful combination of textures and flavours. The saltiness of the cheese is perfectly balanced by the refreshing salad vegetables.

INGREDIENTS

Serves 4

1 cos or romaine lettuce heart
1 green (bell) pepper
1 red (bell) pepper
½ cucumber
4 tomatoes
1 red onion
225g/8oz/2 cups feta cheese, crumbled
black olives, to garnish

For the dressing
45ml/3 tbsp olive oil
45ml/3 tbsp lemon juice
1 garlic clove, crushed
15ml/1 tbsp chopped fresh parsley
15ml/1 tbsp chopped fresh mint
salt and ground black pepper

1 Chop the lettuce into bitesize pieces. Seed the peppers, remove the cores and the bitter white membrane and cut the flesh into thin strips. Chop the cucumber and slice or chop the tomatoes. Cut the onion in half, then slice it very finely.

2 Place the chopped lettuce, peppers, cucumber, tomatoes and onion in a large serving bowl. Scatter the feta over the top and toss together lightly.

3 To make the dressing, blend together the olive oil, lemon juice and garlic in a small bowl. Stir in the chopped parsley and mint and season to taste with salt and pepper.

4 Pour the dressing over the salad and toss lightly. Garnish with a handful of black olives and serve immediately.

Persian Salad

This very simple salad can be served with almost any dish. Don't add the dressing until just before you are ready to serve.

INGREDIENTS

Serves 4

4 tomatoes
½ cucumber
1 onion
1 cos or romaine lettuce heart

For the dressing
30ml/2 tbsp olive oil
juice of 1 lemon
1 garlic clove, crushed
salt and ground black pepper

1 Cut the tomatoes and cucumber into small cubes. Finely chop the onion and tear the lettuce into pieces.

2 Place the prepared tomatoes, cucumber, onion and lettuce in a large salad bowl and mix lightly together.

3 To make the dressing, pour the olive oil into a small bowl. Add the lemon juice, garlic and seasoning and blend together well.

4 Pour over the salad and toss lightly to mix. Sprinkle with extra black pepper and serve.

Turkish: Energy 302kcal/1250kJ; Protein 11g; Carbohydrate 12g, of which sugars 11g; Fat 24g, of which saturates 10g; Cholesterol 39mg; Calcium 246mg; Fibre 4g; Sodium 825mg.
Persian: Energy 108kcal/447kJ; Protein 2g; Carbohydrate 7g, of which sugars 6g; Fat 8g, of which saturates 1g; Cholesterol 0mg; Calcium 33mg; Fibre 3g; Sodium 11mg.

Spinach and Mushroom Salad

This nutritious salad goes well with strongly flavoured dishes. If served alone as a light lunch, it could be dressed with a French vinaigrette and served with warm, crusty French bread.

INGREDIENTS

Serves 4

10 baby corn cobs
2 medium tomatoes
115g/4oz/1½ cups mushrooms
1 medium onion, cut into rings
20 small spinach leaves
25g/1oz salad cress (optional)
salt and ground black pepper

1 Halve the baby corn cobs lengthways and slice the tomatoes into rounds.

2 Trim the mushrooms and cut them into thin slices.

3 Arrange all the salad ingredients attractively in a large bowl. Season with salt and pepper and serve.

Nutty Salad

A delicious salad with a tangy bite to it which can be served as an accompaniment to a main meal, or as an appetizer. For wholesome finger food at a party, serve mini pitta breads stuffed with the salad.

INGREDIENTS

Serves 4

1 medium onion, cut into 12 rings
115g/4oz/¾ cup canned red kidney beans, drained
1 medium green and 1 medium yellow courgette (zucchini), sliced
50g/2oz pasta shells, cooked
50g/2oz/½ cup cashew nuts
25g/1oz/¼ cup peanuts
lime wedges and fresh coriander (cilantro) sprigs, to garnish

For the dressing
120ml/4fl oz/½ cup fromage frais or natural (plain) yogurt
30ml/2 tbsp natural yogurt
1 green chilli, chopped
15ml/1 tbsp chopped fresh coriander (cilantro)
2.5ml/½ tsp crushed black peppercorns
2.5ml/½ tsp crushed dried red chillies
15ml/1 tbsp lemon juice
2.5ml/½ tsp salt

1 Arrange the onion, red kidney beans, courgette and pasta in a salad dish. Sprinkle the cashew nuts and peanuts over the top.

2 In a separate bowl, blend together the fromage frais, yogurt, green chilli, coriander and salt and beat well using a fork.

3 Sprinkle the crushed black pepper, red chillies and lemon juice over the dressing. Garnish the salad with the lime wedges and coriander sprigs and serve with the dressing in a separate bowl or poured over the salad.

Spinach: Energy 21kcal/89kJ; Protein 2g; Carbohydrate 2.4g, of which sugars 2.2g; Fat 0.5g, of which saturates 0.1g; Cholesterol 0mg; Calcium 29mg; Fibre 1.5g; Sodium 309mg.
Nutty: Energy 236kcal/980kJ; Protein 9.2g; Carbohydrate 15.1g, of which sugars 6.1g; Fat 15.8g, of which saturates 4.3g; Cholesterol 3mg; Calcium 102mg; Fibre 3.5g; Sodium 167mg.

Fresh Ceps Salad

To capture the just-picked flavour of a cep, this delicious salad is enriched with an egg yolk and walnut oil dressing. Choose small ceps which will have a firm texture and the very best flavour.

INGREDIENTS

Serves 4

350g/12oz fresh ceps
175g/6oz mixed salad leaves, including Batavia, young spinach and frisée
50g/2oz/½ cup broken walnut pieces, toasted
50g/2oz piece Parmesan cheese
salt and ground black pepper

For the dressing
2 egg yolks
2.5ml/½ tsp French mustard
75ml/5 tbsp groundnut (peanut) oil
45ml/3 tbsp walnut oil
30ml/2 tbsp lemon juice
30ml/2 tbsp chopped fresh parsley
a pinch of caster (superfine) sugar

2 Trim the ceps and cut them into thin slices.

3 Place the ceps in a large salad bowl and combine with the dressing. Leave for 10–15 minutes for the flavours to mingle.

4 Wash and dry the salad leaves, then toss them together with the ceps.

5 Turn the ceps out on to four large serving plates. Season well, scatter with the toasted walnuts and shavings of Parmesan cheese, then serve.

1 To make the dressing, place the egg yolks in a screw-top jar with the mustard, groundnut and walnut oils, lemon juice, parsley and sugar. Shake well.

Energy 388kcal/1603kJ; Protein 10.1g; Carbohydrate 1.5g, of which sugars 1.3g; Fat 38g, of which saturates 6.8g; Cholesterol 113mg; Calcium 191mg; Fibre 1.8g; Sodium 147mg.

Classic Greek Salad

If you have ever visited Greece, you'll know that this salad accompanied by a chunk of bread makes a delicious first course.

INGREDIENTS

Serves 4

1 cos or romaine lettuce
½ cucumber, halved lengthways
4 tomatoes
8 spring onions (scallions), sliced
black olives
115g/4oz feta cheese

For the dressing
90ml/6 tbsp white wine vinegar
150ml/¼ pint/⅔ cup extra virgin olive oil
salt and ground black pepper

1 Tear the lettuce leaves into pieces and place in a large bowl. Slice the cucumber and add to the bowl.

2 Cut the tomatoes into wedges and put them into the bowl.

3 Add the spring onions to the bowl together with the olives, and toss well.

4 Cut the feta cheese into cubes and add to the salad.

5 Put the vinegar, olive oil and seasoning into a small bowl and whisk well. Pour the dressing over the salad and toss to combine. Serve immediately, with extra olives and some bread, if liked.

COOK'S TIP

The salad can be assembled in advance and chilled, but should be dressed only just before serving. Keep the dressing at room temperature as chilling deadens the flavour.

Energy 225kcal/935kJ; Protein 11.2g; Carbohydrate 11.8g, of which sugars 11.1g; Fat 15.1g, of which saturates 8.3g; Cholesterol 39mg; Calcium 249mg; Fibre 3.4g; Sodium 827mg.

Orange and Red Onion Salad with Cumin

Cumin and mint give this refreshing salad a very Middle Eastern flavour. Small, seedless oranges are most suitable, if available.

INGREDIENTS

Serves 6

6 oranges
2 red onions
15ml/1 tbsp cumin seeds
5ml/1 tsp coarsely ground black pepper
15ml/1 tbsp chopped fresh mint
90ml/6 tbsp olive oil
salt
fresh mint sprigs and black olives, to serve

1 Slice the oranges thinly, working over a bowl to catch any juice. Then, holding each orange slice in turn over the bowl, cut round with scissors to remove the peel and pith. Reserve the juice. Slice the onions thinly and separate into rings.

2 Arrange the orange and onion slices in layers in a shallow dish, sprinkling each layer with cumin seeds, black pepper, chopped mint, olive oil and salt to taste. Pour over the reserved orange juice.

3 Leave the salad to marinate in a cool place for about 2 hours. Sprinkle over the mint sprigs and black olives, and serve.

Spanish Salad with Capers and Olives

Make this refreshing salad in the summer when tomatoes are at their sweetest and full of flavour.

INGREDIENTS

Serves 4

4 tomatoes
½ cucumber
1 bunch spring onions (scallions), trimmed and chopped
1 bunch watercress
8 stuffed olives
30ml/2 tbsp drained capers

For the dressing
30ml/2 tbsp red wine vinegar
5ml/1 tsp paprika
2.5ml/½ tsp ground cumin
1 garlic clove, crushed
75ml/5 tbsp olive oil
salt and ground black pepper

1 Peel the tomatoes and finely dice the flesh. Put them in a salad bowl.

2 Peel the cucumber, dice it finely and add it to the tomatoes. Add half the spring onions to the salad bowl and mix lightly. Break the watercress into sprigs. Add to the tomato mixture, with the olives and capers.

3 To make the dressing, mix the wine vinegar, paprika, cumin and garlic in a bowl. Whisk in the oil and add salt and pepper to taste. Pour over the salad and toss lightly. Serve immediately with the remaining spring onions.

Orange: Energy 161kcal/672kJ; Protein 2g; Carbohydrate 14.1g, of which sugars 13.2g; Fat 11.2g, of which saturates 1.6g; Cholesterol 0mg; Calcium 76mg; Fibre 2.7g; Sodium 8mg.
Spanish: Energy 179kcal/739kJ; Protein 3g; Carbohydrate 6.2g, of which sugars 6g; Fat 16g, of which saturates 2.4g; Cholesterol 0mg; Calcium 74mg; Fibre 3g; Sodium 303mg.

Carrot and Orange Salad

A fruit and a vegetable that could have been made for each other form the basis of this wonderful, fresh-tasting salad.

INGREDIENTS

Serves 4

450g/1lb carrots
2 large oranges
15ml/1 tbsp olive oil
30ml/2 tbsp lemon juice
a pinch of sugar (optional)
30ml/2 tbsp chopped pistachio nuts or toasted pine nuts
salt and ground black pepper

1 Peel the carrots and grate them into a large bowl.

2 Peel the oranges with a sharp knife and cut into segments, catching the juice in a small bowl.

3 Blend together the olive oil, lemon juice and orange juice. Season with a little salt and pepper to taste, and sugar if liked.

4 Toss the orange segments together with the carrots and pour the dressing over. Scatter the salad with the pistachio nuts or pine nuts before serving.

Energy 170kcal/720kJ; Protein 2g; Carbohydrate 41g, of which sugars 40g; Fat 1g, of which saturates 0g; Cholesterol 0mg; Calcium 69mg; Fibre 7.7g; Sodium 56mg.

Spinach and Roast Garlic Salad

Don't worry about the amount of garlic in this salad. During roasting, the garlic becomes sweet and subtle and loses its pungent taste.

INGREDIENTS

Serves 4

12 garlic cloves, unpeeled
60ml/4 tbsp extra virgin olive oil
450g/1lb baby spinach leaves
50g/2oz/½ cup pine nuts, lightly toasted
juice of ½ lemon
salt and ground black pepper

1 Preheat the oven to 190°C/ 375°F/Gas 5. Place the garlic in a small roasting pan, toss in 30ml/ 2 tbsp of the olive oil and roast for about 15 minutes, until the garlic cloves are slightly charred around the edges.

2 While still warm, tip the garlic into a salad bowl. Add the spinach, pine nuts, lemon juice, remaining olive oil and a little salt. Toss well and add black pepper to taste. Serve immediately, inviting guests to squeeze the softened garlic purée out of the skin to eat.

Energy 258kcal/1065kJ; Protein 6g; Carbohydrate 4g, of which sugars 2g; Fat 25g, of which saturates 3g; Cholesterol 6mg; Calcium 195mg; Fibre 4.4g; Sodium 256mg.

Mixed Green Salad

A good combination of leaves for this salad would be rocket, radicchio, lamb's lettuce and frisée, along with herbs such as chervil, basil, parsley and tarragon.

INGREDIENTS

Serves 4–6

1 garlic clove, peeled
30ml/2 tbsp red wine or sherry vinegar
5ml/1 tsp Dijon mustard (optional)
75–120ml/5–8 tbsp extra virgin olive oil
200–225g/7–8oz mixed salad leaves and herbs
salt and ground black pepper

1 Rub a large salad bowl with the garlic clove. Leave the garlic clove in the bowl.

2 Add the vinegar, salt and pepper and mustard, if using. Stir to mix the ingredients and dissolve the salt, then whisk in the olive oil slowly.

3 Remove the garlic clove and stir the vinaigrette to combine.

4 Add the salad leaves to the bowl and toss well. Serve the salad immediately before it starts to wilt.

VARIATION

A salad like this should always contain some pungent leaves. Try young dandelion leaves when they are in season, but be sure to pick them well away from traffic routes and agricultural crop spraying.

Apple and Celeriac Salad

Celeriac, despite its coarse appearance, has a sweet and subtle flavour. Traditionally par-boiled in lemony water, in this salad it is served raw, allowing its unique taste and texture to come through.

INGREDIENTS

Serves 3–4

675g/1½lb celeriac, peeled
10–15ml/2–3 tsp lemon juice
5ml/1 tsp walnut oil (optional)
1 apple
45ml/3 tbsp mayonnaise
10ml/2 tsp Dijon mustard
15ml/1 tbsp chopped fresh parsley
salt and ground black pepper

1 Using a food processor or coarse cheese grater, shred the celeriac. Alternatively, cut it into very thin julienne strips.

2 Place the prepared celeriac in a bowl and sprinkle with the lemon juice and the walnut oil, if using. Stir well to mix.

3 Peel the apple if desired. Cut the apple into quarters and remove the core. Slice the apple quarters thinly crossways and toss together with the celeriac.

4 Mix together the mayonnaise, mustard, parsley and salt and pepper to taste. Add to the celeriac mixture and stir well. Chill for several hours until ready to serve.

Mixed: Energy 88kcal/362kJ; Protein 0.8g; Carbohydrate 1.6g, of which sugars 1.6g; Fat 8.7g, of which saturates 1.3g; Cholesterol 0mg; Calcium 32mg; Fibre 1g; Sodium 4mg.
Apple: Energy 99kcal/410kJ; Protein 1.2g; Carbohydrate 3.5g, of which sugars 3.4g; Fat 9.1g, of which saturates 1.3g; Cholesterol 8mg; Calcium 73mg; Fibre 2.1g; Sodium 226mg.

Chicory, Fruit and Nut Salad

The mildly bitter taste of the attractive white chicory leaves combines wonderfully well with sweet fruit, and is especially delicious when complemented by a creamy curry sauce.

INGREDIENTS

Serves 4

45ml/3 tbsp mayonnaise
15ml/1 tbsp Greek (US strained plain) yogurt
15ml/1 tbsp mild curry paste
90ml/6 tbsp single (light) cream
½ iceberg lettuce
2 chicory (Belgian endive) heads
50g/2oz/½ cup cashew nuts
50g/2oz/1¼ cups flaked coconut
2 red apples
75g/3oz/⅓ cup currants

1 Mix the mayonnaise, yogurt, curry paste and single cream in a small bowl. Cover and chill until required.

2 Tear the lettuce into pieces and put into a mixing bowl.

3 Cut the root end off each head of chicory, separate the leaves and add them to the lettuce. Preheat the grill (broiler).

4 Grill (broil) the cashew nuts for 2 minutes, until golden. Tip into a bowl and set aside. Spread out the coconut on a baking sheet. Grill for 1 minute, until golden.

5 Quarter the apples and cut out the cores. Slice the apples and add them to the lettuce with the toasted coconut and cashew nuts and the currants.

6 Spoon the dressing over the salad, toss lightly and serve.

COOK'S TIP

Watch the coconut flakes and cashew nuts with great care when they are under the grill (broiler), as they brown very fast.

Energy 319kcal/1327kJ; Protein 5.1g; Carbohydrate 20.9g, of which sugars 18.2g; Fat 24.5g, of which saturates 9.3g; Cholesterol 21mg; Calcium 84mg; Fibre 3.4g; Sodium 120mg.

Fennel, Orange and Rocket Salad

This light and refreshing salad is an ideal accompaniment to serve with spicy or rich foods.

INGREDIENTS

Serves 4

2 oranges
1 fennel bulb
115g/4oz rocket (arugula) leaves
50g/2oz/⅓ cup black olives

For the dressing
30ml/2 tbsp extra virgin olive oil
15ml/1 tbsp balsamic vinegar
1 small garlic clove, crushed
salt and ground black pepper

1 With a vegetable peeler, cut thin strips of rind from the oranges, leaving the pith behind. Cut the rind into thin julienne strips. Cook in boiling water for a few minutes, then drain.

2 Peel the oranges, removing all the white pith. Slice them into thin rounds and discard any seeds.

3 Cut the fennel bulb in half lengthways. Slice across the bulb as thinly as possible, using a food processor fitted with a slicing disc. Alternatively you can use a mandoline.

4 Combine the oranges and fennel in a serving bowl and toss with the rocket leaves.

5 Mix together the oil, vinegar, garlic and seasoning. Pour over the salad, toss together well and leave to stand for a few minutes. Sprinkle with the black olives and the julienne strips of orange and serve.

Aubergine, Lemon and Caper Salad

This cooked vegetable relish is lovely served as an accompaniment to cold meats, with pasta, or simply on its own with some good, crusty bread. Make sure the aubergine is well cooked until it is meltingly soft.

INGREDIENTS

Serves 4

1 large aubergine (eggplant), about 675g/1½lb
60ml/4 tbsp olive oil
grated rind and juice of 1 lemon
30ml/2 tbsp capers, rinsed
12 pitted green olives
30ml/2 tbsp chopped fresh flat leaf parsley
salt and ground black pepper

1 Cut the aubergine into 2.5cm/1in cubes. Heat the olive oil in a large frying pan and cook the aubergine cubes over a medium heat for about 10 minutes, tossing regularly, until golden and softened. You may need to do this in two batches. Drain on kitchen paper and sprinkle with a little salt.

2 Place the aubergine cubes in a large serving bowl. Toss with the lemon rind and juice, capers, olives and chopped parsley, and season well with salt and pepper. Serve at room temperature.

COOK'S TIP

This will taste even better when made the day before. It will store, covered, in the refrigerator, for up to 4 days.

Fennel: Energy 113kcal/469kJ; Protein 2.5g; Carbohydrate 9.9g, of which sugars 9.8g; Fat 7.3g, of which saturates 1g; Cholesterol 0mg; Calcium 116mg; Fibre 3.9g; Sodium 332mg .
Aubergine: Energy 172kcal/712kJ; Protein 2g; Carbohydrate 4g, of which sugars 4g; Fat 17g, of which saturates 2g; Cholesterol 0mg; Calcium 25mg; Fibre 4g; Sodium 740mg.

Apple Coleslaw

The term coleslaw stems from the Dutch koolsla, meaning "cool cabbage". There are many variations of this salad; this recipe combines the sweet flavours of apple and carrot with celery salt. Coleslaw is traditionally served with cold ham.

INGREDIENTS

Serves 4

450g/1lb white cabbage
1 medium onion
2 apples, peeled and cored
175g/6oz carrots, peeled
150ml/¼ pint/⅔ cup mayonnaise
5ml/1 tsp celery salt
ground black pepper

1 Discard the outside leaves of the white cabbage if they are dirty, cut the cabbage into 5cm/2in wedges, then remove the stem section.

2 Feed the cabbage and the onion through a food processor fitted with a slicing blade. Change to a grating blade and grate the apples and carrots. Alternatively use a hand grater and vegetable slicer.

3 Combine all the salad ingredients in a large serving bowl. Fold in the mayonnaise and season with the celery salt and black pepper.

VARIATION

For a richer coleslaw, add 115g/4oz/½ cup grated Cheddar cheese. You may find you will need smaller portions, as the cheese makes a more sustaining dish.

Energy 340kcal/1408kJ; Protein 3g; Carbohydrate 18g, of which sugars 17g; Fat 29g, of which saturates 4g; Cholesterol 28mg; Calcium 81mg; Fibre 6g; Sodium 583mg.

Carrot, Raisin and Apricot Coleslaw

A tasty variation on classic coleslaw, this colourful salad combines cabbage, carrots and two kinds of dried fruit in a yogurt dressing.

INGREDIENTS

Serves 6

350g/12oz/3 cups white cabbage, finely shredded
225g/8oz/1½ cups carrots, grated
1 red onion, finely sliced
3 celery sticks, sliced
175g/6oz/generous 1 cup raisins
75g/3oz/¾ cup dried apricots, chopped

For the dressing
120ml/4fl oz/½ cup mayonnaise
90ml/6 tbsp natural (plain) yogurt
30ml/2 tbsp chopped fresh mixed herbs
salt and ground black pepper

1 Put the cabbage and carrots in a large bowl.

2 Add the onion, celery, raisins and apricots and mix well.

3 In a small bowl, mix together the mayonnaise, yogurt, herbs and seasoning.

4 Add the mayonnaise dressing to the coleslaw ingredients and toss together to mix. Cover and chill before serving.

VARIATION

Use other dried fruit such as sultanas (golden raisins) and ready-to-eat dried pears or peaches in place of the raisins and apricots.

Energy 263kcal/1099kJ; Protein 3g; Carbohydrate 29.4g, of which sugars 28.8g; Fat 15.7g, of which saturates 2.4g; Cholesterol 15mg; Calcium 92mg; Fibre 3.2g; Sodium 143mg.

Fennel Coleslaw

Another variation on traditional coleslaw in which the aniseed flavour of fennel plays a major role.

INGREDIENTS

Serves 4

175g/6oz fennel
2 spring onions (scallions), plus shreds, to garnish
175g/6oz white cabbage
115g/4oz celery
175g/6oz carrots
50g/2oz/scant ½ cup sultanas (golden raisins)
2.5ml/½ tsp caraway seeds (optional)
15ml/1 tbsp chopped fresh parsley
45ml/3 tbsp extra virgin olive oil
5ml/1 tsp lemon juice

VARIATION

Use sour cream instead of olive oil for a creamier dressing.

3 Stir in the chopped parsley, olive oil and lemon juice and mix all the ingredients very thoroughly. Cover and chill for 3 hours to allow the flavours to mingle. Serve garnished with shreds of spring onion.

1 Cut the fennel and spring onions into thin slices.

2 Slice the cabbage and celery finely and cut the carrots into fine strips. Place in a serving bowl together with the fennel and spring onions. Add the sultanas and caraway seeds, if using, and toss lightly to mix.

Energy 145kcal/604kJ; Protein 1.9g; Carbohydrate 15.6g, of which sugars 15.3g; Fat 8.7g, of which saturates 1.2g; Cholesterol 0mg; Calcium 70mg; Fibre 3.8g; Sodium 46mg.

Beansprout and Mooli Salad

Ribbon-thin slices of fresh, crisp vegetables mixed with beansprouts make the perfect foil for an unusual oriental dressing.

INGREDIENTS

Serves 4

225g/8oz/1 cup beansprouts
1 cucumber
2 carrots
1 small mooli (daikon)
1 small red onion, thinly sliced
2.5cm/1in fresh root ginger, peeled and cut into thin matchsticks
1 small red chilli, seeded and thinly sliced
handful of fresh coriander (cilantro) or mint leaves

For the oriental dressing
15ml/1 tbsp rice-wine vinegar
15ml/1 tbsp light soy sauce
15ml/1 tbsp Thai fish sauce
1 garlic clove, finely chopped
15ml/1 tbsp sesame oil
45ml/3 tbsp groundnut (peanut) oil
30ml/2 tbsp sesame seeds, lightly toasted

1 First make the dressing. Place all the dressing ingredients in a bottle or screw-top jar and shake well. The dressing may be made in advance and will keep well for a couple of days if stored in the refrigerator or a cool place.

2 Wash the beansprouts and drain thoroughly in a colander.

3 Peel the cucumber, cut in half lengthways and scoop out the seeds. Peel the cucumber flesh into long ribbon strips using a potato peeler or mandoline.

4 Peel the carrots and radish into long strips in the same way as for the cucumber.

5 Place the carrots, radish and cucumber in a large, shallow serving dish, add the onion, ginger, chilli and coriander or mint and toss to mix. Pour the dressing over just before serving.

Energy 176kcal/728kJ; Protein 3.8g; Carbohydrate 6.7g, of which sugars 5.2g; Fat 15.1g, of which saturates 1.6g; Cholesterol 0mg; Calcium 82mg; Fibre 2.6g; Sodium 371mg.

Tzatziki

Tzatziki is a Greek cucumber salad dressed with yogurt, mint and garlic. It is typically served with grilled lamb and chicken, but is also good with salmon and trout.

INGREDIENTS

Serves 4

1 cucumber
5ml/1 tsp salt
45ml/3 tbsp finely chopped fresh mint, plus a few sprigs to garnish
1 garlic clove, crushed
5ml/1 tsp caster (superfine) sugar
200ml/7fl oz/scant 1 cup Greek (US strained plain) yogurt
paprika, to garnish (optional)

1 Peel the cucumber. Reserve a little to use as a garnish if you wish and cut the rest in half, lengthways. Remove the seeds with a teaspoon and discard. Slice the cucumber thinly and combine with the salt. Leave for about 15–20 minutes. The salt will soften the cucumber and draw out any bitter juices.

2 Place the chopped mint, garlic, sugar and yogurt in a bowl. Stir well to combine.

3 Rinse the cucumber in a sieve (strainer) under cold running water to flush away the salt. Drain well and combine with the yogurt mixture in a serving bowl. Decorate with sprigs of mint. Garnish with paprika, if you wish.

COOK'S TIP

If preparing tzatziki in a hurry, do not salt the cucumber. The cucumber will have a more crunchy texture, and will be slightly less sweet.

Energy 67kcal/279kJ; Protein 4g; Carbohydrate 2.3g, of which sugars 1.6g; Fat 5.3g, of which saturates 2.6g; Cholesterol 0mg; Calcium 107mg; Fibre 0.3g; Sodium 39mg.

Marinated Cucumber Salad

A wonderfully cooling salad for the summer, with the distinctive flavour of fresh dill.

INGREDIENTS

Serves 4–6

2 medium cucumbers
15ml/1 tbsp salt
90g/3½oz/½ cup sugar
175ml/6fl oz/¾ cup dry (hard) cider
15ml/1 tbsp cider vinegar
45ml/3 tbsp chopped fresh dill
ground black pepper

1 Slice the cucumbers thinly and place them in a colander, sprinkling salt between each layer. Put the colander over a bowl and leave to drain for 1 hour.

2 Thoroughly rinse the cucumber under cold running water to remove excess salt, then pat dry with kitchen paper.

3 Gently heat the sugar, cider and vinegar in a pan, until the sugar has dissolved. Remove from the heat and leave to cool. Put the cucumber slices in a bowl, pour over the cider mixture and leave to marinate for 2 hours.

4 Drain the cucumber and sprinkle with the dill and pepper to taste. Mix well and transfer to a serving dish. Chill until ready to serve.

COOK'S TIP

The salad would be a perfect accompaniment for fresh salmon.

Energy 80kcal/336kJ; Protein 1g; Carbohydrate 18g, of which sugars 18g; Fat 0g, of which saturates 0g; Cholesterol 0mg; Calcium 22mg; Fibre 1g; Sodium 988mg.

Flower Garden Salad

Dress a colourful mixture of salad leaves with good olive oil and freshly squeezed lemon juice, then top it with crispy bread crostini.

INGREDIENTS

Serves 4–6

3 thick slices day-old bread, such as ciabatta
120ml/4fl oz/½ cup extra virgin olive oil
1 garlic clove, halved
½ small cos or romaine lettuce
½ small oak-leaf lettuce
25g/1oz rocket (arugula) leaves or salad cress
25g/1oz fresh flat leaf parsley
a small handful of young dandelion leaves
juice of 1 lemon
a few nasturtium leaves and flowers
pansy and pot marigold flowers
sea salt flakes and ground black pepper

1 Cut the slices of bread into 1cm/½in cubes.

2 Heat half the oil gently in a frying pan and fry the bread cubes in it, tossing them until they are well coated and lightly browned. Remove and cool.

3 Rub the inside of a large salad bowl with the cut sides of the garlic clove, then discard. Pour the remaining oil into the bottom of the bowl.

4 Tear all the salad leaves into bitesize pieces and pile them into the bowl with the oil. Season with salt and pepper. Cover and keep chilled until you are ready to serve the salad.

5 To serve, toss the leaves in the oil at the bottom of the bowl, then sprinkle with the lemon juice and toss again. Sprinkle the crostini and the flowers over the top and serve immediately.

Energy 174kcal/722kJ; Protein 2.4g; Carbohydrate 11.3g, of which sugars 1.5g; Fat 13.5g, of which saturates 2g; Cholesterol 0mg; Calcium 38mg; Fibre 0.9g; Sodium 109mg.

Fresh Spinach and Avocado Salad

Young, tender spinach leaves make a change from lettuce. They are delicious served with avocado, cherry tomatoes and radishes in an unusual tofu sauce.

INGREDIENTS

Serves 2–3

1 large avocado
juice of 1 lime
225g/8oz baby spinach leaves
115g/4oz cherry tomatoes
4 spring onions (scallions), sliced
½ cucumber
50g/2oz radishes, sliced

For the dressing
115g/4oz soft silken tofu
45ml/3 tbsp milk
10ml/2 tsp mustard
2.5ml/½ tsp white wine vinegar
cayenne pepper
salt and ground black pepper
radish roses and fresh herb sprigs, to garnish

1 Cut the avocado in half, remove the stone (pit) and strip off the skin. Cut the flesh into slices. Transfer to a plate, drizzle over the lime juice and set aside.

2 Wash and dry the baby spinach leaves. Put them in a mixing bowl.

3 Cut the larger tomatoes in half and add all the tomatoes to the mixing bowl with the spring onions. Cut the cucumber into chunks and add to the bowl with the sliced radishes. Toss gently to combine everything.

COOK'S TIP

Use soft silken tofu rather than the firm block variety. It can be found in most supermarkets in long-life cartons.

4 To make the dressing, put the tofu, milk, mustard, vinegar and a pinch of cayenne in a food processor or blender. Add salt and pepper to taste. Process for 30 seconds, until smooth. Scrape the dressing into a bowl and add a little extra milk if you like a thinner dressing. Sprinkle with a little extra cayenne, garnish with radish roses and herb sprigs and serve separately.

5 Transfer the spinach and tomato mixture to a serving dish, top with the avocado slices and serve with the dressing.

Energy 200kcal/828kJ; Protein 8g; Carbohydrate 6g, of which sugars 5g; Fat 16g, of which saturates 3g; Cholesterol 2mg; Calcium 383mg; Fibre 4g; Sodium 279mg.

Radish, Mango and Apple Salad

Radish is a year-round vegetable and this salad, with its clean, crisp tastes and mellow flavours, can be served at any time of year. Serve with smoked fish, such as rolls of smoked salmon, or with continental ham or salami.

INGREDIENTS

Serves 4

10–15 radishes
1 apple, peeled, cored and thinly sliced
2 celery sticks, thinly sliced
1 small ripe mango
fresh dill sprigs, to garnish

For the dressing
120ml/4fl oz/½ cup sour cream
10ml/2 tsp creamed horseradish
15ml/1 tbsp chopped fresh dill
salt and ground black pepper

1 To prepare the dressing, blend together the sour cream, horseradish and dill in a small bowl and season with a little salt and pepper.

2 Top and tail the radishes and slice them thinly. Put in a bowl together with the apple and celery.

3 Halve the mango lengthways, cutting either side of the stone (pit). Make even, criss-cross cuts through the flesh of each side section and bend it back to separate the cubes. Remove the cubes with a small knife and add to the bowl.

4 Pour the dressing over the vegetables and fruit and stir gently so that all the ingredients are well coated. Garnish with dill sprigs and serve.

Energy 77kcal/324kJ; Protein 1.4g; Carbohydrate 7.6g, of which sugars 7g; Fat 4.9g, of which saturates 3.1g; Cholesterol 0mg; Calcium 44mg; Fibre 1.4g; Sodium 46mg.

Mango, Tomato and Red Onion Salad

This salad makes a delicious appetizer. The under-ripe mango blends well with the tomato.

INGREDIENTS

Serves 4

1 firm under-ripe mango
2 large tomatoes or 1 beef tomato, sliced
½ red onion, sliced into rings
½ cucumber, peeled and thinly sliced

For the dressing
30ml/2 tbsp sunflower or vegetable oil
15ml/1 tbsp lemon juice
1 garlic clove, crushed
2.5ml/½ tsp hot pepper sauce
salt and ground black pepper
snipped chives, to garnish

1 Have the mango lengthways, cutting either side of the stone (pit). Cut the flesh into slices and peel the skin away.

2 Arrange the mango, tomato, onion and cucumber on a large serving plate.

3 Blend the oil, lemon juice, garlic, pepper sauce and seasoning in a blender or food processor, or place in a small screw-top jar and shake vigorously.

4 Pour the dressing over the salad and serve garnished with snipped chives.

Energy 89kcal/369kJ; Protein 1.1g; Carbohydrate 8.6g, of which sugars 7.9g; Fat 5.8g, of which saturates 0.8g; Cholesterol 0mg; Calcium 17mg; Fibre 1.9g; Sodium 7mg.

Orange and Water Chestnut Salad

Crunchy water chestnuts combine with radicchio or red lettuce and oranges in this unusual salad.

INGREDIENTS

Serves 4

1 medium red onion, thinly sliced into rings
2 oranges, peeled and cut into segments
1 can drained water chestnuts, peeled and cut into strips
2 radicchio heads, cored, or 1 red-leaf lettuce, leaves separated
45ml/3 tbsp chopped fresh parsley
45ml/3 tbsp chopped fresh basil
15ml/1 tbsp white wine vinegar
50ml/2fl oz/¼ cup walnut oil
salt and ground black pepper
1 fresh basil sprig, to garnish

1 Put the onion in a colander and sprinkle with 5ml/1 tsp salt. Allow to drain for 15 minutes.

2 In a large mixing bowl combine the oranges and water chestnuts.

3 Spread out the radicchio or red-leaf lettuce leaves in a large, shallow bowl or on a serving platter.

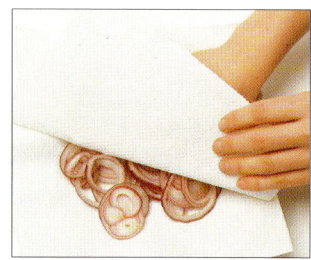

4 Rinse the onion to remove excess salt and dry on kitchen paper. Toss it with the water chestnuts and oranges.

5 Arrange the water chestnut, orange and onion mixture on top of the radicchio or lettuce leaves. Sprinkle with the chopped parsley and basil.

6 Put the vinegar, oil and salt and pepper to taste in a screw-top jar and shake well to combine. Pour the dressing over the salad and serve immediately, garnished with a sprig of basil.

Energy 110kcal/458kJ; Protein 1.5g; Carbohydrate 6.9g, of which sugars 6.6g; Fat 8.8g, of which saturates 0.8g; Cholesterol 0mg; Calcium 59mg; Fibre 2g; Sodium 20mg.

Coleslaw with Pesto Mayonnaise

Both the pesto and the mayonnaise can be made for this dish. However, if time is short, you can buy them ready-prepared and it will taste almost as good. Add the dressing just before serving to keep the cabbage crisp.

INGREDIENTS

Serves 4–6

1 small or ½ medium white cabbage
3–4 carrots, grated
4 spring onions (scallions), finely sliced
25–40g/1–1½oz/¼–⅓ cup pine nuts
15ml/1 tbsp chopped fresh mixed herbs such as parsley, basil, chervil

For the pesto mayonnaise
1 egg yolk
about 10ml/2 tsp lemon juice
200ml/7fl oz/scant 1 cup sunflower oil
10ml/2 tsp pesto
60ml/4 tbsp natural (plain) yogurt
salt and ground black pepper

1 To make the mayonnaise, place the egg yolk in a blender or food processor and process with the lemon juice. With the machine running, very slowly add the oil, pouring it more quickly as the mayonnaise emulsifies.

2 Season to taste with salt and pepper and a little more lemon juice if necessary. Alternatively, you could make the mayonnaise by hand using a balloon whisk.

3 Spoon 75ml/5 tbsp of the mayonnaise into a bowl and stir in the pesto and yogurt, beating well to make a fairly thin dressing.

4 Remove the outer leaves of the cabbage and discard. Using a food processor or a sharp knife, thinly slice the cabbage and place in a large salad bowl.

5 Add the carrots and spring onions, together with the pine nuts and herbs, mixing thoroughly with your hands. Stir the pesto dressing into the salad or serve separately in a small dish.

Energy 292kcal/1202kJ; Protein 2.7g; Carbohydrate 5.1g, of which sugars 5g; Fat 29g, of which saturates 3.5g; Cholesterol 34mg; Calcium 61mg; Fibre 1.8g; Sodium 17mg.

Pepper and Cucumber Salad

Generous quantities of fresh herbs transform ordinary ingredients.

INGREDIENTS

Serves 4

1 yellow or red (bell) pepper
1 large cucumber
4–5 tomatoes
1 bunch spring onions (scallions)
30ml/2 tbsp fresh parsley
30ml/2 tbsp fresh mint
30ml/2 tbsp fresh coriander (cilantro)
2 pitta breads, to serve

For the dressing
2 garlic cloves, crushed
75ml/5 tbsp olive oil
juice of 2 lemons
salt and ground black pepper

1 Slice the pepper, discard the seeds and core. Roughly chop the cucumber and tomatoes. Place in a large salad bowl.

2 Trim and slice the spring onions. Add to the cucumber, tomatoes and pepper. Finely chop the parsley, mint and coriander and add to the bowl. If you have plenty of herbs, you can add as much as you like.

3 To make the dressing, blend the garlic with the olive oil and lemon juice in a jug (pitcher), then season to taste with salt and pepper. Pour the dressing over the salad and toss lightly to mix.

4 Toast the pitta breads in a toaster or under a hot grill (broiler) until crisp and serve them alongside the salad.

VARIATION

If you prefer, make this oriental salad in the traditional way. After toasting the pitta breads, crush them in your hand and then sprinkle over the salad before serving.

Energy 159kcal/656kJ; Protein 1.8g; Carbohydrate 5.8g, of which sugars 5.6g; Fat 14.4g, of which saturates 2.1g; Cholesterol 0mg; Calcium 46mg; Fibre 2.4g; Sodium 13mg.

Guacamole Salsa in Red Leaves

This lovely, light, summery appetizer looks especially attractive arranged in individual cups of radicchio leaves. Serve with chunks of warm garlic bread.

INGREDIENTS

Serves 4

2 tomatoes
15ml/1 tbsp grated onion
1 garlic clove, crushed
1 green chilli, halved, seeded and chopped
2 ripe avocados
30ml/2 tbsp olive oil
2.5ml/½ tsp ground cumin
30ml/2 tbsp chopped fresh coriander (cilantro) or parsley
juice of 1 lime
radicchio leaves
salt and ground black pepper
fresh coriander (cilantro) sprigs, to garnish
crusty garlic bread and lime wedges, to serve

2 Put the tomato flesh into a bowl together with the onion, garlic and chilli. Halve the avocados, remove the stones (pits), then scoop the flesh into the bowl, mashing it with a fork.

3 Add the oil, cumin, coriander or parsley and lime juice. Mix well together, seasoning to taste.

4 Lay the radicchio leaves on a platter and spoon in the salsa. Serve garnished with coriander sprigs and accompanied by garlic bread and lime wedges.

1 Using a sharp knife, slash a small cross on the top of the tomatoes, then place them in a bowl of boiling water for 30 seconds. The skins will slip off easily. Remove the core of each tomato and chop the flesh.

Energy 189kcal/783kJ; Protein 2.4g; Carbohydrate 4.2g, of which sugars 3.2g; Fat 18.1g, of which saturates 3.5g; Cholesterol 0mg; Calcium 50mg; Fibre 3.8g; Sodium 14mg.

Thai Fruit and Vegetable Salad

A cooling, refreshing salad served with a coconut dipping sauce that has a slight kick.

INGREDIENTS

Serves 4–6
1 small pineapple
1 small mango, peeled and sliced
1 green apple, cored and sliced
6 lychees, peeled and stoned (pitted)
115g/4oz French (green) beans, topped, tailed and halved
1 medium red onion, sliced
1 small cucumber, cut into short fingers
115g/4oz/½ cup beansprouts
2 spring onions (scallions), sliced
1 ripe tomato, quartered
225g/8oz cos or iceberg lettuce leaves

For the coconut dipping sauce
30ml/2 tbsp coconut cream
30ml/2 tbsp sugar
75ml/5 tbsp/⅓ cup boiling water
1.5ml/¼ tsp chilli sauce
15ml/1 tbsp Thai fish sauce
juice of 1 lime

1 To make the coconut dipping sauce, put the coconut cream, sugar and boiling water in a screw-top jar. Add the chilli and fish sauces and lime juice and shake.

2 Trim both ends of the pineapple with a serrated knife, then cut away the outer skin.

Remove the central core with an apple corer. Alternatively, cut the pineapple into quarters down the middle and remove the core with a knife. Roughly chop the pineapple and set aside with the other fruits.

3 Bring a small pan of salted water to the boil and cook the beans for 3–4 minutes. Refresh under cold running water and set aside.

4 To serve, arrange the fruits and vegetables in small heaps in a wide, shallow bowl. Serve the coconut sauce separately as a dip.

Sweet Cucumber Cooler

Sweet dipping sauces such as this bring instant relief to the hot chilli flavours of Thai food.

INGREDIENTS

Makes 120ml/4fl oz/½ cup
75ml/5 tbsp water
30ml/2 tbsp sugar
2.5ml/½ tsp salt
15ml/1 tbsp rice or white wine vinegar
¼ small cucumber
2 shallots, or 1 small red onion

1 With a small sharp knife, thinly slice the cucumber and cut into quarters. Thinly slice the shallots or red onion.

2 Measure the water, sugar, salt and vinegar into a stainless steel or enamel pan, bring to the boil and simmer until the sugar has dissolved, for less than 1 minute. Allow to cool.

3 Add the cucumber and shallots or onion and serve at room temperature.

Thai: Energy 159kcal/673kJ; Protein 3.5g; Carbohydrate 32.2g, of which sugars 31g; Fat 2.7g, of which saturates 1.7g; Cholesterol 0mg; Calcium 69mg; Fibre 4.7g; Sodium 188mg.
Cucumber: Energy 147kcal/624kJ; Protein 1.4g; Carbohydrate 37.2g, of which sugars 35.8g; Fat 0.2g, of which saturates 0g; Cholesterol 0mg; Calcium 44mg; Fibre 1.3g; Sodium 6mg.

Tricolour Salad

This can be a simple appetizer if served on individual salad plates, or part of a light buffet meal laid out on a platter. When lightly salted, tomatoes make their own flavoursome dressing with their natural juices.

INGREDIENTS

Serves 4–6

1 small red onion, thinly sliced
6 large full-flavoured tomatoes
extra virgin olive oil, to sprinkle
50g/2oz rocket (arugula) or watercress leaves, roughly chopped
175g/6oz mozzarella cheese, thinly sliced or grated
30ml/2 tbsp pine nuts (optional)
salt and ground black pepper

1 Soak the onion slices in a bowl of cold water for 30 minutes, then drain and pat dry. Skin the tomatoes by cutting a cross in the skin and plunging into boiling water for 30 seconds: the skins can then be easily slipped off.

2 Slice the tomatoes and arrange half on a large platter, or divide them between small plates.

3 Sprinkle liberally with olive oil, then layer with the chopped rocket or watercress, onion slices and cheese, sprinkling over more oil and seasoning well between the layers.

4 Season well to finish and complete with some oil and a good scattering of pine nuts, if you wish. Cover the salad and chill for at least 2 hours before serving.

Energy 480kcal/1992kJ; Protein 16g; Carbohydrate 9g, of which sugars 9g; Fat 42g, of which saturates 14g; Cholesterol 44mg; Calcium 296mg; Fibre 4g; Sodium 323mg.

Tuscan Tuna and Bean Salad

A great store-cupboard (pantry) dish that can be put together in very little time. Served with crusty bread, this salad makes a meal in itself.

INGREDIENTS

Serves 4

1 red onion
30ml/2 tbsp smooth French mustard
300ml/½ pint/1¼ cups olive oil
60ml/4 tbsp white wine vinegar
30ml/2 tbsp chopped fresh parsley
30ml/2 tbsp chopped fresh chives
30ml/2 tbsp chopped fresh tarragon or chervil
400g/14oz can haricot (navy) beans
400g/14oz can kidney beans
225g/8oz canned tuna in oil, drained and lightly flaked
fresh chives and tarragon sprigs, to garnish

1 Chop the red onion finely, using a sharp knife.

2 To make the dressing, whisk together the mustard, oil, vinegar, parsley, chives and tarragon or chervil.

3 Drain the haricot and kidney beans through a colander, then rinse in fresh water.

4 Mix the chopped onion, beans and dressing together thoroughly, then carefully fold in the tuna. Garnish with chives and tarragon sprigs and serve.

Energy 764kcal/3177kJ; Protein 28.5g; Carbohydrate 37.9g, of which sugars 8.9g; Fat 56.5g, of which saturates 8.2g; Cholesterol 25mg; Calcium 182mg; Fibre 13.2g; Sodium 1151mg.

Rocket, Pear and Parmesan Salad

For a sophisticated start to an elaborate meal, try this simple salad of honey-rich pears, fresh Parmesan and aromatic rocket leaves.

INGREDIENTS

Serves 4

3 ripe pears (Williams or Packhams)
10ml/2 tsp lemon juice
45ml/3 tbsp hazelnut or walnut oil
115g/4oz rocket (arugula) leaves
75g/3oz piece Parmesan cheese
ground black pepper

1 Peel and core the pears and slice thickly. Moisten with lemon juice to keep the flesh white.

2 Combine the hazelnut or walnut oil with the pears. Add the rocket leaves and toss.

3 Turn the salad out on to four small plates and top with shavings of Parmesan cheese. Season with pepper and serve.

COOK'S TIP

Parmesan cheese is a delicious main ingredient in a salad. Buy a chunk of fresh Parmesan and shave strips off the side, using a vegetable peeler. The distinctive flavour is quite strong. Store the rest of the Parmesan uncovered in the refrigerator.

Energy 248kcal/1033kJ; Protein 8g; Carbohydrate 16g, of which sugars 16g; Fat 17g, of which saturates 5g; Cholesterol 17mg; Calcium 258mg; Fibre 4g; Sodium 187mg.

Tomato and Feta Cheese Salad

Sweet, sun-ripened tomatoes are rarely more delicious than when served with feta cheese and olive oil.

INGREDIENTS

Serves 4

900g/2lb tomatoes
200g/7oz feta cheese
120ml/4fl oz/½ cup olive oil
12 black olives
4 fresh basil sprigs
ground black pepper

2 Slice the tomatoes thickly and arrange them attractively in a shallow serving dish.

3 Crumble the feta over the tomatoes, sprinkle with oil, then strew with the olives and basil sprigs. Season to taste with pepper and serve at room temperature.

1 Remove the tough cores from the tomatoes, using a small, sharp knife.

COOK'S TIP

Feta cheese has a strong flavour and can be salty. The least salty variety is imported from Greece and Turkey, and is available from specialist delicatessens.

Energy 442kcal/1830kJ; Protein 9g; Carbohydrate 8g, of which sugars 8g; Fat 42g, of which saturates 12g; Cholesterol 35mg; Calcium 201mg; Fibre 3g; Sodium 943mg.

COOKED SIDE SALADS

Simple Cooked Salad

This version of a popular Mediterranean recipe is served as a side dish to accompany a main course.

INGREDIENTS

Serves 4

2 well-flavoured tomatoes, quartered
2 onions, chopped
½ cucumber, halved lengthways, seeded and sliced
1 green (bell) pepper, halved, seeded and chopped

For the dressing
30ml/2 tbsp lemon juice
45ml/3 tbsp olive oil
2 garlic cloves, crushed
30ml/2 tbsp chopped fresh coriander (cilantro)
salt and ground black pepper

1 Put the prepared tomatoes, onions, cucumber and green pepper into a large pan, add 60ml/4 tbsp water and simmer for 5 minutes. Leave to cool.

2 For the dressing, mix together the lemon juice, olive oil and garlic. Strain the vegetables, then transfer to a serving bowl. Pour over the dressing, season to taste with salt and pepper and stir in the chopped coriander.

3 Serve immediately, garnished with coriander sprigs.

Energy 131kcal/540kJ; Protein 2.2g; Carbohydrate 11g, of which sugars 9.1g; Fat 8.9g, of which saturates 1.3g; Cholesterol 0mg; Calcium 55mg; Fibre 3g; Sodium 14mg.

Sweet-and-sour Artichoke Salad

A sweet-and-sour sauce, poured over lightly cooked summer vegetables, works perfectly in this delicious salad.

INGREDIENTS

Serves 4

6 small globe artichokes
juice of 1 lemon
30ml/2 tbsp olive oil
2 medium onions, roughly chopped
175g/6oz/1½ cups fresh or frozen broad (fava) beans (shelled weight)
175g/6oz/1½ cups fresh or frozen peas (shelled weight)
salt and ground black pepper
fresh mint leaves, to garnish

For the sweet-and-sour sauce
120ml/4fl oz/½ cup white wine vinegar
15ml/1 tbsp caster (superfine) sugar
a handful of fresh mint leaves, roughly torn

1 Peel the outer leaves from the artichokes and discard. Cut the artichokes into quarters and place them in a bowl of water with the lemon juice.

2 Heat the olive oil in a large pan and add the onions. Cook until the onions are golden. Add the beans and stir, then drain the artichokes and add to the pan.

3 Pour in about 300ml/½ pint/ 1¼ cups water and cook, covered, for 10–15 minutes more.

4 Add the peas, season with salt and pepper and cook for a further 5 minutes, stirring from time to time, until the vegetables are tender. Strain through a sieve (strainer) or colander and place all the vegetables in a bowl. Leave to cool, then cover with clear film (plastic wrap) and chill.

5 To make the sweet-and-sour sauce, mix all the ingredients in a small pan. Heat gently for 2–3 minutes, until the sugar has dissolved. Simmer gently for about 5 minutes, stirring occasionally. Leave to cool. To serve, drizzle the sauce over the vegetables and garnish with mint leaves.

Energy 172kcal/717kJ; Protein 8g; Carbohydrate 21g, of which sugars 10.8g; Fat 6.8g, of which saturates 1g; Cholesterol 0mg; Calcium 106mg; Fibre 7.3g; Sodium 82mg .

Tomato, Savory and French Bean Salad

Savory and beans could have been invented for each other. This salad mixes them with ripe tomatoes, making a superb accompaniment for cold meats.

INGREDIENTS

Serves 4

450g/1lb French (green) beans
1kg/2¼lb ripe tomatoes
3 spring onions (scallions), roughly sliced
15ml/1 tbsp pine nuts
4 fresh savory sprigs

For the dressing
30ml/2 tbsp extra virgin olive oil
juice of 1 lime
75g/3oz Dolcelatte cheese
1 garlic clove, peeled and crushed
salt and ground black pepper

1 Prepare the dressing first so that it can stand for a while before use. Place all the dressing ingredients in the bowl of a food processor, season to taste and blend until the cheese is finely chopped and you have a smooth dressing. Pour it into a jug (pitcher).

2 Top and tail the beans, and boil in salted water until they are just cooked.

3 Drain the beans in a sieve (strainer) and run cold water over them until they have completely cooled. Slice the tomatoes, or, if they are fairly small, cut them into quarters.

4 Toss the beans, tomatoes and spring onions. Pour on the dressing, sprinkle the pine nuts and savory sprigs over the top and serve immediately.

Squash à la Grecque

This recipe, usually made with mushrooms, also works well with patty-pan squash. Make sure that you cook the baby squash until they are quite tender, so they absorb the delicious flavours of the marinade.

INGREDIENTS

Serves 4

175g/6oz patty-pan squash
250ml/8fl oz/1 cup white wine
juice of 2 lemons
1 fresh thyme sprig
1 bay leaf, plus extra to garnish
small bunch of fresh chervil,
 roughly chopped
1.5ml/¼ tsp crushed coriander seeds
1.5ml/¼ tsp crushed black peppercorns
75ml/5 tbsp olive oil
extra bay leaves, to garnish

1 Blanch the patty-pan squash in boiling water for 3 minutes, then refresh them in cold water.

2 Place all the remaining ingredients in a pan, add 150ml/¼ pint/⅔ cup water and simmer for 10 minutes, covered. Add the squash and cook for 10 minutes until they are tender. Remove with a slotted spoon and set aside.

3 Reduce the liquid by boiling it hard for 10 minutes. Strain through a sieve (strainer) and pour it over the squash. Leave until cool for the flavours to be absorbed.

4 Serve cold, garnished with bay leaves.

Energy 171kcal/704kJ; Protein 0.4g; Carbohydrate 1.4g, of which sugars 1.1g; Fat 13.8g, of which saturates 2g; Cholesterol 0mg; Calcium 18mg; Fibre 0.5g; Sodium 3mg .

Warm Broad Bean and Feta Salad

This medley of fresh-tasting salad ingredients is lovely warm or cold as an appetizer or accompaniment to a main course.

INGREDIENTS

Serves 4–6

900g/2lb broad (fava) beans, shelled, or 350g/12oz shelled frozen beans
60ml/4 tbsp olive oil
175g/6oz fresh plum tomatoes, halved, or quartered if large
4 garlic cloves, crushed
115g/4oz firm feta cheese, cut into chunks
45ml/3 tbsp chopped fresh dill
12 black olives
salt and ground black pepper
chopped fresh dill, to garnish

1 Cook the broad beans in boiling, salted water until just tender. Drain and set aside.

2 Meanwhile, heat the olive oil in a large, heavy frying pan and add the tomatoes and garlic. Cook for about 5 minutes, until the tomatoes are beginning to change colour.

3 Add the feta to the pan and toss the ingredients together for 1 minute. Mix with the drained beans, dill, olives and salt and pepper. Serve garnished with chopped dill.

COOK'S TIP

Plum tomatoes are now widely available fresh as well as tinned in supermarkets. Their deep red, oval shapes are very attractive in salads and they have a sweet, rich flavour.

Halloumi and Grape Salad

In this recipe firm, salty halloumi cheese is fried and then tossed with sweet, juicy grapes which really complement its distinctive flavour.

INGREDIENTS

Serves 4

150g/5oz mixed green salad leaves
75g/3oz seedless green grapes
75g/3oz seedless black grapes
250g/9oz halloumi cheese
45ml/3 tbsp olive oil
fresh young thyme leaves or fresh dill, to garnish

For the dressing
60ml/4 tbsp olive oil
15ml/1 tbsp lemon juice
2.5ml/½ tsp caster (superfine) sugar
15ml/1 tbsp chopped fresh thyme or dill
salt and ground black pepper

1 To make the dressing, mix together the olive oil, lemon juice and sugar. Season with salt and pepper. Stir in the chopped thyme or dill and set aside.

2 Toss together the salad leaves and the green and black grapes, then transfer to a large serving plate.

3 Thinly slice the cheese. Heat the oil in a large frying pan. Add the cheese and fry briefly until golden on the underside. Turn the cheese with a fish slice or metal spatula and cook the other side.

4 Arrange the cheese over the salad. Pour over the dressing and garnish with sprigs of fresh thyme or dill.

Bean: Energy 172kcal/715kJ; Protein 7.8g; Carbohydrate 7.5g, of which sugars 1.4g; Fat 12.5g, of which saturates 3.9g; Cholesterol 13mg; Calcium 108mg; Fibre 4.2g; Sodium 469mg.
Halloumi: Energy 362kcal/1497kJ; Protein 12.1g; Carbohydrate 6.4g, of which sugars 6.4g; Fat 32.2g, of which saturates 11.4g; Cholesterol 36mg; Calcium 242mg; Fibre 0.6g; Sodium 249mg.

Rocket and Goat's Cheese Salad

For this recipe, look out for a cylinder-shaped goat's cheese or for small rolls that can be cut into halves, weighing about 50g/2oz. Serve as an appetizer or a lunch.

INGREDIENTS

Serves 4

15ml/1 tbsp olive oil
15ml/1 tbsp vegetable oil
4 slices French bread
225g/8oz cylinder-shaped goat's cheese
a generous handfuls of rocket (arugula)
115g/4oz frisée leaves
salt and ground black pepper

For the sauce
45ml/3 tbsp apricot jam
60ml/4 tbsp white wine
5ml/1 tsp Dijon mustard

For the dressing
45ml/3 tbsp walnut oil
15ml/1 tbsp lemon juice

1 Heat the olive oil and vegetable oil in a frying pan and fry the slices of French bread on one side only, until lightly golden. Transfer to a plate lined with kitchen paper.

2 To make the sauce, heat the jam in a small pan until warm but not boiling. Push through a sieve (strainer) into a clean pan, to remove the pieces of fruit, then stir in the white wine and mustard. Heat gently and keep warm until ready to serve.

3 Blend the walnut oil and lemon juice and season with a little salt and pepper.

4 Preheat the grill (broiler) a few minutes before serving the salad. Cut the goat's cheese in 50g/2oz rounds and place each piece on a piece of French bread, untoasted side up. Place under the grill and cook for 3–4 minutes, until the cheese melts.

5 Toss the rocket and frisée leaves in the walnut oil dressing and arrange attractively on four individual serving plates.

6 When the cheese croûtons are ready, arrange on each plate, pour over a little of the apricot sauce and serve.

Energy 453kcal/1890kJ; Protein 15.9g; Carbohydrate 31.7g, of which sugars 10.4g; Fat 29.3g, of which saturates 11.7g; Cholesterol 52mg; Calcium 139mg; Fibre 1.4g; Sodium 592mg.

Russian Salad

Russian salad became fashionable in the hotel dining rooms of the 1920s and 1930s. Originally it consisted of lightly-cooked vegetables, egg, shellfish and mayonnaise. Today we find it diced in plastic pots in supermarkets. This version recalls better days and plays on the theme of the Fabergé egg.

INGREDIENTS

Serves 4

115g/4oz large button (white) mushrooms
120ml/4fl oz/½ cup mayonnaise
15ml/1 tbsp lemon juice
350g/12oz shelled cooked prawns (shrimp)
1 large gherkin, chopped, or
 30ml/2 tbsp capers
115g/4oz broad (fava) beans
 (shelled weight)
115g/4oz small new potatoes, scrubbed
 or scraped
115g/4oz young carrots, trimmed
 and peeled
115g/4oz baby corn
115g/4oz baby turnips, trimmed
15ml/1 tbsp olive oil
4 eggs, hard-boiled and shelled
25g/1oz canned anchovy fillets, drained
 and cut into fine strips
ground paprika
salt, and ground black pepper

1 Slice the mushrooms thinly, then cut into matchsticks. Combine the mayonnaise and lemon juice. Fold the mayonnaise into the mushrooms, then add the prawns, gherkin or capers, and seasoning to taste.

2 Bring a large pan of salted water to the boil, add the broad beans and cook for 3 minutes, until tender. Drain and cool under running water, then pinch the beans between thumb and forefinger to release them from their tough skins.

3 Boil the potatoes for about 15 minutes, and the remaining vegetables for 6 minutes. Drain and cool under running water. Moisten the vegetables with oil and divide between four shallow bowls.

4 Spoon on the prawn mixture and place a hard-boiled egg in the centre. Decorate the egg with strips of anchovy, sprinkle with paprika and serve.

Poached Egg Salad with Croûtons

Soft poached eggs, hot garlic croûtons and cool, crisp salad leaves make a great combination.

INGREDIENTS

Serves 2

½ small loaf white bread
75ml/5 tbsp/⅓ cup extra virgin olive oil
2 eggs
115g/4oz mixed salad leaves
2 garlic cloves, crushed
7.5ml/1½ tbsp white wine vinegar
25g/1oz piece Parmesan cheese
ground black pepper

1 Remove the crust from the loaf of bread. Cut the bread into 2.5cm/1in cubes.

2 Heat 30ml/2 tbsp of the oil in a frying pan. Cook the bread for about 5 minutes, tossing the cubes occasionally, until they are golden brown.

3 Meanwhile, bring a pan of water to the boil. Carefully slide in the eggs, one at a time. Gently poach the eggs for 4 minutes until lightly cooked.

4 Divide the salad leaves between two plates. Remove the croûtons from the frying pan and arrange them over the leaves. Wipe the frying pan clean with kitchen paper.

5 Heat the remaining oil in the pan, add the garlic and vinegar and cook over a high heat for 1 minute. Pour the warm dressing over each salad.

6 Place a poached egg on each plate of salad. Scatter with shavings of Parmesan and a little black pepper.

COOK'S TIP

Add a dash of vinegar to the water before poaching the eggs. This helps to keep the whites together and produce a neat egg.

To ensure that a poached egg has a good shape, swirl the water with a spoon, whirlpool-fashion, before sliding in the egg.

Before serving trim the edges of the egg for a neat finish.

Energy 707kcal/2947kJ; Protein 22g; Carbohydrate 44g, of which sugars 4g; Fat 51g, of which saturates 10g; Cholesterol 243mg; Calcium 287mg; Fibre 8g; Sodium 669mg.

Roasted Pepper and Tomato Salad

A lovely, colourful recipe which perfectly combines several red ingredients. Eat this dish at room temperature with a green salad.

INGREDIENTS

Serves 4

3 red (bell) peppers
6 large plum tomatoes
2.5ml/½ tsp dried red chilli flakes
1 red onion, finely sliced
3 garlic cloves, finely chopped
grated rind and juice of 1 lemon
45ml/3 tbsp chopped fresh
  flat leaf parsley
30ml/2 tbsp extra virgin olive oil
salt and ground black pepper
black and green olives and extra chopped
  flat leaf parsley, to garnish

1 Preheat the oven to 220°C/ 425°F/Gas 7. Place the peppers on a baking sheet and roast, turning occasionally, for 10 minutes or until the skins are almost blackened. Add the tomatoes to the baking sheet and bake for 5 minutes more.

2 Place the peppers in a strong plastic bag, close the top loosely, trapping in the steam. Set aside, with the tomatoes, until cool enough to handle.

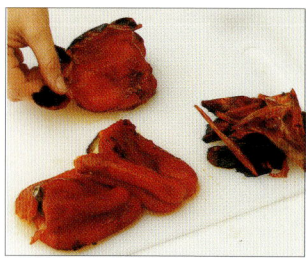

3 Carefully pull the skin off the peppers. Remove the core and seeds, then chop the peppers and tomatoes roughly and place in a mixing bowl.

4 Add the chilli flakes, onion, garlic, lemon rind and juice. Sprinkle over the parsley. Mix well, then transfer to a serving dish. Sprinkle with salt and black pepper, drizzle over the oil and scatter the olives and extra parsley over the top. Serve at room temperature.

Marinated Courgettes

This is a simple vegetable dish which uses the best of the season's courgettes. It can be eaten either hot or cold.

INGREDIENTS

Serves 4

4 courgettes (zucchini)
60ml/4 tbsp extra virgin olive oil
30ml/2 tbsp chopped fresh mint
30ml/2 tbsp white wine vinegar
salt and ground black pepper
fresh mint leaves, to garnish
wholemeal (whole-wheat) Italian bread
  and green olives, to serve

1 Cut the courgettes into thin slices. Heat 30ml/2 tbsp of the oil in a wide, heavy pan.

2 Fry the courgettes in batches, for 4–6 minutes, until tender and brown around the edges. Transfer the courgettes to a serving bowl. Season well with salt and ground black pepper.

3 Heat the remaining oil in the pan, then add the chopped mint and vinegar and let it bubble for a few seconds. Pour the mixture over the courgettes.

4 Marinate for 1 hour, then serve garnished with mint leaves and accompanied by bread and olives.

Pepper: Energy 122kcal/510kJ; Protein 2.5g; Carbohydrate 14.3g, of which sugars 13.5g; Fat 6.5g, of which saturates 1.1g; Cholesterol 0mg; Calcium 24mg; Fibre 3.8g; Sodium 18mg.
Courgettes: Energy 155kcal/638kJ; Protein 2g; Carbohydrate 2g, of which sugars 2g; Fat 15g, of which saturates 2g; Cholesterol 0mg; Calcium 14mg; Fibre 2.2g; Sodium 114mg.

Green Bean and Sweet Red Pepper Salad

A galaxy of colour and texture, with a jolt of heat from the chilli, will make this a favourite salad.

INGREDIENTS

Serves 4

350g/12oz cooked green beans, quartered
2 red (bell) peppers, seeded and chopped
2 spring onions (scallions), chopped
1 or more drained pickled serrano chillies, well rinsed, seeded and chopped
1 iceberg lettuce, coarsely shredded, or mixed salad leaves
green olives, to garnish

For the dressing
45ml/3 tbsp red wine vinegar
135ml/9 tbsp olive oil
salt and ground black pepper

1 Combine the green beans, peppers, spring onions and chilli(es) in a salad bowl.

2 To make the dressing, pour the vinegar into a bowl or jug (pitcher). Add salt and pepper to taste, then gradually whisk in the olive oil until well combined and emulsified.

3 Pour the dressing over the prepared vegetables and toss lightly together to combine and coat thoroughly.

4 Line a large serving platter with the shredded lettuce or mixed salad leaves and arrange the vegetable mixture attractively on top. Garnish with olives and serve.

Energy 362kcal/1498kJ; Protein 3g; Carbohydrate 10g, of which sugars 8g; Fat 34g, of which saturates 5g; Cholesterol 0mg; Calcium 85mg; Fibre 3g; Sodium 63mg.

Green Green Salad

You could make this dish at any time of the year with frozen vegetables and still create a pretty salad.

INGREDIENTS

Serves 4

175g/6oz shelled broad (fava) beans
115g/4oz French (green) beans, quartered
115g/4oz mangetouts (snow peas)
8–10 small fresh mint leaves
3 spring onions (scallions), chopped

For the dressing
60ml/4 tbsp green olive oil
15ml/1 tbsp cider vinegar
15ml/1 tbsp chopped fresh mint
1 garlic clove, crushed
salt and ground black pepper

1 Plunge the broad beans into a pan of boiling water and bring back to the boil. Remove from the heat immediately and plunge into cold water. Drain. Repeat with the French beans.

2 In a large mixing bowl, gently mix together the blanched broad beans and French beans with the raw mangetouts, mint leaves and spring onions, until well combined.

3 In another mixing bowl, whisk together the olive oil, vinegar, chopped or dried mint, garlic and seasoning. Pour the dressing over the salad and toss well. Chill until ready to serve.

COOK'S TIP

Frozen broad (fava) beans are a good stand-by, but for this salad it is worth shelling fresh beans for the extra flavour.

Energy 153kcal/637kJ; Protein 5.3g; Carbohydrate 7.6g, of which sugars 2.6g; Fat 11.5g, of which saturates 1.7g; Cholesterol 0mg; Calcium 53mg; Fibre 4.3g; Sodium 5mg.

Leek and Egg Salad

Smooth-textured leeks are especially delicious warm when partnered with an earthy-rich sauce of parsley, olive oil and walnuts. Serve as a side salad with grilled (broiler) or poached fish and new potatoes.

INGREDIENTS

Serves 4

675g/1½lb young leeks
1 egg
fresh parsley sprigs, to garnish

For the dressing
25g/1oz fresh parsley
30ml/2 tbsp olive oil
juice of ½ lemon
50g/2oz/½ cup broken walnuts, toasted
5ml/1 tsp caster (superfine) sugar
salt and ground black pepper

2 Lower the egg into boiling water and cook for 12 minutes. Cool under running water, shell and set aside.

5 Adjust the consistency with about 90ml/6 tbsp water. Add the sugar and season to taste with salt and pepper.

3 To make the dressing, finely chop the parsley in a food processor.

6 Place the leeks on an attractive plate, then spoon on the sauce. Finely grate the hard-boiled egg and scatter over the sauce. Garnish with the reserved parsley sprigs and serve while the leeks are still warm.

1 Bring a pan of salted water to the boil. Cut the leeks into 10cm/4in lengths and rinse well to flush out any grit or soil. Cook the leeks for 8 minutes. Drain and part-cool under running water.

4 Add the olive oil, lemon juice and toasted walnuts. Blend for 1–2 minutes, until smooth.

Energy 197kcal/817kJ; Protein 6.3g; Carbohydrate 6.5g, of which sugars 5.2g; Fat 16.4g, of which saturates 2.1g; Cholesterol 48mg; Calcium 73mg; Fibre 4.5g; Sodium 24mg .

Winter Vegetable Salad

This simple side salad is made with leeks, cauliflower and celery, flavoured with white wine, herbs and juniper berries.

INGREDIENTS

Serves 4

175ml/6fl oz/¾ cup white wine
5ml/1 tsp olive oil
30ml/2 tbsp lemon juice
2 bay leaves
1 fresh thyme sprig
4 juniper berries
450g/1lb leeks, trimmed and cut into 2.5cm/1in lengths
1 small cauliflower, broken into florets
4 celery sticks, sliced on the diagonal
30ml/2 tbsp chopped fresh parsley
salt and ground black pepper

1 Put the wine, olive oil, lemon juice, bay leaves, thyme and juniper berries into a large, heavy pan and bring to the boil. Cover the pan and leave to simmer for 20 minutes.

2 Add the leeks, cauliflower and celery. Simmer very gently for 5–6 minutes, or until just tender.

3 Remove the vegetables with a slotted spoon and transfer them to a serving dish. Boil the cooking liquid for 15–20 minutes, or until reduced by half. Strain through a sieve (strainer).

4 Stir the parsley into the liquid and season to taste. Pour over the vegetables and leave to cool. Chill in the refrigerator for at least 1 hour before serving.

VARIATION

Change the vegetables used for this salad according to the season.

Energy 110kcal/460kJ; Protein 6.9g; Carbohydrate 8g, of which sugars 6.5g; Fat 2.7g, of which saturates 0.5g; Cholesterol 0mg; Calcium 99mg; Fibre 5.8g; Sodium 44mg.

Avocado and Smoked Fish Salad

Avocado and smoked fish make a good combination and, flavoured with herbs and spices, create a delectable salad.

INGREDIENTS

Serves 4

2 avocados
½ cucumber
15ml/1 tbsp lemon juice
2 firm tomatoes
1 green chilli
salt and ground black pepper

For the fish

15g/½oz/1 tbsp butter or margarine
½ onion, finely sliced
5ml/1 tsp mustard seeds
225g/8oz smoked mackerel, flaked
30ml/2 tbsp fresh chopped
   coriander (cilantro) leaves
2 firm tomatoes, peeled and chopped
15ml/1 tbsp lemon juice

1 For the fish, melt the butter or margarine in a frying pan, add the onion and mustard seeds and fry for about 5 minutes, until the onion is soft.

2 Add the mackerel, coriander, tomatoes and lemon juice and cook over a low heat for 2–3 minutes. Remove from the heat and leave to cool.

3 To make the salad, slice the avocados and cucumber thinly. Place together in a bowl and sprinkle with the lemon juice. Slice the tomatoes and seed them. Finely chop the chilli.

4 Place the fish mixture in the centre of a serving plate.

5 Arrange the avocados, cucumber and tomatoes decoratively around the outside. Alternatively, spoon a quarter of the fish mixture on to each of four serving plates and divide the avocados, cucumber and tomatoes equally between them. Sprinkle with the chopped chilli and a little salt and pepper and serve.

VARIATION

Smoked haddock or cod can also be used in this salad, or a mixture of mackerel and haddock.

Energy 386kcal/1596kJ; Protein 12.8g; Carbohydrate 4.6g, of which sugars 3.1g; Fat 35.2g, of which saturates 8.6g; Cholesterol 67mg; Calcium 32mg; Fibre 3.4g; Sodium 455mg.

Tomato and Bread Salad

This salad, which conveniently uses up stale bread, is best made with flavourful, sun-ripened tomatoes.

INGREDIENTS

Serves 4

400g/14oz stale white or brown bread
4 large tomatoes
1 large red onion or 6 spring onions (scallions)
a few fresh basil leaves, to garnish

For the dressing
60ml/4 tbsp extra virgin olive oil
30ml/2 tbsp white wine vinegar
salt and ground black pepper

1 Cut the bread into thick slices. Place in a shallow bowl and soak with cold water. Leave for at least 30 minutes.

2 Cut the tomatoes into bitesize chunks and place in a serving bowl. Finely slice the onion or spring onions and add them to the tomatoes.

3 Squeeze as much water out of the bread as possible and add it to the vegetables.

4 To make the dressing, mix the oil and vinegar. Season with salt and pepper, pour over the salad and mix well.

5 Garnish with the basil leaves. Allow to stand in a cool place for at least 2 hours to enable the flavours to develop before serving.

Grilled Pepper Salad

Ideally this salad should be made with a combination of red and yellow peppers for the most jewel-like, colourful effect and the sweetest flavour.

INGREDIENTS

Serves 6

4 large (bell) peppers, red or yellow or a combination of both
30ml/2 tbsp capers, rinsed
18–20 black or green olives

For the dressing
90ml/6 tbsp extra virgin olive oil
2 garlic cloves, finely chopped
30ml/2 tbsp balsamic or wine vinegar
salt and ground black pepper

1 Place the peppers under a hot grill (broiler) and turn occasionally until they are black and blistered on all sides. Remove from the heat, place in a strong plastic bag and close the top loosely. Set aside until they are cool enough to handle. Carefully peel the peppers.

2 Cut the peppers into quarters. Remove and discard the stems and seeds.

3 Cut the peppers into strips, and arrange them on a serving dish. Distribute the capers and olives evenly over the peppers.

4 For the dressing, mix the oil and garlic in a small bowl, crushing the garlic with a spoon to release the flavour. Mix in the vinegar and season with salt and pepper. Pour over the salad, mix well and allow to stand for at least 30 minutes before serving.

Tomato: Energy 354kcal/1496kJ; Protein 9.4g; Carbohydrate 52.9g, of which sugars 6.1g; Fat 13.3g, of which saturates 1.7g; Cholesterol 0mg; Calcium 123mg; Fibre 2.7g; Sodium 530mg.
Pepper: Energy 113kcal/469kJ; Protein 2.2g; Carbohydrate 12.3g, of which sugars 11.9g; Fat 6.4g, of which saturates 1g; Cholesterol 0mg; Calcium 19mg; Fibre 3.3g; Sodium 15mg.

Frisée Salad with Bacon

This delicious salad may also be sprinkled with chopped hard-boiled egg.

INGREDIENTS

Serves 4

50g/2oz white bread
225g/8oz frisée or escarole leaves
75–90ml/5–6 tbsp extra virgin olive oil
175g/6oz piece smoked bacon, diced, or
   6 thick-cut smoked bacon rashers
   (strips), cut crossways into thin strips
1 small garlic clove, finely chopped
15ml/1 tbsp red wine vinegar
10ml/2 tsp Dijon mustard
salt and ground black pepper

1 Cut the bread into small cubes. Tear the frisée or escarole into bitesize pieces and put into a salad bowl.

2 Heat 15ml/1 tbsp of the oil in a medium, non-stick frying pan over a medium-low heat and add the bacon. Fry gently until well browned, stirring occasionally. Remove the bacon with a slotted spoon and drain on kitchen paper.

3 Add another 30ml/2 tbsp of the oil to the pan and fry the bread cubes over a medium-high heat, turning frequently, until evenly browned.

4 Remove the bread cubes with a slotted spoon and drain on kitchen paper. Discard any remaining fat.

5 Stir the garlic, vinegar and mustard into the pan with the remaining oil and heat until just warm, whisking to combine.

6 Season to taste, then pour the dressing over the salad and sprinkle with the fried bacon and croûtons. Serve immediately while still warm.

Energy 226kcal/940kJ; Protein 10g; Carbohydrate 8.1g, of which sugars 1.5g; Fat 17.3g, of which saturates 3.2g; Cholesterol 14mg; Calcium 38mg; Fibre 0.8g; Sodium 721mg.

Asparagus and Orange Salad

A slightly unusual combination of ingredients with a simple dressing based on good-quality olive oil.

INGREDIENTS

Serves 4

225g/8oz asparagus, trimmed and cut into 5cm/2 in lengths
2 large oranges
2 well-flavoured tomatoes, cut into eighths
50g/2oz cos or romaine lettuce leaves
30ml/2 tbsp extra virgin olive oil
2.5ml/½ tsp sherry vinegar
salt and ground black pepper

1 Cook the asparagus in boiling, salted water for 3–4 minutes, until just tender. The cooking time may vary according to the size of the asparagus stems. Drain and refresh under cold water, then leave on one side to cool.

2 Grate the rind from half an orange and reserve. Peel both the oranges and cut into segments. Squeeze the juice from the membrane and reserve.

3 Put the asparagus, orange segments, tomatoes and lettuce into a salad bowl.

4 Combine the oil and vinegar. Add 15ml/1 tbsp of the orange juice and 5ml/1 tsp of the rind.

5 Season with salt and pepper. Just before serving, pour the dressing over the salad and mix gently to coat all the ingredients.

Energy 92kcal/384kJ; Protein 2.6g; Carbohydrate 7.1g, of which sugars 7.1g; Fat 6.1g, of which saturates 0.9g; Cholesterol 0mg; Calcium 46mg; Fibre 2.4g; Sodium 8mg.

Hard-boiled Eggs with Tuna Sauce

A tasty tuna mayonnaise poured over hard-boiled eggs makes a nourishing first course that is quick and easy to prepare.

INGREDIENTS

Serves 6

6 large (US extra large) eggs
200g/7oz can tuna in olive oil
3 canned anchovy fillets
15ml/1 tbsp capers, drained
30ml/2 tbsp lemon juice
60ml/4 tbsp olive oil
salt and ground black pepper
capers and anchovy fillets, to garnish

For the mayonnaise
1 egg yolk
5ml/1 tsp Dijon mustard
5ml/1 tsp white wine vinegar or
    lemon juice
150ml/¼ pint/⅔ cup olive oil

1 Boil the eggs for 12–14 minutes. Drain them under cold water. Shell the eggs carefully and set aside.

2 Make the mayonnaise by whisking the egg yolk, mustard and vinegar or lemon juice together in a small bowl.

3 Whisk in the oil a few drops at a time until 3–4 tablespoons have been incorporated. Pour in the remaining oil in a slow stream, whisking constantly. It is easiest if you use a blender.

4 Place the tuna with its oil, the anchovies, capers, lemon juice and olive oil in a blender or food processor. Process until the mixture is smooth.

5 Fold the tuna mixture carefully into the mayonnaise. Season with black pepper to taste, and salt if necessary. Chill for at least 1 hour.

6 Cut the eggs in half lengthways. Arrange on a serving platter. Spoon on the mayonnaise and garnish with capers and anchovy fillets. Serve chilled.

Energy 369kcal/1529kJ; Protein 16.6g; Carbohydrate 0.1g, of which sugars 0.1g; Fat 33.8g, of which saturates 5.8g; Cholesterol 242mg; Calcium 46mg; Fibre 0g; Sodium 311mg.

Artichoke and Egg Salad

Artichoke hearts are best when cut from fresh artichokes, but can also be bought frozen. This salad is easily assembled for a light lunch.

INGREDIENTS

Serves 4

4 large artichokes or 4 frozen artichoke hearts, thawed
½ lemon
4 eggs, hard-boiled and shelled
fresh parsley sprigs, to garnish

For the mayonnaise
1 egg yolk
10ml/2 tsp Dijon mustard
15ml/1 tbsp white wine vinegar
250ml/8fl oz/1 cup olive or vegetable oil
30ml/2 tbsp chopped fresh parsley
salt and ground black pepper

1 If using fresh artichokes, wash them. Squeeze the lemon and put the juice and the squeezed half in a bowl of cold water.

2 Prepare the artichokes one at a time. Cut off only the tip from the stem. Peel the stem with a small knife, pulling upwards towards the leaves. Pull off the small leaves around the stem and continue snapping off the upper part of the dark outer leaves until you reach the taller inner leaves. Cut the tops off the leaves with a sharp knife. Place the artichoke in the acidulated water. Repeat with the other artichokes.

3 Boil or steam fresh artichokes until they are just tender (when a leaf comes away quite easily when pulled). Cook frozen artichoke hearts according to the packet instructions, until tender. Allow to cool.

4 To make the mayonnaise, combine the egg yolk, mustard and vinegar in a large mixing bowl. Add salt and pepper to taste. Add the oil in a thin stream while beating vigorously with a wire whisk or a with a hand-held blender.

5 When the mixture is thick and smooth, stir in the chopped parsley. Blend well. Cover and refrigerate until needed.

6 If using fresh artichokes, pull off the leaves. Cut the stems off level with the base. Scrape off the hairy "choke" with a knife or spoon, removing all the fine hairs.

7 Cut the eggs and artichokes into wedges. Arrange on a serving plate, spoon the parsley mayonnaise over the top, garnish with parsley sprigs and serve.

Energy 493kcal/2034kJ; Protein 7.9g; Carbohydrate 1.3g, of which sugars 1.2g; Fat 51g, of which saturates 7.1g; Cholesterol 241mg; Calcium 100mg; Fibre 1.7g; Sodium 137mg.

Panzanella

In this lively salad, a sweet, tangy blend of tomato juice, rich olive oil and red wine vinegar is soaked up by a colourful mixture of roasted peppers, anchovies and toasted ciabatta bread.

INGREDIENTS

Serves 4–6

225g/8oz ciabatta (about 2/3 loaf)
150ml/1/4 pint/2/3 cup olive oil
3 red and 3 yellow (bell) peppers
50g/2oz can anchovy fillets, drained
675g/1 1/2lb ripe plum tomatoes
4 garlic cloves, crushed
60ml/4 tbsp red wine vinegar
50g/2oz capers
115g/4oz/1 cup pitted black olives
salt and ground black pepper
fresh basil leaves, to garnish

1 Preheat the oven to 200°C/400°F/Gas 6. Cut the ciabatta into 2cm/3/4in chunks and drizzle with 50ml/2fl oz/1/4 cup of the olive oil. Grill (broil) lightly until just golden.

2 Put the peppers on a foil-lined baking sheet and bake for about 45 minutes, until the skins begin to char. Remove the peppers from the oven, place in a strong plastic bag, close the end and leave to cool slightly.

3 Pull the skins off the peppers and cut them into quarters, discarding the stalk ends and seeds. Roughly chop the anchovies and set aside.

4 To make the tomato dressing, peel and halve the tomatoes. Scoop the seeds and pulp into a sieve (strainer) set over a bowl. Using the back of a spoon, press the tomato pulp in the sieve to extract as much juice as possible. Discard the pulp and add the remaining oil, the garlic and vinegar to the juices.

5 Layer the toasted ciabatta, peppers, tomatoes, anchovies, capers and olives in a large salad bowl. Season the tomato dressing and pour it over the salad.

6 Leave to stand for about 30 minutes. Serve garnished with plenty of basil leaves.

Radicchio, Artichoke and Walnut Salad

The distinctive, earthy taste of Jerusalem artichokes makes a lovely contrast to the sharp freshness of radicchio and lemon. Serve warm or cold as an accompaniment to grilled (broiled) steak or barbecued meats.

INGREDIENTS

Serves 4

1 large radicchio or 150g/5oz radicchio leaves
40g/1 1/2oz/1/3 cup walnut pieces
45ml/3 tbsp walnut oil
500g/1 1/4lb Jerusalem artichokes
thinly pared rind and juice of 1 lemon
coarse sea salt and ground black pepper
fresh flat leaf parsley, to garnish

1 If using a whole radicchio, cut it into 8–10 wedges. Put the wedges or leaves in a flameproof dish. Scatter over the walnuts, then spoon over the oil and season to taste with salt and pepper. Grill (broil) for 2–3 minutes, until slightly softened.

2 Peel the artichokes and cut up any large ones so that the pieces are all about the same size. Add the artichokes to a pan of boiling salted water with half the lemon juice and cook for 5–7 minutes, until tender. Drain. Preheat the grill (broiler) to high.

3 Toss the artichokes into the salad with the remaining lemon juice and the pared rind. Season with coarse salt and pepper. Grill until beginning to brown.

4 Serve immediately, garnished with torn pieces of parsley, if you like.

Panzanella: Energy 237kcal/987kJ; Protein 6.3g; Carbohydrate 15.4g, of which sugars 3.5g; Fat 17.1g, of which saturates 4.5g; Cholesterol 11mg; Calcium 105mg; Fibre 1.3g; Sodium 213mg.
Radicchio: Energy 179kcal/739kJ; Protein 2.7g; Carbohydrate 7.3g, of which sugars 7.1g; Fat 15.7g, of which saturates 1.4g; Cholesterol 0mg; Calcium 87mg; Fibre 3.1g; Sodium 21mg.

Egg, Bacon and Avocado Salad

A glorious medley of colours, flavours and textures to delight the eye and the taste buds.

INGREDIENTS

Serves 4

1 large cos or romaine lettuce
8 bacon rashers (strips), fried until crisp
2 large avocados, peeled and diced
6 hard-boiled eggs, chopped
2 beefsteak tomatoes, peeled, seeded and chopped
175g/6oz blue cheese, crumbled

For the dressing
1 garlic clove, crushed
5ml/1 tsp sugar
7.5ml/1½ tsp lemon juice
25ml/1½ tbsp red wine vinegar
120ml/4fl oz/½ cup groundnut (peanut) oil
salt and ground black pepper

1 Slice the lettuce into strips across the leaves. Crumble the fried bacon rashers.

2 To make the dressing, combine all the ingredients in a screw-top jar and shake well. On a large, rectangular or oval platter, spread out the strips of lettuce to make a bed.

3 Arrange the avocados, eggs, tomatoes and cheese neatly in rows on top of the lettuce. Sprinkle the bacon on top.

4 Pour the dressing carefully and evenly over the salad just before serving.

Spicy Corn Salad

This brilliant, sweet-flavoured salad is served warm with a delicious, spicy dressing.

INGREDIENTS

Serves 4

30ml/2 tbsp vegetable oil
450g/1lb drained canned corn, or frozen corn, thawed
1 green (bell) pepper, seeded and diced
1 small red chilli, seeded and finely diced
4 spring onions (scallions), sliced
45ml/3 tbsp chopped fresh parsley
225g/8oz cherry tomatoes, halved
salt and ground black pepper

For the dressing
2.5ml/½ tsp sugar
30ml/2 tbsp white wine vinegar
2.5ml/½ tsp Dijon mustard
15ml/1 tbsp chopped fresh basil
15ml/1 tbsp mayonnaise
1.5ml/¼ tsp chilli sauce

1 Heat the oil in a frying pan. Add the corn, green pepper, chilli and spring onions. Cook over a medium heat for about 5 minutes, until softened, stirring frequently.

2 Transfer the vegetables to a salad bowl. Stir in the parsley and the cherry tomatoes.

3 To make the dressing, combine all the ingredients in a small bowl and whisk together.

4 Pour the dressing over the corn mixture. Season with salt and pepper. Toss well to combine, then serve immediately, while the salad is still warm.

Egg: Energy 730kcal/3025kJ; Protein 30.8g; Carbohydrate 7.7g, of which sugars 6.7g; Fat 64.4g, of which saturates 20.2g; Cholesterol 348mg; Calcium 310mg; Fibre 4.7g; Sodium 1522mg.
Corn: Energy 205kcal/863kJ; Protein 4.3g; Carbohydrate 32.5g, of which sugars 15.3g; Fat 7.3g, of which saturates 1.1g; Cholesterol 3mg; Calcium 39mg; Fibre 3.4g; Sodium 298mg.

Tofu and Cucumber Salad

A nutritious and refreshing salad with a hot, sweet-and-sour dressing, this is ideal for buffets.

INGREDIENTS

Serves 4–6

1 small cucumber
115g/4oz square tofu
oil, for frying
115g/4oz/½ cup beansprouts
salt
celery leaves, to garnish

For the dressing
1 small onion, grated
2 garlic cloves, crushed
5–7.5ml/1–1½ tsp chilli sauce
30–45ml/2–3 tbsp dark soy sauce
15–30ml/1–2 tbsp rice-wine vinegar
10ml/2 tsp soft dark brown sugar

1 Cut the cucumber into neat cubes and place in a bowl. Sprinkle with salt to extract excess liquid. Set aside, while preparing the remaining ingredients.

2 Cut the tofu into cubes. Heat a little oil in a pan and fry on both sides until golden brown. Drain on kitchen paper.

3 To make the dressing, blend together the onion, garlic and chilli sauce in a screw-top jar. Stir in the soy sauce, vinegar, sugar and salt to taste.

4 Just before serving, rinse the cucumber under cold running water. Drain and dry thoroughly. Toss the cucumber, tofu and beansprouts together in a serving bowl and pour over the dressing. Garnish with the celery leaves and serve the salad immediately.

Energy 52kcal/215kJ; Protein 2.6g; Carbohydrate 4.3g, of which sugars 3.6g; Fat 2.8g, of which saturates 0.3g; Cholesterol 0mg; Calcium 109mg; Fibre 0.5g; Sodium 537mg.

Plantain and Green Banana Salad

Cook the plantains and bananas in their skins to retain their soft texture. They will then absorb all the flavour of the dressing.

INGREDIENTS

Serves 4

2 firm yellow plantains
3 green bananas
1 garlic clove, crushed
1 red onion
15–30ml/1–2 tbsp chopped fresh coriander (cilantro)
45ml/3 tbsp sunflower oil
25ml/1½ tbsp malt vinegar
salt and ground black pepper

1 Slit the plantains and bananas lengthways along their natural ridges, then cut in half and place in a large pan.

2 Cover the plantains and bananas with water, add a little salt and bring to the boil. Boil gently for 20 minutes, until tender, then remove from the water. When they are cool enough to handle, peel and cut into medium slices.

3 Put the plantain and banana slices into a large mixing bowl and add the garlic, turning them with a wooden spoon to distribute the garlic evenly, without breaking up the plantain or banana.

4 Halve the onion and slice it thinly. Add the onion slices to the bowl with the coriander, oil, vinegar and seasoning. Toss together to mix, then transfer to a serving bowl.

Energy 328kcal/1386kJ; Protein 3g; Carbohydrate 56g, of which sugars 9g; Fat 12g, of which saturates 2g; Cholesterol 0mg; Calcium 25mg; Fibre 5g; Sodium 8mg.

French Bean Salad

French beans are delicious served with a simple vinaigrette dressing, but this dish is a little more elaborate.

INGREDIENTS

Serves 4

450g/1lb French (green) beans
15ml/1 tbsp olive oil
25g/1oz butter
½ garlic clove, crushed
50g/2oz/1 cup fresh white breadcrumbs
15ml/1 tbsp chopped fresh parsley
1 hard-boiled egg, finely chopped

For the dressing
30ml/2 tbsp olive oil
30ml/2 tbsp sunflower oil
10ml/2 tsp white wine vinegar
½ garlic clove, crushed
1.5ml/¼ tsp Dijon mustard
a pinch of sugar
a pinch of salt

3 Heat the oil and butter in a frying pan and fry the garlic for 1 minute. Stir in the breadcrumbs and fry over a moderate heat for about 3–4 minutes, until golden brown, stirring frequently.

4 Remove the pan from the heat and stir in the parsley and then the egg. Sprinkle the breadcrumb mixture over the French beans. Serve warm or at room temperature.

1 Cook the French beans in boiling salted water for 5–6 minutes, until tender. Drain, refresh under cold running water and place in a serving bowl.

2 To make the dressing, mix all the ingredients thoroughly together. Pour over the beans and toss.

Energy 260kcal/1076kJ; Protein 5.2g; Carbohydrate 13.3g, of which sugars 3g; Fat 21.1g, of which saturates 5.6g; Cholesterol 61mg; Calcium 65mg; Fibre 2.8g; Sodium 151mg.

Coronation Salad

The famous salad dressing used in this dish was created especially for the coronation dinner of Queen Elizabeth II. It is a wonderful accompaniment to hard-boiled eggs and vegetables.

INGREDIENTS

Serves 6

450g/1lb new potatoes
45ml/3 tbsp French Dressing
3 spring onions (scallions), chopped
salt and ground black pepper
6 eggs, hard-boiled and halved
frilly lettuce leaves
¼ cucumber, cut into thin strips
6 large radishes, sliced
1 carton salad cress

For the coronation dressing
30ml/2 tbsp olive oil
1 small onion, chopped
15ml/1 tbsp mild curry powder or korma spice mix
10ml/2 tsp tomato purée (paste)
30ml/2 tbsp lemon juice
30ml/2 tbsp sherry
300ml/½ pint/1¼ cups mayonnaise
150ml/¼ pint/⅔ cup natural (plain) yogurt

1 Boil the potatoes until tender. Drain them, transfer to a large bowl and toss in the French dressing while they are still warm.

2 Stir in the spring onions and the salt and pepper, and allow to cool thoroughly.

3 Meanwhile, make the coronation dressing. Heat the oil in a small pan and fry the onion for 3 minutes, until soft. Stir in the curry powder or spice mix and fry for a further 1 minute. Remove from the heat and mix in all the other dressing ingredients.

4 Stir the dressing into the potatoes, add the eggs, then chill. Line a serving platter with lettuce leaves and pile the salad in the centre. Scatter over the cucumber, radishes and cress.

Energy 587kcal/2429kJ; Protein 10.1g; Carbohydrate 17.1g, of which sugars 4.7g; Fat 51.6g, of which saturates 8.8g; Cholesterol 228mg; Calcium 97mg; Fibre 1.1g; Sodium 401mg.

Sweet Potato and Carrot Salad

This warm salad has a sweet-and-sour taste, and several unusual ingredients. It is attractively garnished with whole walnuts, sultanas and onion rings.

INGREDIENTS

Serves 4

1 medium sweet potato
2 carrots, cut into thick diagonal slices
3 medium tomatoes
8–10 iceberg lettuce leaves
75g/3oz/½ cup canned
   chickpeas, drained

For the dressing
15ml/1 tbsp clear honey
90ml/6 tbsp natural (plain) yogurt
2.5ml/½ tsp salt
5ml/1 tsp ground black pepper

For the garnish
15ml/1 tbsp walnuts
15ml/1 tbsp sultanas (golden raisins)
1 small onion, cut into rings

1 Peel the sweet potato and cut roughly into cubes. Boil it until it is soft but not mushy, then cover the pan and set aside.

2 Boil the carrots for just a few minutes, making sure that they remain crunchy. Add the carrots to the sweet potato.

3 Drain the water from the sweet potato and carrots and place them together in a bowl.

4 Slice the tops off the tomatoes, then scoop out the seeds with a spoon and discard. Roughly chop the flesh. Slice the lettuce into strips across the leaves.

5 Line a salad bowl with the shredded lettuce leaves. Mix together the sweet potato, carrots, chickpeas and tomatoes and place the mixture in the centre.

6 To make the dressing, mix together all the ingredients and beat well, using a fork.

7 Garnish the salad with the walnuts, sultanas and onion rings. Pour the dressing over the top just before serving, or serve it in a separate bowl.

COOK'S TIP

This salad makes an excellent main course for lunch or a family supper. Serve it with a sweet mango chutney and warm naan bread.

Energy 153kcal/648kJ; Protein 4.7g; Carbohydrate 26.7g, of which sugars 15.4g; Fat 3.9g, of which saturates 0.6g; Cholesterol 0mg; Calcium 88mg; Fibre 3.9g; Sodium 95mg.

Potato Salads

Most people adore home-made potato salad made with a creamy mayonnaise. These two versions are lighter and more summery. The first salad should be served warm; the second can be prepared a day ahead and served cold.

INGREDIENTS

Serves 4
900g/2lb new potatoes
5ml/1 tsp salt

For the dressing for the warm salad
30ml/2 tbsp hazelnut or walnut oil
60ml/4 tbsp sunflower oil
juice of 1 lemon
15 pistachio nuts
salt and ground black pepper
flat leaf parsley, to garnish

For the dressing for the cold salad
75ml/5 tbsp olive oil
10ml/2 tsp white wine vinegar
1 garlic clove, crushed
90ml/6 tbsp finely chopped fresh parsley
2 large spring onions (scallions), chopped
salt and ground black pepper

1 Scrub the potatoes but don't peel them. Cover with cold water and bring to the boil. Add the salt and simmer for about 15 minutes, until tender. Drain the potatoes well and set aside.

2 For the warm salad, mix together the hazelnut or walnut oil with the sunflower oil and lemon juice and season well.

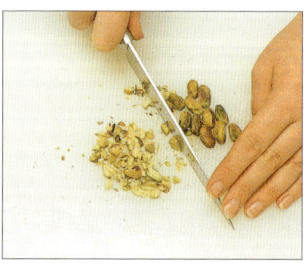

3 Use a knife to crush the pistachio nuts roughly.

4 When the potatoes have cooled slightly, pour over the dressing and sprinkle with the chopped nuts. Serve garnished with a sprig of parsley.

5 For the cold salad, cook the potatoes as above, drain and leave to cool.

6 Whisk together the oil, vinegar, garlic, parsley, spring onions and seasoning and pour over the potatoes. Cover tightly and chill overnight. Allow to come to room temperature before serving.

Warm: Energy 283kcal/1182kJ; Protein 3.7g; Carbohydrate 32.4g, of which sugars 3.4g; Fat 16.2g, of which saturates 2.5g; Cholesterol 11mg; Calcium 18mg; Fibre 2.1g; Sodium 147mg.
Cold: Energy 253kcal/1057kJ; Protein 3g; Carbohydrate 27g, of which sugars 2g; Fat 16g, of which saturates 2g; Cholesterol 0mg; Calcium 13mg; Fibre 2g; Sodium 19mg.

Cooked Side Salads • 111

Potato Salad with Egg and Lemon Dressing

Potato salads are a popular addition to any salad spread and are enjoyed with an assortment of cold meats and fish. This recipe draws on the contrasting flavours of egg and lemon. Chopped parsley provides a fresh green finish.

INGREDIENTS

Serves 4

900g/2lb new potatoes
1 medium onion, finely chopped
1 hard-boiled egg
300ml/½ pint/1¼ cups mayonnaise
1 garlic clove, crushed
finely grated rind and juice of 1 lemon
60ml/4 tbsp chopped fresh parsley
salt and ground black pepper
fresh parsley sprig, to garnish

1 Scrub or scrape the potatoes, cover with cold water and bring to the boil. Add salt and simmer for 15 minutes, until tender. Drain and allow to cool. Cut the potatoes into large dice, season well and combine with the chopped onion.

VARIATION

Fresh chives make an excellent alternative to parsley.

2 Shell the hard-boiled egg and grate into a mixing bowl, then add the mayonnaise. Combine the garlic and lemon rind and juice in a small bowl and stir them carefully into the mayonnaise.

3 Mix the mayonnaise mixture thoroughly into the potatoes, then fold in the chopped parsley.

4 Serve warm or cold, garnished with a sprig of parsley.

Energy 714kcal/2964kJ; Protein 7g; Carbohydrate 41g, of which sugars 6g; Fat 59g, of which saturates 9g; Cholesterol 114mg; Calcium 45mg; Fibre 4g; Sodium 386mg.

Spicy Potato Salad

This tasty salad is quick to prepare, and makes a satisfying accompaniment to grilled (broiled) meat or fish.

INGREDIENTS

Serves 6

900g/2lb potatoes
2 red (bell) peppers
2 celery sticks
1 shallot
2 or 3 spring onions (scallions)
1 green chilli
1 garlic clove, crushed
10ml/2 tsp finely snipped fresh chives
10ml/2 tsp finely chopped fresh basil
15ml/1 tbsp finely chopped fresh parsley
15ml/1 tbsp single (light) cream
30ml/2 tbsp salad cream
15ml/1 tbsp mayonnaise
5ml/1 tsp prepared mild mustard
7.5ml/1½ tsp sugar
salt
snipped fresh chives, to garnish

4 Blend the cream, salad cream, mayonnaise, mustard and sugar in a small bowl, stirring until the mixture is well combined.

5 Pour the dressing over the salad and stir gently to coat evenly. Serve, garnished with the snipped chives.

1 Peel the potatoes. Boil in salted water for 10–12 minutes, until tender. Drain and cool, then cut into cubes and place in a large mixing bowl.

2 Halve the peppers, cut away and discard the core and seeds and cut the flesh into small pieces. Finely chop the celery, shallot and spring onions and slice the chilli very thinly, discarding the seeds.

3 Add the vegetables, garlic and herbs to the potatoes.

Potato Salad with Garlic Sausage

In this delicious potato salad, the potatoes are moistened with a little white wine before adding the vinaigrette.

INGREDIENTS

Serves 4

450g/1lb small waxy potatoes
30–45ml/2–3 tbsp dry white wine
2 shallots, finely chopped
15ml/1 tbsp chopped fresh parsley
15ml/1 tbsp chopped fresh tarragon
175g/6oz cooked garlic sausage
fresh flat leaf parsley sprig, to garnish

For the vinaigrette
10ml/2 tsp Dijon mustard
15ml/1 tbsp tarragon vinegar or white wine vinegar
75ml/5 tbsp extra virgin olive oil
salt and ground black pepper

1 Scrub the potatoes. Boil in salted water for 10–12 minutes, until tender. Drain and refresh under cold running water.

2 Peel the potatoes if you like, or leave in their skins, and cut into 5mm/¼in slices. Sprinkle with the wine and shallots.

VARIATION

The potatoes are also delicious served on their own, simply dressed with vinaigrette, and perhaps accompanied by marinated herrings.

3 To make the vinaigrette, mix the mustard and vinegar in a small bowl, then whisk in the oil, 15ml/1 tbsp at a time. Season and pour over the potatoes.

4 Add the herbs to the potatoes and toss until well mixed.

5 Slice the garlic sausage thinly into rounds and toss with the potatoes.

6 Season the salad with salt and pepper to taste and serve at room temperature, garnished with a sprig of parsley.

Energy 315kcal/1313kJ; Protein 8.3g; Carbohydrate 22.3g, of which sugars 3.1g; Fat 21.6g, of which saturates 4.4g; Cholesterol 50mg; Calcium 45mg; Fibre 2.3g; Sodium 372mg.

Peppery Bean Salad

This pretty salad uses canned beans for speed and convenience.

INGREDIENTS

Serves 4–6

425g/15oz can red kidney beans
425g/15oz can black-eyed beans (peas)
425g/15oz can chickpeas
¼ each red and green (bell) pepper
6 radishes
15ml/1 tbsp finely chopped spring onion (scallion)

For the dressing
5ml/1 tsp ground cumin
15ml/1 tbsp tomato ketchup
30ml/2 tbsp olive oil
15ml/1 tbsp white wine vinegar
1 garlic clove, crushed
2.5ml/½ tsp hot pepper sauce

1 Drain the red kidney beans, black-eyed beans and chickpeas and rinse them under cold running water. Shake off the excess water and tip them into a large bowl.

2 Core, seed and chop the red and green peppers. Trim the radishes and slice thinly. Add the peppers, radishes and spring onion to the beans.

3 Mix together the cumin, ketchup, oil, vinegar and garlic in a small bowl. Add a little salt and hot pepper sauce to taste and stir again thoroughly.

4 Pour the dressing over the salad and mix to combine everything thoroughly.

5 Chill for at least 1 hour before serving, garnished with the sliced spring onion.

Energy 249kcal/1051kJ; Protein 15.6g; Carbohydrate 37g, of which sugars 8.5g; Fat 5.3g, of which saturates 0.7g; Cholesterol 0mg; Calcium 162mg; Fibre 12.5g; Sodium 826mg.

Smoked Ham and Bean Salad

A fairly substantial salad that should be served in small quantities if intended as an accompaniment.

INGREDIENTS

Serves 8

175g/6oz black-eyed beans (peas)
1 onion
1 carrot
225g/8oz smoked ham, diced
3 medium tomatoes, peeled, seeded and diced
salt and ground black pepper

For the dressing

2 garlic cloves, crushed
45ml/3 tbsp olive oil
45ml/3 tbsp red wine vinegar
30ml/2 tbsp vegetable oil
15ml/1 tbsp lemon juice
15ml/1 tbsp chopped fresh or 5ml/1 tsp dried basil
15ml/1 tbsp wholegrain mustard
5ml/1 tsp soy sauce
2.5ml/½ tsp dried oregano
2.5ml/½ tsp caster (superfine) sugar
1.5ml/¼ tsp Worcestershire sauce
2.5ml/½ tsp chilli sauce

1 Soak the beans in cold water to cover overnight. Drain.

2 Put the beans in a large pan and add the onion and carrot. Cover with fresh cold water and bring to the boil. Lower the heat and simmer for about 1 hour, until the beans are tender.

3 Drain the beans, reserving the onion and carrot. Transfer the beans to a salad bowl.

4 Finely chop the onion and carrot. Toss with the beans. Stir in the ham and tomatoes.

5 For the dressing, combine all the ingredients in a small bowl and whisk to mix.

6 Pour the dressing over the ham and beans. Season with salt and pepper. Toss to combine, then serve.

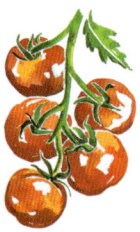

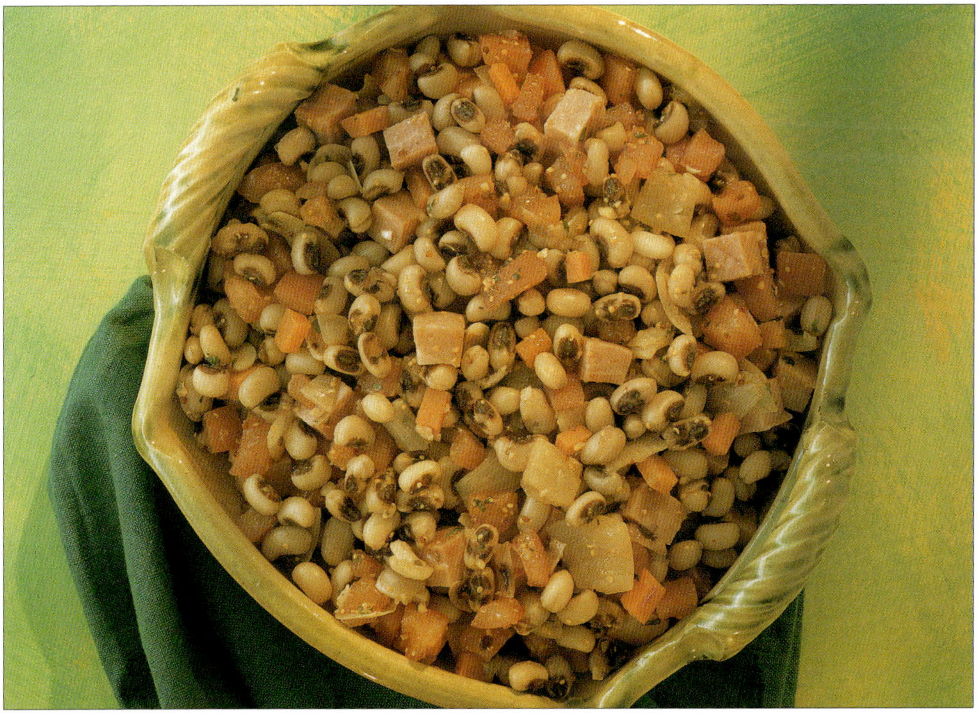

Energy 166kcal/698kJ; Protein 10.6g; Carbohydrate 12.9g, of which sugars 3.5g; Fat 8.5g, of which saturates 1.3g; Cholesterol 16mg; Calcium 34mg; Fibre 4.2g; Sodium 380mg.

White Bean and Celery Salad

This simple bean salad is a delicious alternative to the potato salad that seems to appear on every salad menu. If you do not have time to soak and cook dried beans, you can use canned ones.

INGREDIENTS

Serves 4

450g/1lb dried white beans (haricot (navy), canellini or butter (lima) beans) or 3 x 400g/14oz cans white beans
1 litre/1¾ pints/4 cups vegetable stock
3 celery sticks, cut into 1cm/½in strips
120ml/4fl oz/½ cup French Dressing
45ml/3 tbsp chopped fresh parsley
salt and ground black pepper

1 If you are using dried beans, cover them with plenty of cold water and soak for at least 4 hours. Discard the soaking water, then place the beans in a heavy pan. Cover with water.

2 Bring to the boil and simmer without a lid for 1½ hours, or until the skins are broken. Cooked beans will squash readily between a thumb and forefinger. Drain the beans. If using canned beans, drain and rinse.

3 Place the cooked beans in a large pan. Add the vegetable stock and celery, bring to the boil, cover and simmer for 15 minutes. Drain thoroughly. Moisten the beans with the French dressing and leave to cool.

4 Add the chopped parsley and mix. Season to taste with salt and pepper, transfer to a salad bowl and serve.

Energy 496kcal/2082kJ; Protein 25.1g; Carbohydrate 49.9g, of which sugars 3.1g; Fat 16.5g, of which saturates 3.2g; Cholesterol 0mg; Calcium 125mg; Fibre 17.9g; Sodium 313mg.

Lentil and Cabbage Salad

A warm, crunchy salad that makes a satisfying meal if served with crusty French bread or rolls.

INGREDIENTS

Serves 4–6

225g/8oz/1 cup Puy lentils
3 garlic cloves
1 bay leaf
1 small onion, peeled and studded with 2 cloves
15ml/1 tbsp olive oil
1 red onion, finely sliced
15ml/1 tbsp fresh thyme leaves
350g/12oz cabbage, finely shredded
finely grated rind and juice of 1 lemon
15ml/1 tbsp raspberry vinegar
salt and ground black pepper

1 Rinse the lentils in cold water and place in a large pan with 1.5 litres/2½ pints/6¼ cups cold water, 1 of the garlic cloves, the bay leaf and clove-studded onion.

2 Bring to the boil and cook for 10 minutes. Reduce the heat, cover and simmer gently for 15–20 minutes. Drain and discard the onion, garlic and bay leaf.

3 Crush the remaining garlic cloves. Heat the oil in a large pan. Add the red onion, crushed garlic and thyme and cook for 5 minutes, until softened.

4 Add the cabbage and cook for 3–5 minutes, until just cooked but still crunchy.

5 Stir in the cooked lentils, lemon rind and juice and the raspberry vinegar. Season to taste and serve warm.

Energy 155kcal/656kJ; Protein 9.9g; Carbohydrate 24.8g, of which sugars 4.3g; Fat 2.5g, of which saturates 0.3g; Cholesterol 0mg; Calcium 50mg; Fibre 3.2g; Sodium 18mg.

Brown Bean Salad

Brown beans, sometimes called ful medames, are available from health-food stores and Middle Eastern grocery stores. Dried broad beans or black or red kidney beans make a good substitute.

INGREDIENTS

Serves 6

350g/12oz/1½ cups dried brown beans
3 fresh thyme sprigs
2 bay leaves
1 onion, halved
4 garlic cloves, crushed
7.5ml/1½ tsp crushed cumin seeds
3 spring onions (scallions), finely chopped
90ml/6 tbsp chopped fresh parsley
20ml/4 tsp lemon juice
90ml/6 tbsp olive oil
3 hard-boiled eggs, roughly chopped
1 pickled cucumber, roughly chopped
salt and ground black pepper

1 Put the beans in a bowl with plenty of cold water and leave to soak overnight. Drain, transfer to a pan and cover with fresh water. Bring to the boil and boil rapidly for 10 minutes.

2 Reduce the heat and add the thyme, bay leaves and onion. Simmer very gently for about 1 hour, until tender. Drain and discard the herbs and onion.

> **COOK'S TIP**
>
> The cooking time for dried beans can vary considerably. They may need only 45 minutes, or a lot longer.

3 Place the beans in a large bowl. Mix together the garlic, cumin seeds, spring onions, parsley, lemon juice and oil in a small bowl, and add a little salt and pepper. Pour over the beans and toss the ingredients lightly together.

4 Gently stir in the eggs and pickled cucumber. Transfer the salad to a serving dish and serve immediately.

Energy 385kcal/1613kJ; Protein 17g; Carbohydrate 36g, of which sugars 2g; Fat 19g, of which saturates 3g; Cholesterol 116mg; Calcium 112mg; Fibre 1g; Sodium 119mg.

Cracked Wheat Salad

Fresh herbs, bursting with the flavours of summer, are essential for this salad. Dried herbs will not make a suitable substitute.

INGREDIENTS

Serves 4

225g/8oz/1⅓ cups cracked wheat
350ml/12fl oz/1½ cups vegetable stock
1 cinnamon stick
a generous pinch of ground cumin
a pinch of cayenne pepper
a pinch of ground cloves
5ml/1 tsp salt
10 mangetouts (snow peas), topped and tailed
1 red and 1 yellow (bell) pepper, roasted, skinned, seeded and diced
2 plum tomatoes, peeled, seeded and diced
2 shallots, finely sliced
5 black olives, pitted and cut into quarters
30ml/2 tbsp each shredded fresh basil, mint and parsley
30ml/2 tbsp roughly chopped walnuts
30ml/2 tbsp balsamic vinegar
120ml/4fl oz/½ cup extra virgin olive oil
ground black pepper
onion rings, to garnish

1 Place the cracked wheat in a large bowl. Pour the stock into a pan and bring to the boil with the spices and salt.

2 Cook for 1 minute, then pour the stock, with the cinnamon stick, over the cracked wheat. Leave to stand for 30 minutes.

3 In another bowl, mix together the mangetouts, peppers, tomatoes, shallots, olives, herbs and walnuts. Add the vinegar, olive oil and a little black pepper and stir thoroughly to mix.

4 Strain the cracked wheat of any liquid and discard the cinnamon stick. Place the cracked wheat in a serving bowl, stir in the fresh vegetable mixture and serve, garnished with onion rings.

Energy 254kcal/1060kJ; Protein 7.8g; Carbohydrate 39g, of which sugars 9.8g; Fat 7.9g, of which saturates 0.6g; Cholesterol 0mg; Calcium 96mg; Fibre 3g; Sodium 10mg.

Fruity Brown Rice Salad

An oriental-style dressing accompanies this salad. Brown rice has a nuttier flavour than white rice.

INGREDIENTS

Serves 4–6

115g/4oz/⅔ cup brown rice
1 small red (bell) pepper, seeded and diced
200g/7oz can corn niblets, drained
45ml/3 tbsp sultanas (golden raisins)
225g/8oz can pineapple pieces in fruit juice
15ml/1 tbsp light soy sauce
15ml/1 tbsp sunflower oil
15ml/1 tbsp hazelnut oil
1 garlic clove, crushed
5ml/1 tsp chopped fresh root ginger
salt and ground black pepper
4 spring onions (scallions), sliced, to garnish

1 Cook the brown rice in a large pan of lightly salted boiling water for about 30 minutes, or until it is tender. Drain thoroughly and cool. Meanwhile, prepare the garnish. Slice the spring onions at an angle, as shown, then set aside.

2 Transfer the rice to a large serving bowl and add the red pepper, corn and sultanas. Drain the pineapple pieces, reserving the juice, then add them to the rice mixture and toss lightly.

3 Pour the reserved pineapple juice into a clean screw-top jar. Add the soy sauce, sunflower and hazelnut oils, garlic and root ginger. Season with salt and pepper. Close the jar tightly and shake well to combine.

4 Pour the dressing over the salad and toss well. Scatter the spring onions over the top and serve.

COOK'S TIP

Hazelnut oil gives a wonderfully distinctive flavour to any salad dressing. Like olive oil, it contains mainly mono-unsaturated fats.

Energy 189kcal/799kJ; Protein 3g; Carbohydrate 35.5g, of which sugars 14.4g; Fat 4.9g, of which saturates 0.6g; Cholesterol 0mg; Calcium 20mg; Fibre 2g; Sodium 94mg.

Couscous Salad

There are many ways of serving couscous. This salad has a delicate flavour and is excellent with grilled (broiled) chicken or kebabs.

INGREDIENTS

Serves 4

275g/10oz/1⅔ cups couscous
550ml/18fl oz/2¼ cups boiling vegetable stock
16–20 black olives
2 small courgettes (zucchini)
25g/1oz/¼ cup flaked (sliced) almonds, toasted
60ml/4 tbsp olive oil
15ml/1 tbsp lemon juice
15ml/1 tbsp chopped fresh coriander (cilantro)
15ml/1 tbsp chopped fresh parsley
a good pinch of ground cumin
a good pinch of cayenne pepper
salt

3 Carefully mix the courgettes, olives and toasted almonds into the couscous without breaking up the piece too much.

4 Mix together the olive oil, lemon juice, herbs, spices and a pinch of salt in a jug (pitcher) or bowl. Stir into the salad.

1 Place the couscous in a heatproof bowl and pour over the boiling stock. Stir with a fork and then set aside for 10 minutes for the stock to be absorbed. Fluff up with a fork.

2 Halve the olives, discarding the pits. Top and tail the courgettes and cut them into small julienne strips.

Energy 123kcal/509kJ; Protein 1g; Carbohydrate 4g, of which sugars 4g; Fat 12g, of which saturates 2g; Cholesterol 0mg; Calcium 44mg; Fibre 1g; Sodium 176mg.

Orange and Cracked Wheat Salad

Cracked wheat makes an excellent alternative to rice or pasta as a sustaining side salad.

INGREDIENTS

Serves 4

1 small green (bell) pepper
150g/5oz/scant 1 cup cracked wheat
1/4 cucumber, diced
15g/1/2oz/1/2 cup chopped fresh mint
40g/11/2oz/1/3 cup flaked (sliced) almonds, toasted
grated rind and juice of 1 lemon
2 seedless oranges, peeled
salt and ground black pepper
fresh mint sprigs, to garnish

1 Using a sharp vegetable knife, carefully halve and seed the green pepper. Cut into small cubes and put to one side.

2 Place the cracked wheat in a pan and add 600ml/1 pint/ 2 1/2 cups water. Bring to the boil, lower the heat, cover and simmer for 10–15 minutes, until tender. Alternatively, place the cracked wheat in a heatproof bowl, pour over boiling water and leave to soak for 30 minutes. Most, if not all, of the water should be absorbed; drain off any excess.

3 Toss the cracked wheat with the cucumber, green pepper, mint and toasted almonds in a serving bowl. Add the grated lemon rind and juice.

4 Working over the salad bowl to catch the juice, cut the oranges into neat segments, leaving the membrane behind. Add the segments to the cracked wheat mixture, then season with salt and pepper and toss lightly.

5 Garnish with mint sprigs and serve immediately.

VARIATION
CRACKED WHEAT SALAD WITH FENNEL AND POMEGRANATE

This version uses the added crunchiness of fennel and the sweetness of pomegranate seeds. Perfect for a summer lunch.

INGREDIENTS

Serves 6

225g/8oz/1 1/3 cups cracked wheat
2 fennel bulbs
1 small red chilli, seeded and chopped
1 celery stick, finely sliced
30ml/2 tbsp olive oil
finely grated rind and juice of 2 lemons
6–8 spring onions (scallions), chopped
90ml/6 tbsp chopped fresh mint
90ml/6 tbsp chopped fresh parsley
the seeds from 1 pomegranate
salt and ground black pepper
lettuce leaves, to serve

1 Place the cracked wheat in a bowl and pour over enough boiling water to cover. Leave to stand for 30 minutes.

2 Drain through a sieve (strainer), pressing out excess water with the back of a spoon.

3 Halve the fennel bulbs and cut into very fine slices.

4 Mix all the remaining ingredients together, then stir in the cracked wheat and fennel.

5 Season well with salt and pepper, cover and set aside for 30 minutes before serving with lettuce leaves.

Orange: Energy 254kcal/1060kJ; Protein 7.8g; Carbohydrate 39g, of which sugars 9.8g; Fat 7.9g, of which saturates 0.6g; Cholesterol 0mg; Calcium 96mg; Fibre 3g; Sodium 10mg.
Fennel: Energy 286kcal/1192kJ; Protein 6g; Carbohydrate 47g, of which sugars 4g; Fat 9g, of which saturates 1g; Cholesterol 0mg; Calcium 76mg; Fibre 1g; Sodium 18mg.

MAIN COURSE
SALADS

Salade Niçoise

Served with good French bread, this regional classic makes a wonderful summer lunch or light supper dish.

INGREDIENTS
Serves 4–6

225g/8oz French (green) beans
450g/1lb new potatoes, peeled and cut into 2.5cm/1in pieces
white wine vinegar and olive oil, for sprinkling
1 small cos, romaine or round lettuce, torn into bitesize pieces
4 ripe plum tomatoes, quartered
1 small cucumber, peeled, seeded and diced
1 green or red (bell) pepper, seeded and thinly sliced
4 hard-boiled eggs, peeled and quartered
24 black olives
225g/8oz can tuna in brine, drained
50g/2oz can anchovy fillets in olive oil, drained
basil leaves, to garnish
garlic croûtons, to serve

For the anchovy vinaigrette
20ml/4 tsp Dijon mustard
50g/2oz can anchovy fillets in olive oil, drained
1 garlic clove, crushed
60ml/4 tbsp lemon juice or white wine vinegar
120ml/4fl oz/½ cup sunflower oil
120ml/4fl oz/½ cup extra virgin olive oil
ground black pepper

1 First make the anchovy vinaigrette. Place the mustard, anchovies and garlic in a bowl and mix together by pressing the garlic and anchovies against the sides of the bowl. Season generously with pepper. Using a small whisk, blend in the lemon juice or vinegar. Slowly whisk in the sunflower oil in a thin stream, followed by the olive oil, whisking until the dressing is smooth and creamy.

2 Alternatively, put all the ingredients except the oils in a food processor fitted with the metal blade and process to combine. With the machine running, slowly add the oils in a thin stream until the vinaigrette is thick and creamy.

3 Put the French beans into a large pan of boiling water and boil for 3 minutes until tender, yet crisp. Transfer the beans to a colander with a slotted spoon, then rinse under cold running water to stop the cooking process. Drain again and set aside.

4 Add the potatoes to the same boiling water, reduce the heat and simmer for 10–15 minutes, until just tender, then drain. Sprinkle with a little vinegar and olive oil and a spoonful of the vinaigrette.

5 Arrange the lettuce on a serving platter, top with the tomatoes, cucumber and red or green pepper, then add the French beans and potatoes.

6 Arrange the eggs around the edge. Place olives, tuna and anchovies on top and garnish with the basil leaves. Drizzle with the remaining vinaigrette and serve with garlic croûtons.

COOK'S TIP

To make garlic croûtons, thinly slice a French stick or cut a larger loaf, such as rustic country bread, into 2.5cm/1in cubes. Place the bread in a single layer on a baking sheet and cook in the oven, preheated to 180°C/350°F/Gas 4, for 7–10 minutes or until golden, turning once. Rub the toast with a garlic clove and serve hot, or allow to cool and store in an airtight container.

Energy 218kcal/903kJ; Protein 12.3g; Carbohydrate 3.4g, of which sugars 3.2g; Fat 17.4g, of which saturates 3.2g; Cholesterol 135mg; Calcium 50mg; Fibre 1.7g; Sodium 256mg.

Moroccan Tuna Salad

This salad is similar to the classic Salade Niçoise but uses tuna or swordfish steaks and fresh broad beans along with the familiar French beans.

INGREDIENTS

Serves 6

about 900g/2lb fresh tuna or swordfish, sliced into 2cm/¾in steaks
olive oil, for brushing

For the salad
450g/1lb French (green) beans, topped and tailed
450g/1lb broad (fava) beans
1 cos or romaine lettuce
450g/1lb cherry tomatoes, halved, unless very tiny
30ml/2 tbsp coarsely chopped fresh coriander (cilantro)
3 hard-boiled eggs
45ml/3 tbsp olive oil
10–15ml/2–3 tsp lime or lemon juice
½ garlic clove, crushed
175–225g/6–8oz/1½–2 cups pitted black olives

For the marinade
1 onion
2 garlic cloves
½ bunch fresh parsley
½ bunch fresh coriander (cilantro)
10ml/2 tsp paprika
45ml/3 tbsp olive oil
30ml/2 tbsp white wine vinegar
15ml/1 tbsp lime or lemon juice

1 First make the marinade. Place all the ingredients in a food processor, add 45ml/3 tbsp water and process for 30–40 seconds, until finely chopped.

2 Prick the fish all over with a fork, place in a shallow dish and pour over the marinade, turning the fish to coat. Cover with clear film (plastic wrap) and leave in a cool place for 2–4 hours.

3 To prepare the salad, cook the French beans and broad beans in boiling salted water until tender. Drain and refresh under cold water. Discard the outer shells from the broad beans and place in a large serving bowl with the French beans.

4 Discard the outer lettuce leaves and tear the inner leaves into pieces. Add to the salad with the tomatoes and coriander. Shell the eggs and cut into eighths. Mix the olive oil, lime or lemon juice and garlic to make a dressing.

5 Preheat the grill (broiler) and arrange the tuna or swordfish steaks in a grill pan. Brush with the marinade together with a little extra olive oil and grill (broil) for 5–6 minutes on each side, until the fish is tender and flakes easily. Brush again with marinade and more olive oil when turning the fish over.

6 Allow the fish to cool a little then break the steaks into large pieces. Toss into the salad with the olives and the dressing. Decorate with the eggs and serve.

Energy 402kcal/1677kJ; Protein 35.4g; Carbohydrate 14.9g, of which sugars 6.2g; Fat 22.8g, of which saturates 4.3g; Cholesterol 123mg; Calcium 134mg; Fibre 8.6g; Sodium 752mg.

Warm Fish Salad with Mango Dressing

This salad is best served during the summer months, preferably out of doors. The dressing combines the flavour of rich mango with hot chilli, ginger and lime.

INGREDIENTS

Serves 4

1 French loaf
4 redfish, black bream or porgy, each about 275g/10oz
15ml/1 tbsp vegetable oil
1 mango
1cm/½in fresh root ginger
1 red chilli, seeded and finely chopped
30ml/2 tbsp lime juice
30ml/2 tbsp chopped fresh coriander (cilantro)
175g/6oz young spinach
150g/5oz pak choi (bok choy)
175g/6oz cherry tomatoes, halved

1 Preheat the oven to 180°C/350°F/Gas 4. Cut the French loaf into 20cm/8in lengths. Slice lengthways, then cut into fingers. Place on a baking sheet and leave to dry in the oven for 15 minutes.

2 Preheat the grill (broiler) or light the barbecue and allow the embers to settle. Slash the fish deeply on both sides and moisten with oil. Grill (broil) or barbecue the fish for 6 minutes, turning once.

3 Peel the mango and cut in half, discarding the stone (pit). Thinly slice one half and set aside. Place the other half in a food processor. Peel the ginger, grate finely, then add to the mango with the chilli, lime juice and coriander. Process until smooth.

4 Adjust to a pouring consistency with 30–45ml/2–3 tbsp water.

5 Wash the spinach and pak choi leaves and spin dry, then distribute them among four serving plates. Place the fish over the leaves. Spoon on the mango dressing and finish with the reserved slices of mango and the tomato halves.

6 Serve with the fingers of crispy French bread.

Energy 457kcal/1937kJ; Protein 33.7g; Carbohydrate 64.1g, of which sugars 10.6g; Fat 9.1g, of which saturates 0.8g; Cholesterol 48mg; Calcium 317mg; Fibre 5.5g; Sodium 872mg.

Grilled Salmon and Spring Vegetable Salad

Spring is the time to enjoy sweet, young vegetables. Cook them briefly, cool to room temperature, dress and serve with a piece of lightly grilled (broiled) salmon topped with sorrel and quail's eggs.

INGREDIENTS

Serves 4

350g/12oz small new potatoes, scrubbed or scraped
4 quail's eggs
115g/4oz young carrots, peeled
115g/4oz baby corn
115g/4oz sugar snap peas, topped and tailed
115g/4oz fine green beans, topped and tailed
115g/4oz young courgettes (zucchini)
115g/4oz patty-pan squash (optional)
120ml/4fl oz/½ cup French Dressing
4 salmon fillets, each about 150g/5oz, skinned
115g/4oz sorrel, stems removed
salt and ground black pepper

1 Bring the potatoes to the boil in salted water and cook for about 15 minutes, until tender. Drain, cover and keep warm.

2 Cover the quail's eggs with boiling water and cook for 8 minutes. Refresh under cold water, shell and cut in half.

3 Bring a pan of salted water to the boil, add the carrots, corn, sugar snap peas, beans, courgettes and squash, if using, and cook for 2–3 minutes. Drain well.

4 Place the hot vegetables and potatoes in a bowl, moisten with a little French Dressing and allow to cool.

5 Brush the salmon fillets with some of the French Dressing and grill (broil) for 6 minutes, turning once.

6 Place the sorrel in a stainless-steel or enamel pan with 30ml/2 tbsp French Dressing. Cover and soften over a gentle heat for 2 minutes. Strain in a small sieve (strainer) and leave to cool to room temperature.

7 Divide the potatoes and vegetables among four large serving plates, then position a piece of salmon to one side of each plate. Place a spoonful of sorrel on each piece of salmon and top with two pieces of quail's egg. Season and serve at room temperature.

VARIATION

If sorrel is unavailable, use young spinach leaves instead. Cook it gently in the same way as the sorrel.

Energy 545kcal/2264kJ; Protein 32.3g; Carbohydrate 20.1g, of which sugars 6.3g; Fat 31g, of which saturates 6g; Cholesterol 110mg; Calcium 131mg; Fibre 4.2g; Sodium 739mg.

Noodles with Pineapple, Ginger and Chillies

A coconut, lime and fish sauce dressing is the perfect partner to this fruity and spicy salad.

INGREDIENTS
Serves 4
275g/10oz dried udon noodles
½ pineapple, peeled, cored and sliced into 4cm/1½in rings
45ml/3 tbsp soft light brown sugar
60ml/4 tbsp lime juice
60ml/4 tbsp coconut milk
30ml/2 tbsp Thai fish sauce
30ml/2 tbsp grated fresh root ginger
2 garlic cloves, finely chopped
1 ripe mango or 2 peaches, stoned (pitted), skinned and finely diced
ground black pepper
2 spring onions (scallions), finely sliced, 2 red chillies, seeded and finely shredded, and fresh mint leaves, to garnish

1 Cook the noodles in a large pan of boiling water until tender, following the directions on the packet. Drain, refresh under cold water and drain again.

2 Place the pineapple rings in a flameproof dish, sprinkle with 30ml/2 tbsp of the sugar and grill (broil) for about 5 minutes, or until golden. Cool slightly and cut into small dice.

3 Mix the lime juice, coconut milk and fish sauce in a salad bowl. Add the remaining brown sugar with the ginger, garlic and black pepper and whisk well. Add the noodles and pineapple.

4 Add the diced mango or peaches and toss gently to combine thoroughly. Sprinkle over the spring onions, chillies and mint leaves just before serving.

Buckwheat Noodles with Smoked Salmon

Young pea sprouts are available for only a short time. You can substitute watercress, salad cress, young leeks or your favourite green vegetable or herb in this dish.

INGREDIENTS
Serves 4
225g/8oz buckwheat or soba noodles
15ml/1 tbsp oyster sauce
juice of ½ lemon
30–45ml/2–3 tbsp light olive oil
115g/4oz smoked salmon, cut into fine strips
115g/4oz young pea sprouts
2 ripe tomatoes, peeled, seeded and cut into strips
15ml/1 tbsp snipped chives
ground black pepper

1 Cook the buckwheat or soba noodles in a large pan of boiling water until tender, following the directions on the packet. Drain, then rinse under cold running water and drain well.

2 Tip the noodles into a large bowl. Add the oyster sauce and lemon juice and season with pepper to taste. Moisten the noodles with the olive oil.

3 Add the smoked salmon, pea sprouts, tomatoes and chives. Mix well and serve immediately.

Pineapple: Energy 380kcal/1604kJ; Protein 4.5g; Carbohydrate 89.4g, of which sugars 33.1g; Fat 0.5g, of which saturates 0.1g; Cholesterol 0mg; Calcium 48mg; Fibre 3.2g; Sodium 29mg .
Buckwheat: Energy 330kcal/1394kJ; Protein 15.1g; Carbohydrate 46.6g, of which sugars 4.6g; Fat 10.6g, of which saturates 1.1g; Cholesterol 10mg; Calcium 28mg; Fibre 2.6g; Sodium 609mg.

Smoked Trout and Noodle Salad

It is important to use ripe, juicy tomatoes for this fresh-tasting salad. For a special occasion you could use smoked salmon.

INGREDIENTS

Serves 4

225g/8oz somen noodles
2 smoked trout, skinned and boned
2 hard-boiled eggs, coarsely chopped
30ml/2 tbsp snipped fresh chives
lime halves, to serve (optional)

For the dressing
6 ripe plum tomatoes
2 shallots, finely chopped
30ml/2 tbsp tiny capers, rinsed
30ml/2 tbsp chopped fresh tarragon
finely grated rind and juice of ½ orange
60ml/4 tbsp extra virgin olive oil
salt and ground black pepper

1 To make the dressing, cut the tomatoes in half, remove the cores and cut the flesh into chunks.

2 Place in a bowl with the shallots, capers, tarragon, orange rind and juice and olive oil. Season with salt and pepper and mix well. Cover with clear film (plastic wrap) and leave to marinate at room temperature for 1–2 hours.

3 Cook the noodles in a pan of boiling water, following the packet directions, until just tender. Drain and rinse under cold running water. Drain well.

4 Toss the cooked noodles with the dressing, then adjust the seasoning to taste. Arrange the noodles on a large serving platter or individual plates.

5 Flake the smoked trout over the noodles, then sprinkle the eggs and chives over the top. Serve, with lime halves on the side of the plate, if you like.

Energy 619kcal/2597kJ; Protein 41g; Carbohydrate 49g, of which sugars 8g; Fat 30g, of which saturates 5g; Cholesterol 216mg; Calcium 74mg; Fibre 5g; Sodium 139mg.

Smoked Trout and Horseradish Salad

In the summer, when lettuce leaves are sweet and crisp, partner them with fillets of smoked trout, warm new potatoes and a creamy horseradish dressing.

INGREDIENTS

Serves 4

675g/1½lb new potatoes
4 smoked trout fillets
115g/4oz mixed lettuce leaves
4 slices dark rye bread, cut into fingers
salt and ground black pepper

For the dressing
60ml/4 tbsp creamed horseradish
60ml/4 tbsp groundnut (peanut) oil
15ml/1 tbsp white wine vinegar
10ml/2 tsp caraway seeds

1 Scrub the potatoes. Bring to the boil in a pan of salted water and simmer for about 15 minutes, until tender. Remove the skin from the trout fillets and lift the flesh from the bone.

2 To make the dressing, place all the ingredients in a screw-top jar and shake vigorously. Season the lettuce leaves and moisten them with the dressing. Distribute among four serving plates.

3 Flake the trout fillets and cut the potatoes in half. Scatter them together with the rye bread fingers over the salad leaves and toss to mix. Season the salad to taste and serve.

COOK'S TIP

In some cases it is better to season the leaves rather than the dressing when making a salad.

Energy 428kcal/1797kJ; Protein 25.3g; Carbohydrate 41.8g, of which sugars 5.4g; Fat 18.9g, of which saturates 2.6g; Cholesterol 28mg; Calcium 84mg; Fibre 3.7g; Sodium 1712mg

Prawn and Artichoke Salad

The mild flavours of prawns and artichoke hearts are complemented by a zingy herb dressing.

INGREDIENTS

Serves 4

1 garlic clove
10ml/2 tsp Dijon mustard
60ml/4 tbsp red wine vinegar
150ml/¼ pint/⅔ cup olive oil
45ml/3 tbsp shredded fresh basil leaves or 30ml/2 tbsp finely chopped fresh parsley
1 red onion, very finely sliced
350g/12oz shelled cooked prawns (shrimp)
400g/14oz can artichoke hearts
½ iceberg lettuce
salt and ground black pepper

1 Chop the garlic, then crush it to a pulp with 5ml/1 tsp salt, using the flat edge of a heavy knife blade. Mix the garlic and mustard to a paste in a small bowl.

2 Beat in the vinegar and finally the olive oil, beating hard to make a thick, creamy dressing. Season with black pepper and, if necessary, additional salt.

3 Stir the basil or parsley into the dressing, followed by the sliced onion. Leave the mixture to stand for 30 minutes at room temperature, then stir in the prawns and chill for 1 hour, or until ready to serve.

4 Drain the artichoke hearts and halve each one. Shred the lettuce finely.

5 Make a bed of lettuce on a serving platter or four individual salad plates and spread the artichoke hearts over it.

6 Immediately before serving, pour the prawns and their marinade over the top of the salad.

Energy 319kcal/1319kJ; Protein 17g; Carbohydrate 3.5g, of which sugars 3.1g; Fat 26.4g, of which saturates 3.7g; Cholesterol 171mg; Calcium 155mg; Fibre 2.4g; Sodium 306mg.

Ghanaian Prawn Salad

The addition of plantain, which is first cooked in its skin, brings an unusual flavour to this salad.

INGREDIENTS

Serves 4

115g/4oz cooked shelled prawns (shrimp)
1 garlic clove, crushed
7.5ml/1½ tsp vegetable oil
2 eggs
1 yellow plantain, halved
4 lettuce leaves
2 tomatoes
1 red pepper, seeded
1 avocado
juice of 1 lemon
1 carrot
200g/7oz can tuna or sardines, drained
1 green chilli, finely chopped
30ml/2 tbsp chopped spring onion (scallion)
salt and ground black pepper

1 Put the prawns and garlic in a small bowl. Add a little seasoning.

2 Heat the oil in a small pan, add the prawns and cook over a low heat for a few minutes. Transfer to a plate to cool.

VARIATION

To vary this salad, use other types of canned fish and a mixture of interesting lettuce leaves.

3 Hard-boil the eggs, place in cold water to cool, then shell and cut into slices.

4 Boil the unpeeled plantain in a pan of water for 15 minutes, cool, then peel and cut into thick slices.

5 Shred the lettuce and arrange on a large serving plate. Slice the tomatoes and red pepper and peel and slice the avocado, sprinkling it with a little lemon juice.

6 Cut the carrot into matchsticks and arrange over the lettuce with the other vegetables.

7 Add the plantain, eggs, prawns and tuna or sardines. Sprinkle with the remaining lemon juice, scatter the chilli and spring onion on top, season and serve.

Energy 263kcal/1103kJ; Protein 23.6g; Carbohydrate 12.7g, of which sugars 6.3g; Fat 13.5g, of which saturates 2.8g; Cholesterol 176mg; Calcium 62mg; Fibre 2.6g; Sodium 245mg.

Prawn Salad with Curry Dressing

Curry spices add an unexpected twist to this salad. The warm flavours combine especially well with the sweet prawns and grated apple. Curry paste is needed here rather than curry powder as there is no cooking, which is necessary for bringing out the flavours of powdered spices.

INGREDIENTS

Serves 4

1 ripe tomato
1/2 iceberg lettuce
1 small onion
1 small bunch fresh coriander (cilantro)
15ml/1 tbsp lemon juice
450g/1lb shelled cooked prawns (shrimp)
1 apple
8 whole prawns, 8 lemon wedges and
    4 fresh coriander sprigs, to garnish
salt

For the curry dressing
75ml/5 tbsp mayonnaise
5ml/1 tsp mild curry paste
15ml/1 tbsp tomato ketchup
sake

3 Finely shred the lettuce and put in a large bowl, then finely chop the onion and coriander. Add to the bowl together with the tomato, moisten with lemon juice and season with salt.

4 To make the dressing, combine the mayonnaise, curry paste and tomato ketchup in a small bowl. Add 30ml/2 tbsp water to thin the dressing and season to taste with salt.

5 Combine the prawns with the dressing and stir gently so that all the prawns are evenly coated with the dressing.

6 Quarter and core the apple and grate into the prawn and dressing mixture.

7 Distribute the shredded lettuce mixture among four serving plates or bowls. Pile the prawn mixture in the centre of each and decorate each with two whole prawns, two lemon wedges and a sprig of coriander.

1 To peel the tomato, cut a cross in the skin with a knife and immerse in boiling water for 30 seconds. Drain and cool under running water. Peel off the skin.

2 Halve the tomato, push the seeds out with your thumb and discard them. Cut the flesh into large dice.

COOK'S TIP

Fresh coriander (cilantro) is inclined to wilt if it is kept out of water. Put it in a jar of water, cover with a plastic bag and place in the refrigerator and it will stay fresh for several days.

Energy 271kcal/1129kJ; Protein 5g; Carbohydrate 5g, of which sugars 5g; Fat 16g, of which saturates 2g; Cholesterol 329mg; Calcium 153mg; Fibre 2g; Sodium 1958mg.

Prawn and Mint Salad

Fresh, uncooked prawns make all the difference to this salad as cooking them in butter adds to the piquant flavour. Garnish with shavings of fresh coconut for a tropical topping, if you wish.

INGREDIENTS

Serves 4

12 large fresh, uncooked prawns (shrimp)
15ml/1 tbsp unsalted butter
15ml/1 tbsp Thai fish sauce
juice of 1 lime
45ml/3 tbsp thin coconut milk
5ml/1 tsp caster (superfine) sugar
1 garlic clove, crushed
2.5cm/1 in fresh root ginger, peeled and grated
2 red chillies, seeded and finely chopped
30ml/2 tbsp fresh mint leaves
225g/8oz light green lettuce leaves
ground black pepper

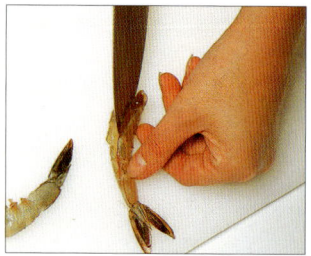

1 Carefully peel the uncooked prawns, removing and discarding the heads and outer shells, but leaving the tails intact.

2 Using a sharp knife, carefully remove the dark-coloured vein that runs along the back of each prawn.

3 Melt the butter in a large frying pan. When the melted butter is foaming add the prawns and toss on a high heat until they turn pink. Remove from the heat; it is important not to cook them for too long or their tenderness will not be retained and they will be rubbery and overcooked.

4 In a small bowl mix the fish sauce, lime juice, coconut milk, sugar, garlic, ginger and chillies together. Season to taste with freshly ground black pepper.

5 Toss the warm prawns into the sauce with the mint leaves. Arrange the lettuce leaves on a serving plate and place the prawn and mint mixture in the centre.

VARIATION

Instead of prawns (shrimp), this dish also works very well with lobster tails if you are feeling very extravagant.

COOK'S TIP

If you can't find any fresh, uncooked prawns (shrimp) you could use frozen ones. To make the most of their flavour, toss them very quickly in the hot butter once they are completely thawed.

Energy 83kcal/347kJ; Protein 9.8g; Carbohydrate 2.5g, of which sugars 1.7g; Fat 3.8g, of which saturates 2.1g; Cholesterol 106mg; Calcium 86mg; Fibre 0.5g; Sodium 144mg.

Mixed Shellfish Salad

Use fresh shellfish that is in season, or you can use a combination of fresh and frozen shellfish.

INGREDIENTS

Serves 6–8

350g/12oz small squid
1 small onion, cut into quarters
1 bay leaf
200g/7oz uncooked prawns (shrimp), in their shells
750g/1½lb fresh mussels, in their shells
450g/1lb fresh small clams
175ml/6fl oz/¾ cup white wine
1 fennel bulb

For the dressing
75ml/5 tbsp extra virgin olive oil
45ml/3 tbsp lemon juice
1 garlic clove, finely chopped
salt and ground black pepper

1 Working near the sink, clean the squid by first peeling off the thin skin from the body section. Rinse well.

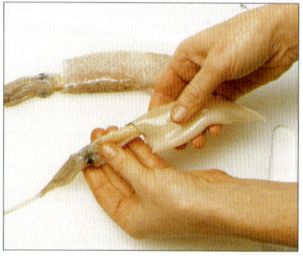

2 Pull the head and tentacles away from the sac section. Remove and discard the translucent quill and any remaining insides from the sac. Sever the tentacles and head.

3 Discard the head and intestines. Remove the small, hard beak from the base of the tentacles. Rinse the tentacles and sac under cold water. Drain.

4 Bring a large pan of water to the boil. Add the onion and bay leaf. Drop in the squid and cook for about 10 minutes, or until tender. Remove with a slotted spoon and allow to cool before slicing into rings 1cm/½in wide. Cut each tentacle section into two pieces. Set aside.

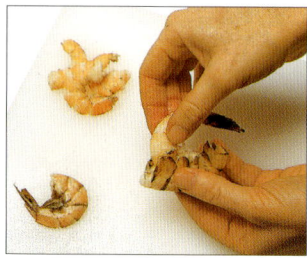

5 Drop the prawns into the same boiling water and cook for about 2 minutes, until they turn pink. Remove with a slotted spoon. Shell and devein. (The cooking liquid may be strained and kept for soup.)

6 Cut the "beards" from the mussels. Scrub and rinse the mussels and clams well in several changes of cold water. Any that are open should close if given a sharp tap; if they fail to do so, discard. Place in a large pan with the wine. Cover and steam until all the shells have opened. (Discard any that do not open.) Lift the clams and mussels out of the pan.

7 Remove all the clams from their shells with a small spoon. Place in a large serving bowl. Remove all but eight of the mussels from their shells and add them to the clams in the bowl. Leave the remaining mussels in their half-shells, and set aside.

8 Cut the green, ferny part of the fennel away from the bulb. Chop finely and set aside. Chop the bulb into bitesize pieces and add it to the serving bowl together with the squid and prawns.

9 To make the dressing, combine the oil, lemon juice and garlic in a bowl. Add the reserved chopped fennel green and salt and pepper to taste.

10 Pour the dressing over the salad in the serving bowl, and toss well to combine. Decorate the top of the salad with the remaining mussels in their half-shells. Serve at room temperature or just lightly chilled.

Energy 166kcal/693kJ; Protein 19.3g; Carbohydrate 2.9g, of which sugars 1g; Fat 8.6g, of which saturates 1.3g; Cholesterol 177mg; Calcium 65mg; Fibre 0.9g; Sodium 480mg.

Avocado, Crab and Herb Salad

The sweet richness of crab combines especially well with ripe avocado, fresh herbs and tomato.

INGREDIENTS

Serves 4

675g/1½lb small new potatoes
1 fresh mint sprig
900g/2lb boiled crabs or 275g/10oz frozen crab meat
1 endive (US chicory) or round (butterhead) lettuce
175g/6oz lamb's lettuce or young spinach leaves
1 large ripe avocado, peeled and sliced
175g/6oz cherry tomatoes
salt, ground black pepper and freshly grated nutmeg

For the dressing
75ml/5 tbsp olive oil
15ml/1 tbsp lime juice
45ml/3 tbsp chopped fresh coriander (cilantro)
2.5ml/½ tsp caster (superfine) sugar

1 Scrape or peel the potatoes. Cover with water, add a good pinch of salt and a sprig of mint. Bring to the boil and simmer for about 15 minutes, until tender. Drain the potatoes, cover and keep warm until needed.

2 Remove the legs and claws from each crab. Crack these open with the back of a chopping knife and remove the white meat.

3 Turn the crab on its back and push the rear leg section away with the thumb and forefinger of each hand. Remove the flesh from inside the shell.

4 Discard the "dead men's fingers", the soft gills which the crab uses to filter impurities in its diet. Apart from these and the shell, everything else is edible, both white and dark meat.

5 Split the central body section open with a knife and remove the white and dark flesh with a pick or skewer.

6 Combine all the dressing ingredients in a screw-top jar and shake. Put the salad leaves in a large bowl, pour the dressing over and toss well.

7 Distribute the leaves among four serving plates. Top with the avocado, crab, tomatoes and warm new potatoes. Season with salt, pepper and freshly grated nutmeg and serve.

COOK'S TIP

Young crabs offer the sweetest meat, but are more fiddly to prepare than older, larger ones. The hen crab carries more flesh than the cock, which is considered to have a better overall flavour. The cock crab, shown here, is identified by his narrow apron flap at the rear.

The hen has a broad flap, under which she carries her eggs. Frozen crab meat is a good alternative to fresh and retains much of its original sweetness.

Energy 444kcal/1848kJ; Protein 21.2g; Carbohydrate 31.1g, of which sugars 5.5g; Fat 26.6g, of which saturates 4.3g; Cholesterol 56mg; Calcium 128mg; Fibre 5.3g; Sodium 429mg.

Thai Noodle Salad

The addition of coconut milk and sesame oil gives an unusual nutty flavour to the dressing for this colourful noodle salad.

INGREDIENTS

Serves 4–6

350g/12oz somen noodles
1 large carrot, cut into thin strips
1 bunch asparagus, trimmed and cut into 4cm/1½in lengths
1 red (bell) pepper, seeded and cut into fine strips
115g/4oz mangetouts (snow peas), topped, tailed and halved
115g/4oz baby corn cobs, halved lengthways
115g/4oz beansprouts
115g/4oz can water chestnuts, drained and finely sliced
1 lime, cut into wedges, 50g/2oz/½ cup roasted peanuts, roughly chopped, and fresh coriander (cilantro) leaves, to garnish

For the dressing

45ml/3 tbsp roughly torn fresh basil
75ml/5 tbsp roughly chopped fresh mint
250ml/8fl oz/1 cup coconut milk
30ml/2 tbsp dark sesame oil
15ml/1 tbsp grated fresh root ginger
2 garlic cloves, finely chopped
juice of 1 lime
2 spring onions (scallions), finely chopped
salt and cayenne pepper

1 To make the dressing, combine all the ingredients in a bowl and mix well. Season to taste.

2 Cook the noodles in a pan of boiling water, following the directions on the packet, until just tender. Drain, rinse under cold running water and drain again.

3 Cook all the vegetables, except the water chestnuts, in separate pans of boiling, lightly salted water until they are tender but still crisp. Drain, plunge them immediately into cold water and drain again.

4 Toss the noodles, vegetables, water chestnuts and dressing together. Arrange on individual serving plates and garnish with the lime wedges, chopped peanuts and coriander leaves.

Energy 428kcal/1799kJ; Protein 18g; Carbohydrate 59g, of which sugars 14g; Fat 15g, of which saturates 2g; Cholesterol 0mg; Calcium 127mg; Fibre 11g; Sodium 105mg.

Prawn Noodle Salad with Fragrant Herbs

A light, refreshing salad with all the tangy flavour of the sea. Instead of prawns, you can also use squid, scallops, mussels or crab.

INGREDIENTS

Serves 4

115g/4oz cellophane noodles, soaked in hot water until soft
1 small green (bell) pepper, seeded and cut into strips
½ cucumber, cut into strips
1 tomato, cut into strips
2 shallots, finely sliced
16 shelled cooked prawns (shrimp)
salt and ground black pepper
fresh coriander (cilantro) leaves, to garnish

For the dressing
15ml/1 tbsp rice wine vinegar
30ml/2 tbsp Thai fish sauce
30ml/2 tbsp lime juice
2.5ml/½ tsp grated fresh root ginger
1 lemon grass stalk, finely chopped
1 red chilli, seeded and finely sliced
30ml/2 tbsp roughly chopped fresh mint
a few sprigs of tarragon, roughly chopped
15ml/1 tbsp snipped fresh chives
a pinch of salt

1 To make the dressing, combine all the ingredients in a small bowl or jug (pitcher) and whisk.

2 Drain the noodles, then plunge them in a pan of boiling water for 1 minute. Drain, rinse under cold running water and drain again well.

3 In a large bowl, combine the noodles with the green pepper, cucumber, tomato and shallots. Lightly season with salt and pepper, then toss with the dressing.

COOK'S TIP

Prawns (shrimp) are available ready-cooked and often shelled. To cook prawns, boil them for 5 minutes. Leave them to cool in the cooking liquid, then gently pull off the tail shell and twist off the head.

4 Spoon the noodles on to individual serving plates, arranging the prawns on top. Garnish with a few coriander leaves and serve at once.

Energy 156kcal/653kJ; Protein 7.4g; Carbohydrate 29.4g, of which sugars 5.4g; Fat 0.7g, of which saturates 0.1g; Cholesterol 49mg; Calcium 68mg; Fibre 2.1g; Sodium 417mg.

Egg Noodle Salad with Sesame Chicken

Quickly stir-fried chicken is served warm in a nest of crunchy salad vegetables and noodles.

INGREDIENTS

Serves 4–6

400g/14oz fresh thin egg noodles
1 carrot, cut into long fine strips
50g/2oz mangetouts (snow peas), topped, tailed, cut into fine strips and blanched
115g/4oz/½ cup beansprouts, blanched
30ml/2 tbsp olive oil
225g/8oz skinless chicken breast fillet, finely sliced
30ml/2 tbsp sesame seeds, toasted
2 spring onions (scallions), finely sliced diagonally, and fresh coriander (cilantro) leaves, to garnish

For the dressing
45ml/3 tbsp sherry vinegar
75ml/5 tbsp soy sauce
60ml/4 tbsp sesame oil
90ml/6 tbsp light olive oil
1 garlic clove, finely chopped
5ml/1 tsp grated fresh root ginger
salt and ground black pepper

1 To make the dressing, whisk together all the ingredients in a small bowl. Season to taste.

2 Cook the noodles in a large pan of boiling water. Stir them occasionally to separate. They will take only a few minutes to cook. Drain the noodles, rinse under cold running water and drain well. Tip into a bowl.

3 Add the carrot, mangetouts and beansprouts to the noodles. Pour in about half of the dressing, then toss the mixture well and adjust the seasoning according to taste.

4 Heat the oil in a large frying pan. Add the chicken and stir-fry for 3 minutes, or until cooked and golden. Remove from the heat. Add the sesame seeds and drizzle in some of the remaining dressing.

5 Arrange the noodle mixture on individual serving plates, making a nest on each plate. Spoon the chicken on top. Sprinkle with the spring onions and coriander leaves and serve any remaining dressing separately.

Energy 546kcal/2286kJ; Protein 19.3g; Carbohydrate 50.9g, of which sugars 3.8g; Fat 30.9g, of which saturates 5.3g; Cholesterol 46mg; Calcium 69mg; Fibre 3.2g; Sodium 860mg.

Chicken and Pasta Salad

This is a delicious way to use up left-over cooked chicken and, with the pasta, it makes a satisfying meal.

INGREDIENTS

Serves 4

225g/8oz tri-coloured pasta twists
30ml/2 tbsp bottled pesto sauce
15ml/1 tbsp olive oil
1 beef tomato
12 pitted black olives
225g/8oz French (green) beans, cooked
350g/12oz cooked chicken, cubed
salt and ground black pepper
fresh basil, to garnish

3 Peel the beef tomato by cutting a cross in the skin and plunging it in boiling water for about 30 seconds. The skin will now pull away easily. Cut the tomato into small cubes.

4 Add the tomato and olives to the pasta. Cut the French beans into 4cm/1½in lengths. Add the beans and chicken and season to taste. Toss gently, transfer to a serving platter, garnish with basil, and serve.

1 Cook the pasta in plenty of boiling, salted water until al dente (for about 12 minutes or as directed on the packet).

2 Drain the pasta and rinse in plenty of cold running water. Put into a bowl and stir in the pesto sauce and olive oil.

Energy 373kcal/1575kJ; Protein 32g; Carbohydrate 44g, of which sugars 3.7g; Fat 8.9g, of which saturates 2.6g; Cholesterol 69mg; Calcium 138mg; Fibre 3.4g; Sodium 419mg.

Corn-fed Chicken Salad with Garlic Bread

This makes a light first course for eight people or a substantial main course for four.

INGREDIENTS

Serves 4

1.75kg/4–4½lb corn-fed chicken
300ml/½ pint/1¼ cups white wine and water, mixed
24 slices French bread, 5mm/¼in thick
1 garlic clove, peeled
225g/8oz French (green) beans
115g/4oz young spinach leaves
2 celery sticks, thinly sliced
2 sun-dried tomatoes, chopped
2 spring onions (scallions), thinly sliced
fresh chives and parsley, to garnish

For the vinaigrette
30ml/2 tbsp red wine vinegar
90ml/6 tbsp olive oil
15ml/1 tbsp wholegrain mustard
15ml/1 tbsp clear honey
30ml/2 tbsp chopped fresh mixed herbs, such as thyme, parsley, chives
10ml/2 tsp finely chopped capers
salt and ground black pepper

1 Preheat the oven to 190°C/375°F/Gas 5. Put the chicken into a casserole with the wine and water. Cook in the oven for 1½ hours, until tender. Leave to cool in the liquid. Discard the skin and bones and cut the flesh into small pieces.

2 To make the vinaigrette, put all the ingredients into a screw-top jar and shake vigorously to combine. Adjust the seasoning to taste if necesary.

3 Toast the French bread under the grill (broiler) or in the oven until dry and golden brown. Rub with the peeled garlic clove.

4 Trim the French beans, cut into 5cm/2in lengths and cook in boiling water until just tender. Drain and rinse under cold running water.

5 Wash the spinach, discarding the stalks, and tear into small pieces. Arrange on individual serving plates with the celery, French beans, sun-dried tomatoes, chicken and spring onions.

6 Spoon over the vinaigrette dressing. Arrange the toasted slices of French bread on top, garnish with fresh chives and parsley and serve immediately.

Energy 462kcal/1939kJ; Protein 38.9g; Carbohydrate 35.4g, of which sugars 34.7g; Fat 19.3g, of which saturates 3g; Cholesterol 105mg; Calcium 119mg; Fibre 3.2g; Sodium 174mg.

Warm Chicken Salad

Succulent chicken pieces are combined with vegetables and rice in a light chilli dressing.

INGREDIENTS

Serves 6

50g/2oz mixed salad leaves
50g/2oz baby spinach leaves
50g/2oz watercress
30ml/2 tbsp chilli sauce
30ml/2 tbsp dry sherry
15ml/1 tbsp light soy sauce
15ml/1 tbsp tomato ketchup
10ml/2 tsp olive oil
8 shallots, finely chopped
1 garlic clove, crushed
350g/12oz skinless chicken breast fillet, cut into thin strips
1 red (bell) pepper, seeded and sliced
175g/6oz mangetouts (snow peas), trimmed
400g/14oz can baby corn cobs, drained and halved
275g/10oz brown rice, cooked
salt and ground black pepper
fresh parsley sprig, to garnish

2 In a small bowl, mix together the chilli sauce, sherry, soy sauce and tomato ketchup. Set the sauce mixture aside.

5 Add the pepper, mangetouts, baby corn cobs and rice, and stir-fry for a further 2–3 minutes.

3 Heat the oil in a large, non-stick frying pan or wok. Add the shallots and garlic and stir-fry over a medium heat for 1 minute.

4 Add the chicken to the pan and stir-fry for a further 3–4 minutes.

6 Pour in the chilli sauce mixture and stir-fry for 2–3 minutes, until hot and bubbling. Season to taste.

7 Spoon the chicken mixture over the salad leaves, toss together to mix and serve immediately, garnished with a sprig of fresh parsley.

VARIATION

Use other lean meat such as turkey breast, beef or pork in place of the chicken breast fillet.

1 If any of the mixed salad leaves are large, tear them into smaller pieces and arrange with the spinach leaves on a serving dish. Add the watercress and toss together to mix.

Spicy Chicken Salad

Marinate the chicken in advance for this tasty salad, which is otherwise quick to prepare.

INGREDIENTS

Serves 6

5ml/1 tsp ground cumin seeds
5ml/1 tsp paprika
5ml/1 tsp ground turmeric
1–2 garlic cloves, crushed
30ml/2 tbsp lime juice
4 skinless chicken breast fillets
225g/8oz rigatoni
1 red (bell) pepper, seeded and chopped
2 celery sticks, thinly sliced
1 shallot or small onion, finely chopped
25g/1oz/¼ cup stuffed green olives, halved
30ml/2 tbsp clear honey
15ml/1 tbsp wholegrain mustard
15–30ml/1–2 tbsp lime juice
mixed salad leaves
salt and ground black pepper

1 Mix the cumin, paprika, turmeric, garlic and lime juice in a bowl. Season with salt and pepper. Rub this mixture over the chicken breast fillet. Lay these in a dish, cover with clear film (plastic wrap) and leave in a cool place for about 3 hours or overnight.

2 Preheat the oven to 200°C/400°F/Gas 6. Put the chicken on a grill (broiler) rack and bake for 20 minutes. (Alternatively, grill (broil) for 8–10 minutes on each side.)

3 Cook the rigatoni pasta in a large pan of boiling, salted water until al dente. Drain and rinse under cold water. Leave to drain thoroughly.

4 Put the red pepper, celery, shallot or small onion and olives into a large bowl with the pasta. Mix together.

5 Mix the honey, mustard and lime juice together in a small bowl and pour over the pasta mixture. Toss to coat.

6 Cut the chicken breast fillets into bitesize pieces. Arrange the mixed salad leaves on a serving dish, spoon the pasta mixture into the centre and top with the spicy chicken pieces.

Energy 137kcal/579kJ; Protein 24.9g; Carbohydrate 4.9g, of which sugars 3.9g; Fat 2.1g, of which saturates 0.5g; Cholesterol 70mg; Calcium 21mg; Fibre 0.8g; Sodium 236mg.

Chicken Maryland Salad

Tender chicken, corn, bacon, banana and watercress combine in a sensational main-course salad. Serve with jacket potatoes topped with a little butter.

INGREDIENTS

Serves 4

4 chicken breast fillets
oil, for brushing
225g/8oz rindless unsmoked bacon
4 corn cobs
45ml/3 tbsp soft butter (optional)
4 ripe bananas, peeled and halved
4 firm tomatoes, halved
1 escarole or round (butterhead) lettuce
1 bunch watercress
salt and ground black pepper

For the dressing

75ml/5 tbsp groundnut (peanut) oil
15ml/1 tbsp white wine vinegar
10ml/2 tsp maple syrup
10ml/2 tsp prepared mild mustard

2 Bring a large pan of salted water to the boil. Shuck and trim the corn cobs or leave the husks on if you prefer. Boil for 20 minutes.

3 For extra flavour, brush the corn cobs with butter and brown over the barbecue or under the grill. Barbecue or grill the bananas and tomatoes for 6–8 minutes; you can brush these with butter too if you wish.

5 Wash the lettuce and watercress leaves and spin dry. Put into a large bowl, pour over the dressing and toss well.

6 Distribute the salad leaves between four large serving plates. Slice the chicken and arrange over the salad leaves together with the bacon, banana, corn and tomatoes.

1 Season the chicken breasts, brush with oil and barbecue or grill (broiler) for 15 minutes, turning once. Barbecue or grill (broil) the bacon for 8–10 minutes, or until crisp.

4 To make the dressing, combine the oil, vinegar, maple syrup and mustard with 15ml/1 tbsp water in a screw-top jar and shake well.

Energy 659kcal/2768kJ; Protein 50.9g; Carbohydrate 56.4g, of which sugars 37.1g; Fat 27.1g, of which saturates 7g; Cholesterol 135mg; Calcium 51mg; Fibre 4.2g; Sodium 1319mg.

Chicken, Tongue and Gruyère Cheese Salad

The rich, sweet flavours of this salad marry well with the tart, peppery watercress. A minted lemon dressing freshens the overall effect. Serve with warm new potatoes.

INGREDIENTS

Serves 4

2 skinless chicken breast fillets
½ chicken stock (bouillon) cube
225g/8oz ox tongue or ham, sliced 5mm/¼in thick
225g/8oz Gruyère cheese
1 lollo rosso lettuce
1 round (butterhead) lettuce or endive (US chicory)
1 bunch watercress
2 green-skinned apples, cored and sliced
3 celery sticks, sliced
60ml/4 tbsp sesame seeds, toasted
salt, ground black pepper and freshly grated nutmeg

For the dressing

75ml/5 tbsp groundnut (peanut) or sunflower oil
5ml/1 tsp sesame oil
45ml/3 tbsp lemon juice
10ml/2 tsp chopped fresh mint
3 drops Tabasco sauce

1 Place the chicken fillets in a shallow pan, cover with 300ml/½ pint/1¼ cups water, add the ½ stock cube and bring to the boil. Put the lid on the pan and simmer for 15 minutes. Drain, reserving the stock for another occasion, then leave the chicken to cool.

2 To make the dressing, measure the oils, lemon juice, mint and Tabasco sauce into a screw-top jar and shake well. Cut the chicken, tongue or ham and cheese into fine strips. Moisten with a little dressing and set aside.

3 Combine the lettuce and watercress leaves with the apple and celery. Add the dressing and toss. Distribute between four large serving plates. Pile the chicken, tongue or ham and cheese in the centre, sprinkle with sesame seeds, season with salt, pepper and freshly grated nutmeg and serve.

Energy 626kcal/2606kJ; Protein 46.8g; Carbohydrate 6.1g, of which sugars 6g; Fat 45.1g, of which saturates 16.2g; Cholesterol 140mg; Calcium 586mg; Fibre 3.1g; Sodium 1155mg.

Curried Chicken Salad

A smooth, mildly spicy sauce with the distinctive tang of fresh coriander leaves blends with lean chicken pieces on a bed of pasta and vegetables.

INGREDIENTS

Serves 4

2 cooked skinless chicken breast fillets
175g/6oz French (green) beans
350g/12oz multi-coloured penne
150ml/¼ pint/⅔ cup natural (plain) yogurt
5ml/1 tsp mild curry powder
1 garlic clove, crushed
1 green chilli, seeded and finely chopped
30ml/2 tbsp chopped fresh
   coriander (cilantro)
4 firm ripe tomatoes, skinned,
   seeded and cut in strips
salt and ground black pepper
fresh coriander leaves, to garnish

1 Cut the chicken into strips. Cut the French beans into 2.5cm/1in lengths and cook for 5 minutes. Drain and rinse under cold water.

2 Cook the pasta in a large pan of boiling, salted water until al dente. Drain and rinse thoroughly.

3 To make the sauce, mix the yogurt, curry powder, garlic, chilli and chopped coriander together in a bowl. Stir in the chicken pieces and leave to stand for 30 minutes.

4 Transfer the pasta to a large serving bowl and toss with the beans and tomatoes. Spoon over the chicken and sauce mixture. Garnish with the coriander leaves and serve.

Energy 430kcal/1828kJ; Protein 32.1g; Carbohydrate 72.5g, of which sugars 9.8g; Fat 3.4g, of which saturates 0.7g; Cholesterol 53mg; Calcium 128mg; Fibre 4.8g; Sodium 94mg.

"Poor Boy" Steak Salad

"Poor Boy" started life in the Italian Creole community of New Orleans when the poor survived on sandwiches filled with left-over scraps. Times have improved since then, and today the "Poor Boy" sandwich is commonly filled with tender beef steak and other goodies. This is a salad version of "Poor Boy".

INGREDIENTS

Serves 4

4 sirloin or rump (round) steaks, each about 175g/6oz
1 escarole lettuce
1 bunch watercress
4 tomatoes, quartered
4 large gherkins, sliced
4 spring onions (scallions), sliced
4 canned artichoke hearts, halved
175g/6oz button (white) mushrooms, sliced
12 green olives
120ml/4fl oz/½ cup French Dressing
salt and ground black pepper

1 Season the steaks with black pepper. Cook under a moderate grill (broiler) for 6–8 minutes, turning once, until medium-rare. Cover with foil and leave to rest in a warm place.

2 Combine the lettuce and watercress leaves with the tomatoes, gherkins, spring onions, artichoke hearts, mushrooms and olives and toss with the French Dressing.

3 Divide the salad between four serving plates. Slice each steak diagonally and arrange over the salad. Adjust the seasoning as required and serve immediately before the leaves wilt.

Energy 573kcal/2379kJ; Protein 43.2g; Carbohydrate 6g, of which sugars 5.8g; Fat 35.1g, of which saturates 10.4g; Cholesterol 102mg; Calcium 105mg; Fibre 3.9g; Sodium 990mg.

Waldorf Ham Salad

Waldorf Salad first appeared at the Waldorf-Astoria Hotel, New York, in the 1890s. Originally it consisted of apples, celery and mayonnaise, and was commonly served with duck, ham and goose. This modern-day version often includes meat and is something of a meal in itself.

INGREDIENTS

Serves 4

3 apples
15ml/1 tbsp lemon juice
2 slices cooked ham, each about 175g/6oz
2 celery stalks
150ml/¼ pint/⅔ cup mayonnaise
1 escarole or endive (US chicory)
1 small radicchio, finely shredded
½ bunch watercress
45ml/3 tbsp walnut or olive oil
50g/2oz/½ cup broken walnuts, toasted
salt and ground black pepper

1 Peel, core, slice and finely shred the apples. Moisten with lemon juice to keep them white. Cut the ham into 5cm/2in strips. Cut the celery stalks into similar-sized pieces. Combine the apples, ham and celery in a bowl.

2 Add the mayonnaise and mix thoroughly.

3 Shred all the salad leaves finely, then moisten with oil. Distribute the leaves between four serving plates. Pile the mayonnaise mixture in the centre, scatter with toasted walnuts, season and serve.

Energy 551kcal/2285kJ; Protein 19.4g; Carbohydrate 9.7g, of which sugars 9.5g; Fat 48.7g, of which saturates 7.2g; Cholesterol 79mg; Calcium 58mg; Fibre 2.6g; Sodium 1233mg.

Chicken Liver, Bacon and Tomato Salad

Warm salads are especially welcome during the autumn months when the days are growing shorter and cooler. This rich salad includes sweet spinach and the bitter leaves of frisée lettuce.

INGREDIENTS

Serves 4

225g/8oz young spinach, stems removed
1 frisée lettuce
105ml/7 tbsp groundnut (peanut) oil
175g/6oz rindless unsmoked bacon, cut into strips
75g/3oz day-old bread, crusts removed and cut into short fingers
450g/1lb chicken livers
115g/4oz cherry tomatoes
salt and ground black pepper

1 Place the spinach and lettuce leaves in a salad bowl.

2 Heat 60ml/4 tbsp of the oil in a large frying pan, add the bacon and cook for 3–4 minutes, or until crisp and brown. Remove the bacon with a slotted spoon and drain on kitchen paper.

3 To make croûtons, fry the bread in the bacon-flavoured oil, tossing until crisp and golden. Drain on kitchen paper.

4 Heat the remaining 45ml/3 tbsp oil in the frying pan, add the chicken livers and fry briskly for 2–3 minutes. Turn the chicken livers out over the salad leaves and add the bacon, croûtons and tomatoes. Season, toss and serve warm.

VARIATION

If you can't find any baby spinach leaves you can use lamb's lettuce. Watercress would make a deliciously peppery substitute, but you should use less of it and bulk the salad out with a milder leaf so that the watercress doesn't overwhelm the other flavours.

Energy 468kcal/1943kJ; Protein 33g; Carbohydrate 11.9g, of which sugars 3.1g; Fat 32.3g, of which saturates 6.7g; Cholesterol 457mg; Calcium 144mg; Fibre 2.2g; Sodium 1132mg.

Curry Fried Pork and Rice Vermicelli Salad

Pork crackling adds a delicious crunch to this popular salad.

INGREDIENTS

Serves 4

225g/8oz lean pork
2 garlic cloves, finely chopped
2 slices fresh root ginger, peeled and finely chopped
30–45ml/2–3 tbsp rice wine
45ml/3 tbsp vegetable oil
2 lemon grass stalks, finely chopped
10ml/2 tsp curry powder
175g/6oz/¾ cup beansprouts
225g/8oz rice vermicelli, soaked in warm water until soft then drained
½ lettuce, finely shredded
30ml/2 tbsp fresh mint leaves
lemon juice and Thai fish sauce, to taste
salt and ground black pepper
2 spring onions (scallions), chopped, 25g/1oz/¼ cup toasted peanuts, chopped, and pork crackling (optional) to garnish

1 Cut the pork into thin strips. Place in a shallow dish with half the garlic and ginger. Season with salt and pepper, pour over 30ml/2 tbsp rice wine and marinate for at least 1 hour.

2 Heat the oil in a frying pan. Add the remaining garlic and ginger and fry for a few seconds until fragrant and golden. Stir in the strips of pork, with the marinade, and add the lemon grass and curry powder.

3 Fry on a high heat until the pork is golden and cooked through, adding more rice wine if the mixture seems too dry.

4 Place the beansprouts in a sieve (strainer). Blanch them by lowering the sieve into a pan of boiling water for 1 minute, then drain and refresh under cold water. Drain again. Using the same water, cook the rice vermicelli for 3–5 minutes, until tender. Drain and rinse under cold running water.

5 Drain the vermicelli well and tip into a large bowl. Add the beansprouts, shredded lettuce and mint leaves. Season with lemon juice and fish sauce to taste. Toss lightly to combine the flavours.

6 Divide the vermicelli mixture among individual serving plates, making a nest on each plate. Arrange the pork mixture on top. Garnish with spring onions, toasted peanuts and pork crackling, if using. Serve.

Energy 409kcal/1705kJ; Protein 20.8g; Carbohydrate 48.7g, of which sugars 2.8g; Fat 14.5g, of which saturates 2.4g; Cholesterol 35mg; Calcium 68mg; Fibre 2.4g; Sodium 60mg.

Sweet Potato, Egg, Pork and Beetroot Salad

This dish is a delicious way to use up left-over roast pork. Sweet flavours balance well with the bitterness of the chicory leaves.

INGREDIENTS

Serve 4

900g/2lb sweet potatoes
4 chicory (Belgian endive) heads
5 eggs, hard-boiled
450g/1lb pickled young beetroot (beets)
175g/6oz cold roast pork
salt

For the dressing
75ml/5 tbsp groundnut (peanut) oil
30ml/2 tbsp white wine vinegar
10ml/2 tsp Dijon mustard
5ml/1 tsp fennel seeds, crushed

1 Peel the sweet potatoes and dice into equal pieces.

2 Add the diced sweet potatoes to a pan of boiling salted water. Bring back to the boil then simmer for 10–15 minutes, or until the potatoes are soft. Drain and allow to cool.

3 To make the dressing, combine the oil, vinegar, mustard and fennel seeds in a screw-top jar and shake.

4 Separate the chicory leaves and arrange them around the edge of four serving plates.

5 Pour two thirds of the dressing over the sweet potatoes, stir in so that all the pieces of potato are coated in the dressing, and spoon on top of the chicory leaves.

6 Shell the hard-boiled eggs. Slice the eggs and beetroot, and arrange to make an attractive circle around the sweet potato.

7 Slice the pork then cut into strips of around 4cm/1½in. Place in a bowl and moisten with the rest of the dressing.

8 Pile the strips of pork into the centre of each salad. Season with salt and serve.

COOK'S TIP

To crush the fennel seeds, grind using a mortar and pestle. If you don't have these use two dessertspoons instead. For extra flavour try toasting the fennel seeds before crushing.

Energy 507kcal/2132kJ; Protein 21.9g; Carbohydrate 56.7g, of which sugars 20.9g; Fat 23.3g, of which saturates 4.4g; Cholesterol 265mg; Calcium 119mg; Fibre 7.7g; Sodium 283mg.

Frankfurter Salad with Mustard Dressing

This is a last-minute salad, which you can put together using mostly store-cupboard (pantry) ingredients.

INGREDIENTS

Serves 4

675g/1½lb small new potatoes, scrubbed or scraped
2 eggs
350g/12oz frankfurters
1 round (butterhead) lettuce or endive (US chicory)
225g/8oz young spinach leaves, stems removed
salt and ground black pepper

For the dressing
45ml/3 tbsp safflower oil
30ml/2 tbsp olive oil
15ml/1 tbsp white wine vinegar
10ml/2 tsp mustard
5ml/1 tsp caraway seeds, crushed

1 Bring the potatoes to the boil in salted water and simmer for about 15 minutes, or until tender. Drain, cover and keep warm. Hard-boil the eggs for 12 minutes. Refresh in cold water, shell and cut into quarters.

2 Score the frankfurter skins cork-screw fashion with a small knife, then cover with boiling water and simmer for about 5 minutes to heat through. Drain well, cover and keep warm.

3 To make the dressing, place all the ingredients in a screw-top jar and shake.

4 Moisten the salad leaves with half of the dressing and distribute between four large serving plates.

5 Moisten the warm potatoes and frankfurters with the remainder of the dressing and scatter over the salad.

6 Finish the salad with sections of hard-boiled egg, season and serve warm.

COOK'S TIP

This salad has a German slant to it and calls for a sweet-and-sour German-style mustard. American mustards have a similar quality.

Energy 561kcal/2336kJ; Protein 20.5g; Carbohydrate 31g, of which sugars 5.9g; Fat 40.4g, of which saturates 11g; Cholesterol 162mg; Calcium 160mg; Fibre 3.9g; Sodium 1014mg.

Smoked Bacon and Green Bean Pasta Salad

A tasty pasta salad, subtly flavoured with smoked bacon and tossed in a light, flavoursome dressing.

INGREDIENTS

Serves 4

350g/12oz whole-wheat pasta twists
225g/8oz green beans
8 rashers (strips) lean smoked back bacon
350g/12oz cherry tomatoes, halved
2 bunches spring onions scallions, chopped
400g/14oz can chickpeas, drained

For the dressing
90ml/6 tbsp tomato juice
30ml/2 tbsp balsamic vinegar
5ml/1 tsp ground cumin
5ml/1 tsp ground coriander
30ml/2 tbsp chopped fresh coriander (cilantro)
salt and ground black pepper

2 Preheat the grill (broiler) and cook the bacon for 2–3 minutes on each side, until cooked. Dice the bacon and add to the beans.

3 Put the tomatoes, spring onions and chickpeas in a large bowl. In a small bowl, mix together the tomato juice, vinegar, spices, chopped fresh coriander and seasoning.

4 Pour the dressing into a large bowl. Drain the cooked pasta thoroughly and add to the tomato mixture along with the green beans and bacon.

5 Toss all the ingredients together to mix thoroughly. Serve warm or cold.

1 Cook the pasta in a large pan of lightly salted, boiling water until al dente. Meanwhile, trim and halve the green beans and cook them in boiling water for about 5 minutes, until tender. Drain thoroughly and keep warm.

COOK'S TIP

Always rinse canned beans, peas and lentils well before using, to remove as much of the brine (salt water) as possible.

Energy 534kcal/2260kJ; Protein 27g; Carbohydrate 85g, of which sugars 8g; Fat 12g, of which saturates 4g; Cholesterol 32mg; Calcium 123mg; Fibre 5g; Sodium 724mg.

Warm Pasta Salad with Asparagus

This warm salad is served with ham, eggs and parmesan cheese. A mustard dressing made from the thick part of the asparagus stalks provides a rich accompaniment.

INGREDIENTS

Serves 4

450g/1lb asparagus
450g/1lb dried tagliatelle
225g/8oz cooked ham, sliced 5mm/¼in thick, and cut into fingers
2 eggs, hard-boiled and sliced
50g/2oz piece Parmesan cheese

For the dressing
50g/2oz cooked potato
75ml/5 tbsp olive oil
15ml/1 tbsp lemon juice
10ml/2 tsp Dijon mustard
120ml/4fl oz/½ cup vegetable stock
salt and ground black pepper

1 Bring a pan of salted water to the boil. Trim and discard the tough, woody part of the asparagus stalks. Cut the asparagus in half and boil the thicker halves for 12 minutes, adding the asparagus tips after 6 minutes. Refresh under cold water until warm, then drain.

2 Finely chop 150g/5oz of the thicker asparagus pieces. Place in a food processor together with the dressing ingredients and process until smooth. Season the dressing to taste.

3 Boil the pasta in a large pan of salted water until al dente. Refresh under cold water.

4 Dress with the asparagus sauce and turn out into four pasta bowls. Top each pile of pasta with some of the ham, eggs and asparagus tips. Finish with shavings of Parmesan cheese and serve warm.

Energy 815kcal/3424kJ; Protein 39g; Carbohydrate 90g, of which sugars 5g; Fat 36g, of which saturates 9g; Cholesterol 174mg; Calcium 213mg; Fibre 8g; Sodium 975mg.

Devilled Ham and Pineapple Salad

This tasty salad, with a crunchy topping of toasted almonds, can be quickly prepared using items from the store cupboard (pantry).

INGREDIENTS

Serves 4

225g/8oz whole-wheat penne
150ml/¼ pint/⅔ cup natural (plain) yogurt
15ml/1 tbsp cider vinegar
5ml/1 tsp wholegrain mustard
a large pinch of caster (superfine) sugar
30ml/2 tbsp hot mango chutney
115g/4oz cooked lean ham, cubed
200g/7oz can pineapple chunks, drained
2 celery sticks, chopped
½ green (bell) pepper, seeded and diced
15ml/1 tbsp toasted flaked (sliced) almonds, chopped roughly
salt and ground black pepper
crusty bread, to serve

1 Cook the pasta in a large pan of salted boiling water until al dente. Drain and rinse thoroughly. Leave to cool.

2 To make the dressing, mix the yogurt, vinegar, mustard, sugar and mango chutney together. Season with salt and pepper. Add the pasta and toss lightly together.

3 Transfer the pasta to a serving dish. Add the ham, pineapple, celery and green pepper.

4 Sprinkle toasted almonds over the top of the salad. Serve with crusty bread.

Energy 311kcal/1319kJ; Protein 15.3g; Carbohydrate 55.5g, of which sugars 15.5g; Fat 4.7g, of which saturates 0.8g; Cholesterol 17mg; Calcium 115mg; Fibre 3.2g; Sodium 402mg.

Pear and Pecan Nut Salad

Toasted pecan nuts have a special affinity with crisp white pears. Their robust flavours combine well with a rich Blue Cheese and Chive dressing to make this a salad to remember.

INGREDIENTS

Serves 4

75g/3oz/½ cup shelled pecan nuts, roughly chopped
3 crisp pears
175g/6oz young spinach, stems removed
1 escarole or round (butterhead) lettuce
1 radicchio
30ml/2 tbsp Blue Cheese and Chive Dressing
salt and ground black pepper
crusty bread, to serve

1 Toast the pecan nuts under a moderate grill (broiler) to bring out their flavour.

2 Cut the pears into even slices, leaving the skins intact but discarding the cores.

3 Place the spinach, lettuce and radicchio leaves into a large bowl. Add the pears and toasted pecans, pour over the Blue Cheese and Chive Dressing and toss well.

4 Distribute among four large serving plates and season with salt and pepper. Serve the salad with warm crusty bread.

COOK'S TIP

The pecan nuts will burn very quickly under the grill (broiler), so keep constant watch over them and remove them as soon as they change colour.

Energy 231kcal/960kJ; Protein 5g; Carbohydrate 15g, of which sugars 15g; Fat 17g, of which saturates 1g; Cholesterol 3mg; Calcium 130mg; Fibre 6g; Sodium 151mg.

Goat's Cheese and Fig Salad

Fresh figs and walnuts are perfect partners for goat's cheese and toasted buckwheat. The olive and nut oil dressing contains no vinegar, depending instead on the acidity of the goat's cheese.

INGREDIENTS

Serves 4

175g/6oz/1 cup couscous
30ml/2 tbsp toasted buckwheat
1 egg, hard-boiled
30ml/2 tbsp chopped fresh parsley
60ml/4 tbsp olive oil
45ml/3 tbsp walnut oil
115g/4oz rocket (arugula) leaves
½ frisée lettuce
175g/6oz crumbly white goat's cheese
50g/2oz/½ cup broken walnuts, toasted
4 ripe figs, trimmed and almost cut into four (leave the pieces joined at the base)

1 Place the couscous and toasted buckwheat in a bowl, cover with boiling water and leave to soak for 15 minutes. Place in a sieve to drain off any remaining water, then spread out on a metal tray and allow to cool.

2 Shell the hard-boiled egg and grate finely.

3 Toss the grated egg, parsley, couscous and buckwheat together in a bowl. Combine the olive and walnut oils using half to moisten the couscous mixture.

4 Toss the salad leaves in the remaining oil and distribute between four large serving plates.

5 Pile the couscous mixture in the centre of each plate and crumble the goat's cheese over the top. Scatter with toasted walnuts, place a fig in the centre of each plate and serve.

COOK'S TIP

Goat's cheeses vary in strength from the youngest, which are soft and mild, to strongly-flavoured, mature (sharp) cheeses, which have a firm and crumbly texture. The crumbly varieties are best suited to salads.

Energy 581kcal/2410kJ; Protein 17g; Carbohydrate 35.9g, of which sugars 13.3g; Fat 41.9g, of which saturates 11.4g; Cholesterol 88mg; Calcium 189mg; Fibre 3.5g; Sodium 301mg.

Avocado, Tomato and Mozzarella Salad

This popular salad is made from ingredients representing the colours of the Italian flag – a sunny, cheerful dish! The addition of pasta turns it into a main course meal for a light lunch.

INGREDIENTS

Serves 4

175g/6oz pasta bows (farfalle)
6 ripe red tomatoes
225g/8oz mozzarella cheese
1 large ripe avocado
30ml/2 tbsp chopped fresh basil
30ml/2 tbsp pine nuts, toasted
fresh basil sprig, to garnish

For the dressing
90ml/6 tbsp olive oil
30ml/2 tbsp wine vinegar
5ml/1 tsp balsamic vinegar (optional)
5ml/1 tsp wholegrain mustard
a pinch of sugar
salt and ground black pepper

1 Cook the pasta bows in plenty of salted, boiling water until al dente.

2 Slice the tomatoes and mozzarella cheese into thin rounds with a sharp knife.

3 Halve the avocado, remove the stone (pit) and peel off the skin. Slice the flesh lengthways.

4 Whisk the dressing ingredients together in a small bowl.

5 Arrange the tomato, mozzarella and avocado slices in overlapping slices around the edge of a flat serving plate.

6 Toss the pasta with half of the dressing and the chopped basil. Pile into the centre of the plate. Pour over the remaining dressing, scatter over the pine nuts and garnish with a sprig of fresh basil. Serve immediately.

COOK'S TIP

The pale green flesh of the avocado quickly discolours once it is cut. Prepare it at the last minute and place immediately in dressing. If you do have to prepare it ahead, squeeze lemon juice over the cut side and cover with clear film (plastic wrap).

Energy 649kcal/2705kJ; Protein 19g; Carbohydrate 39g, of which sugars 6g; Fat 48g, of which saturates 13g; Cholesterol 33mg; Calcium 237mg; Fibre 4g; Sodium 298mg.

Roquefort and Walnut Pasta Salad

This is a simple, earthy salad, relying totally on the quality of the ingredients. There is no real substitute for the Roquefort – a blue-veined ewe's-milk cheese from south-western France.

INGREDIENTS

Serves 4

225g/8oz pasta shapes

selection of salad leaves such as rocket (arugula), frisée, lamb's lettuce, baby spinach, radicchio

30ml/2 tbsp walnut oil

60ml/4 tbsp sunflower oil

30ml/2 tbsp red wine vinegar or sherry vinegar

225g/8oz Roquefort cheese, roughly crumbled

115g/4oz/1 cup walnut halves

salt and ground black pepper

3 Pile the pasta in the centre of the salad leaves, scatter over the crumbled Roquefort and pour over the dressing.

4 Scatter the walnut halves over the top. Toss the salad to combine the ingredients just before serving.

1 Cook the pasta in plenty of salted, boiling water until al dente. Drain well and cool. Place the salad leaves in a bowl.

2 Whisk together the walnut oil, sunflower oil and vinegar. Season with salt and pepper to taste.

COOK'S TIP

Toast the walnuts under the grill (broiler) to add extra flavour.

Energy 812kcal/3376kJ; Protein 22g; Carbohydrate 44g, of which sugars 2g; Fat 62g, of which saturates 16g; Cholesterol 51mg; Calcium 346mg; Fibre 5g; Sodium 949mg.

Pasta, Asparagus and Potato Salad

Made with whole-wheat pasta, this delicious salad is a real treat, especially when made with fresh asparagus just in season.

INGREDIENTS

Serves 4

225g/8oz whole-wheat pasta shapes
60ml/4 tbsp extra virgin olive oil
350g/12oz baby new potatoes
225g/8oz asparagus
115g/4oz piece Parmesan cheese
salt and ground black pepper

1 Cook the pasta in salted, boiling water until al dente.

2 Drain well and toss with the olive oil while the pasta is still warm. Season with salt and ground black pepper.

3 Scrub the potatoes and cook in boiling salted water for about 15 minutes, or until tender. Drain the potatoes and toss together with the pasta.

4 Trim any woody ends off the asparagus and halve the stalks if very long. Blanch in boiling salted water for 6 minutes, until bright green and still crunchy. Drain. Plunge into cold water to stop the asparagus cooking and allow to cool. Drain and dry on kitchen paper.

5 Toss the asparagus with the potatoes and pasta, adjust the seasoning to taste and transfer to a shallow serving bowl. Using a vegetable peeler, shave the Parmesan over the salad.

Energy 512kcal/2146kJ; Protein 21g; Carbohydrate 53g, of which sugars 5g; Fat 26g, of which saturates 8g; Cholesterol 27mg; Calcium 333mg; Fibre 9g; Sodium 301mg.

Courgettes, Carrots and Pecan Salad

Chunks of warm fried courgettes are served with a crisp tangy salad in pockets of pitta bread.

INGREDIENTS

Serves 2

2 carrots
25g/1oz/¼ cup pecan nuts
4 spring onions (scallions), sliced
50ml/2fl oz/¼ cup Greek (US strained plain) yogurt
35ml/7 tsp olive oil
5ml/1 tsp lemon juice
15ml/1 tbsp chopped fresh mint
2 courgettes (zucchini)
25g/1oz/¼ cup plain (all-purpose) flour
2 pitta breads
salt and ground black pepper
shredded lettuce, to serve

1 Top and tail the carrots. Grate them coarsely into a bowl.

2 Stir in the pecans and spring onions and toss well.

3 In a clean bowl, make the dressing. Whisk the yogurt with 7.5ml/1½ tsp of the olive oil, the lemon juice and the mint. Stir the dressing into the carrot mixture and mix well. Cover and chill until required.

4 Top and tail the courgettes. Cut them diagonally into slices. Season the flour with salt and pepper. Spread it out on a plate and turn the courgette slices in it until they are well coated.

5 Heat the remaining oil in a large frying pan. Add the coated courgette slices and cook for 3–4 minutes, turning once, until browned. Drain the courgettes on kitchen paper.

6 Make a slit in each pitta bread to form a pocket. Fill the pittas with the carrot mixture and the courgette slices. Serve on a bed of shredded lettuce.

COOK'S TIP

Warm the pitta breads in the oven or under a medium grill (broiler). Do not fill the pitta breads too soon or the carrot mixture will make the bread soggy.

Energy 770kcal/3210kJ; Protein 14g; Carbohydrate 71.9g, of which sugars 9.7g; Fat 49.4g, of which saturates 6.6g; Cholesterol 0mg; Calcium 209mg; Fibre 5.8g; Sodium 455mg.

Pasta, Olive and Avocado Salad

The ingredients of this salad are united by a wonderful sun-dried tomato and fresh basil dressing.

INGREDIENTS

Serves 6

225g/8oz pasta spirals or other small pasta shapes
115g/4oz can corn, drained, or frozen corn, thawed
½ red (bell) pepper, seeded and diced
8 black olives, pitted and sliced
3 spring onions (scallions), finely chopped
2 medium avocados

For the dressing

2 sun-dried tomato halves, loose-packed (not preserved in oil)
25ml/1½ tbsp balsamic or white wine vinegar
25ml/1½ tbsp red wine vinegar
½ garlic clove, crushed
2.5ml/½ tsp salt
75ml/5 tbsp olive oil
15ml/1 tbsp chopped fresh basil

1 To make the dressing, drop the sun-dried tomatoes into a pan containing 2.5cm/1in boiling water and simmer for about 3 minutes until tender. Drain and chop finely.

2 Combine the sun-dried tomatoes, both vinegars, garlic and salt in a food processor. With the machine on, add the olive oil in a steady stream until a paste forms. Stir in the basil.

3 Cook the pasta in a large pan of salted boiling water until al dente, following the packet instructions. Drain well. In a large bowl, combine the pasta, corn, red pepper, olives and spring onions. Add the dressing and toss well.

4 Just before serving, peel and stone (pit) the avocados and cut the flesh into cubes. Mix these gently into the pasta without breaking them up then place the salad on a serving dish. Serve at room temperature.

Energy 329kcal/1374kJ; Protein 6.5g; Carbohydrate 31.1g, of which sugars 3.7g; Fat 20.6g, of which saturates 3.6g; Cholesterol 0mg; Calcium 26mg; Fibre 3.9g; Sodium 412m.

Roast Pepper and Mushroom Pasta Salad

A combination of grilled (broiled) peppers and two different kinds of mushroom makes this salad colourful as well as nutritious.

INGREDIENTS

Serves 6

1 red, 1 yellow and 1 green (bell) pepper, halved
350g/12oz whole-wheat pasta shells or twists
30ml/2 tbsp olive oil
45ml/3 tbsp balsamic vinegar
75ml/5 tbsp tomato juice
30ml/2 tbsp chopped fresh basil
15ml/1 tbsp chopped fresh thyme
175g/6oz/2¼ cups shiitake mushrooms, diced
175g/6oz/2¼ cups oyster mushrooms, sliced
400g/14oz can black-eyed beans (peas), drained and rinsed
115g/4oz/¾ cup sultanas (golden raisins)
2 bunches spring onions (scallions), finely chopped
salt and ground black pepper

1 Preheat the grill (broiler) to hot. Put the peppers cut-side down on a grill pan rack and place under the grill for 10–15 minutes, until the skins are charred. Cover the peppers with a clean, damp dish towel and set aside to cool.

2 Meanwhile, cook the pasta shells or twists in lightly salted, boiling water until al dente, then drain thoroughly.

3 Mix together the oil, vinegar, tomato juice, basil and thyme, add to the warm pasta and toss.

4 Remove and discard the skins from the peppers. Seed and slice and add to the pasta.

5 Add the mushrooms, beans, sultanas, spring onions and seasoning. Toss the ingredients to mix and serve immediately. Alternatively, cover with clear film (plastic wrap) and chill in the refrigerator before serving.

Energy 390kcal/1650kJ; Protein 15.6g; Carbohydrate 71.8g, of which sugars 25.4g; Fat 6.5g, of which saturates 1g; Cholesterol 0mg; Calcium 126mg; Fibre 12.5g; Sodium 380mg.

Mediterranean Pasta Salad

A type of Salade Niçoise with pasta, conjuring up all the sunny flavours of the Mediterranean.

INGREDIENTS

Serves 4

225g/8oz chunky pasta shapes
175g/6oz fine green beans
2 large ripe tomatoes
50g/2oz fresh basil leaves
200g/7oz can tuna fish in oil, drained
2 hard-boiled eggs, shelled and sliced or quartered
50g/2oz can anchovy fillets, drained
capers and black olives, to taste

For the dressing
90ml/6 tbsp extra virgin olive oil
30ml/2 tbsp white wine vinegar or lemon juice
2 garlic cloves, crushed
2.5ml/½ tsp Dijon mustard
30ml/2 tbsp chopped fresh basil
salt and ground black pepper

1 To make the dressing, whisk all the ingredients together in a small bowl. Leave to infuse while you prepare the salad.

COOK'S TIP

Don't be tempted to chill this salad – the flavour will be dulled.

2 Cook the pasta in plenty of salted, boiling water until al dente. Drain well and cool.

3 Top and tail the green beans and blanch in salted, boiling water for 3 minutes. Drain and refresh in cold water.

4 Slice the tomatoes thinly and arrange on the bottom of a serving bowl. Moisten with a little dressing and cover with a quarter of the basil leaves, then cover with the beans.

5 Moisten with a little more dressing and cover with a third of the remaining basil.

6 Cover the vegetables with the pasta tossed in a little more dressing, half the remaining basil and the roughly flaked tuna.

7 Arrange the eggs on top, then finally scatter over the anchovy fillets, capers and olives. Spoon over the remaining dressing and garnish with the remaining basil. Serve immediately.

Energy 552kcal/2312kJ; Protein 30.9g; Carbohydrate 44.6g, of which sugars 4.4g; Fat 29.2g, of which saturates 5.1g; Cholesterol 223mg; Calcium 105mg; Fibre 3.1g; Sodium 713mg.

Special Occasion Salads

Gado Gado

This classic Indonesian vegetable salad is served with a delicious hot peanut sauce.

INGREDIENTS

Serves 4–6

2 medium potatoes
175g/6oz French (green) beans, topped and tailed
175g/6oz Chinese leaves (Chinese cabbage), shredded
1 iceberg lettuce
175g/6oz beansprouts
½ cucumber, cut into fingers
150g/5oz mooli (daikon), shredded
3 spring onions (scallions)
225g/8oz tofu, cut into large slices
3 hard-boiled eggs, shelled and quartered
1 small bunch fresh coriander (cilantro)
prawn crackers, to serve

For the peanut sauce
150g/5oz/1¼ cups raw peanuts
15ml/1 tbsp vegetable oil
2 shallots or 1 small onion, finely chopped
1 garlic clove, crushed
1–2 small chillies, seeded and finely chopped
1cm/½ in square shrimp paste or 15ml/1 tbsp Thai fish sauce (optional)
30ml/2 tbsp tamarind sauce
120ml/4fl oz/½ cup canned coconut milk
15ml/1 tbsp clear honey

1 Peel the potatoes. Bring to the boil in salted water and simmer for about 15 minutes, or until tender. Cook the French beans for 3–4 minutes. Drain the potatoes and beans and refresh under cold running water.

2 To make the peanut sauce, dry-fry the peanuts in a wok, or place under a moderate grill (broiler), tossing them all the time to prevent burning.

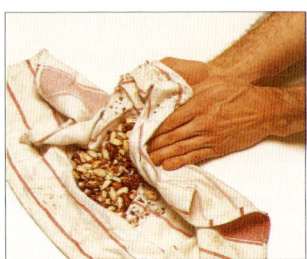

3 Turn the peanuts on to a clean cloth and rub them vigorously with your hands to remove the papery skins. Place the peanuts in a food processor and blend for 2 minutes until finely crushed.

4 Heat the vegetable oil in a wok and soften the shallots or onion, garlic and chillies without letting them colour. Add the shrimp paste or fish sauce, if using, together with the tamarind sauce, coconut milk and honey.

5 Simmer briefly, add to the blended peanuts and process to form a thick sauce. Transfer to a small serving bowl and keep hot.

6 Arrange the potatoes, French beans and all the other salad ingredients on a large serving platter. Serve with the bowl of peanut sauce and prawn crackers.

Energy 232kcal/964kJ; Protein 9g; Carbohydrate 16g, of which sugars 13g; Fat 15g, of which saturates 3g; Cholesterol 0mg; Calcium 87mg; Fibre 8g; Sodium 121mg.

Composed Salads

Composed salads make perfect appetizers. They are light and colourful and lend themselves to endless variation – and the components can often be prepared ahead for quick assembly.

The French are masters of the composed salad. Any combination of ingredients can be used – let your imagination and your palate guide you. Arranged attractively on a plate or in a bowl, this type of salad offers contrasting flavours, textures and colours. Raw or cooked vegetables, fresh fruits, hard-boiled hen's or quail's eggs, smoked or cooked poultry, meat, fish or shellfish can all be used, but it is important that the dressing or other seasoning unites all the elements harmoniously.

Unlike a tossed salad such as Salade de Mesclun, in which the leaves are tossed together with a simple vinaigrette, the components of a composed salad are kept more separate. The ingredients might be arranged in groups, sometimes on a base of lettuce or other leaves, or simply arranged in circles on the plate. Composed salads, such as the famous Salade Niçoise or any of the following salads, are often served as a first course or a light main course, especially in warm weather. A tossed green salad is frequently eaten after the main course and is generally thought to cleanse the palate in preparation for the cheese course or dessert.

PRAWN, AVOCADO AND CITRUS SALAD

INGREDIENTS

Serves 6

15ml/1 tbsp lemon juice
15ml/1 tbsp lime juice
15ml/1 tbsp clear honey
45ml/3 tbsp olive oil
30–45ml/2–3 tbsp walnut oil
30ml/2 tbsp snipped fresh chives
450g/1lb large cooked prawns (shrimp), shelled and deveined
1 avocado, peeled, stoned (pitted) and cut into small dice
1 pink grapefruit, peeled and segmented
1 large navel orange, peeled and segmented
30ml/2 tbsp pine nuts, toasted (optional)
salt and ground black pepper

1 Blend the lemon and lime juices, salt and pepper and honey in a small bowl. Slowly whisk in the olive oil, then the walnut oil, to make a creamy dressing. Stir in the chives.

2 Arrange the prawns with the diced avocado and grapefruit and orange segments on individual serving plates. Drizzle over the dressing, sprinkle with the toasted pine nuts, if using, and serve.

SMOKED SALMON SALAD WITH DILL

INGREDIENTS

Serves 4

225g/8oz smoked salmon, thinly sliced
1 fennel bulb, thinly sliced
1 medium cucumber, seeded and cut into julienne strips
30ml/2 tbsp lemon juice
120ml/4fl oz/½ cup extra virgin olive oil
30ml/2 tbsp chopped fresh dill, plus a few sprigs to garnish
ground black pepper
caviar, to garnish (optional)

1 Arrange the smoked salmon slices on four individual serving plates and arrange the slices of fennel alongside, together with the cucumber strips.

2 Mix together the lemon juice and pepper in a small bowl. Slowly whisk in the oil to make a creamy vinaigrette. Stir in the dill.

3 Spoon a little vinaigrette over the fennel and cucumber. Drizzle the remaining vinaigrette over the smoked salmon and garnish with sprigs of dill. Top each salad with a spoonful of caviar, if you like, before serving.

CHICORY SALAD WITH ROQUEFORT

INGREDIENTS

Serves 4

30ml/2 tbsp red wine vinegar
5ml/1 tsp Dijon mustard
50ml/2oz/¼ cup walnut oil
15–30ml/1–2 tbsp sunflower oil
2 white or red chicory heads
1 celery heart or 4 celery sticks, cut into julienne strips
75g/3oz/¾ cup walnut halves, toasted
115g/4oz Roquefort cheese
salt and ground black pepper
fresh parsley sprigs, to garnish

1 Whisk together the vinegar, mustard and salt and pepper to taste in a small bowl. Slowly whisk in the oils, to make a vinaigrette.

2 Arrange the chicory on individual serving plates. Scatter over the celery and walnut halves. Crumble the Roquefort cheese on top of each salad, drizzle over a little vinaigrette and serve garnished with parsley sprigs.

Clockwise from far right: Prawn, Avocado and Citrus Salad; Smoked Salmon Salad with Dill; and Chicory Salad with Roquefort.

Prawn: Energy 194kcal/806kJ; Protein 14g; Carbohydrate 5.7g, of which sugars 5.5g; Fat 12.9g, of which saturates 1.9g; Cholesterol 146mg; Calcium 77mg; Fibre 1.3g; Sodium 146mg.
Salmon: Energy 258kcal/1070kJ; Protein 15.1g; Carbohydrate 1.2g, of which sugars 1.1g; Fat 21.5g, of which saturates 3.1g; Cholesterol 20mg; Calcium 46mg; Fibre 1.4g; Sodium 1065mg
Chicory: Energy 361kcal/1488kJ; Protein 9.4g; Carbohydrate 1.5g, of which sugars 1.3g; Fat 35.3g, of which saturates 7.9g; Cholesterol 22mg; Calcium 204mg; Fibre 1.8g; Sodium 423mg

Thai Scented Fish Salad

For a tropical taste of the Far East, try this delicious fish salad scented with coconut, exotic fruits and warm Thai spices.

INGREDIENTS

Serves 4

350g/12oz fillet of red mullet, sea bream or snapper
1 cos or romaine lettuce
½ lollo biondo lettuce
1 papaya or mango, peeled and sliced
1 pithaya, peeled and sliced
1 large ripe tomato, cut into wedges
½ cucumber, peeled and cut into strips
3 spring onions (scallions), sliced

For the marinade

5ml/1 tsp coriander seeds
5ml/1 tsp fennel seeds
2.5ml/½ tsp cumin seeds
5ml/1 tsp caster (superfine) sugar
2.5ml/½ tsp hot chilli sauce
30ml/2 tbsp garlic oil
salt

For the dressing

15ml/1 tbsp creamed coconut
60ml/4 tbsp groundnut (peanut) oil
finely grated rind and juice of 1 lime
1 red chilli, seeded and finely chopped
5ml/1 tsp sugar
45ml/3 tbsp chopped fresh coriander (cilantro)
salt

2 To make the marinade, crush the coriander, fennel and cumin seeds together with the sugar. Add the chilli sauce, garlic oil and salt and combine.

3 Spread the marinade over the fish, cover and leave to stand in a cool place for at least 20 minutes – longer if you have time.

4 To make the dressing, place the creamed coconut and salt in a screw-top jar with 45ml/3 tbsp boiling water and allow to dissolve. Add the oil, lime rind and juice, chilli, sugar and chopped coriander. Shake well to combine and set aside.

5 Combine the lettuce leaves with the papaya or mango, pithaya, tomato, cucumber and spring onions. Toss with the dressing, then distribute between four large serving plates.

6 Heat a large non-stick frying-pan, add the fish and cook for 5 minutes, turning once. Place the cooked fish over the salad and serve immediately.

1 Cut the fish into even strips and place them on a plate or in a shallow bowl.

COOK'S TIP

If planning ahead, you can leave the fish in the marinade for up to 8 hours. The dressing can also be made in advance, minus the fresh coriander (cilantro). Store at room temperature and add the coriander when you are ready to assemble the salad.

Energy 339kcal/1410kJ; Protein 18.2g; Carbohydrate 15.7g, of which sugars 15.6g; Fat 23g, of which saturates 5.2g; Cholesterol 0mg; Calcium 119mg; Fibre 3.9g; Sodium 94mg.

San Francisco Salad

California is a salad-maker's paradise and is renowned for the healthiness of its produce. San Francisco has become the salad capital of California, although this recipe is in fact based on a salad served at the Chez Panisse restaurant in Berkeley.

INGREDIENTS

Serves 4

900g/2lb langoustines or Dublin Bay prawns (jumbo shrimp)
50g/2oz bulb fennel, sliced
2 ripe medium tomatoes, quartered, and 4 small tomatoes
30ml/2 tbsp olive oil, plus extra for moistening the salad leaves
60ml/4 tbsp brandy
150ml/¼ pint/⅔ cup dry white wine
200ml/7fl oz can lobster or crab bisque
30ml/2 tbsp chopped fresh tarragon
45ml/3 tbsp double (heavy) cream
225g/8oz green beans, topped and tailed
2 oranges
175g/6oz lamb's lettuce
115g/4oz rocket (arugula) leaves
½ frisée lettuce
salt and cayenne pepper

1 Bring a large pan of salted water to the boil, add the langoustines or Dublin Bay prawns and simmer for 10 minutes. Refresh under cold running water.

2 Pre-heat the oven to 220°C/ 425°F/Gas 7. Twist the tails from all but four of the prawns or langoustines – reserve these to garnish the dish. Peel the outer shell from the tail meat. Put the tail peelings, carapace and claws in a heavy roasting pan with the fennel and medium tomatoes. Toss with the olive oil and roast near the top of the oven for 20 minutes to bring out the flavours.

3 Remove the roasting tray from the oven and place it over a moderate heat on top of the stove. Add the brandy and ignite to release the flavour of the alcohol. Add the wine and simmer briefly.

4 Transfer the contents of the roasting pan to a food processor and reduce to a coarse purée: this will take only 10–15 seconds. Rub the purée through a fine nylon sieve (strainer) into a bowl. Add the bisque, tarragon and cream. Season to taste with salt and a little cayenne pepper.

5 Bring a pan of salted water to the boil and cook the beans for 6 minutes. Drain and cool under running water. To segment the oranges, cut the peel from the top and bottom, and then from the sides, with a serrated knife. Loosen the segments by cutting between the membranes and the flesh with a small knife.

6 Moisten the salad leaves with olive oil and distribute between four serving plates. Fold the langoustine tails into the dressing and distribute between the plates. Add the beans, orange segments and small tomatoes. Garnish each plate with a whole langoustine and serve warm.

Millionaire's Lobster Salad

When money is no object and you're in a decadent mood, this salad will satisfy your every whim.

INGREDIENTS

Serves 4
1 medium lobster, live or cooked
1 bay leaf
1 fresh thyme sprig
675g/1½lb new potatoes, scrubbed
2 ripe tomatoes
4 oranges
½ frisée lettuce
175g/6oz lamb's lettuce leaves
60ml/4 tbsp extra virgin olive oil
200g/7oz can artichokes in brine, quartered
1 small bunch fresh tarragon, chervil or flat leaf parsley
salt

For the dressing
30ml/2 tbsp frozen concentrated orange juice, thawed
75g/3oz/6 tbsp unsalted butter, diced
salt and cayenne pepper

1 If the lobster needs cooking, add to a large pan of boiling salted water with the bay leaf and thyme. Bring back to the boil and simmer for 15 minutes. Cool under running water.

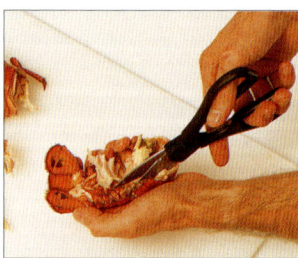

2 Twist off the legs and claws, and separate the tail from the body. Break the claws with a hammer and remove the meat. Cut the tail piece open from the underside, slice the meat and set aside.

3 Bring the potatoes to the boil in salted water and simmer for about 15 minutes, until tender. Drain, cover and keep warm.

4 Cut a cross in the skin of the tomatoes, cover with boiling water and leave for 30 seconds. Cool under running water and slip off the skins. Halve the tomatoes, discard the seeds, then cut the flesh into large dice.

5 To segment the oranges, remove the peel from the top, bottom and sides with a serrated knife. With a small paring knife, loosen the orange segments by cutting between the flesh and the membranes, holding the fruit over a small bowl.

6 To make the dressing, measure the orange juice into a heatproof bowl and set it over a pan containing 2.5cm/1in simmering water. Heat the juice for 1 minute, turn off the heat, then whisk in the butter a little at a time until the dressing reaches a coating consistency.

7 Season to taste with salt and a pinch of cayenne pepper, cover and keep warm.

8 Dress the salad leaves with olive oil, then divide between four large serving plates. Moisten the potatoes, artichokes and orange segments with olive oil and distribute among the leaves.

9 Lay the sliced lobster over the salad, spoon on the warm dressing, add the diced tomato and decorate with the fresh herbs. Serve at room temperature.

Energy 662kcal/2775kJ; Protein 51.5g; Carbohydrate 47.7g, of which sugars 22.7g; Fat 30.7g, of which saturates 12g; Cholesterol 260mg; Calcium 325mg; Fibre 6.9g; Sodium 900mg.

Genoese Squid Salad

This is a good salad for summer, when French beans and new potatoes are at their best. Serve it for a first course or light lunch.

INGREDIENTS

Serves 4–6

450g/1lb prepared squid, cut into rings
4 garlic cloves, roughly chopped
300ml/½ pint/1¼ cups Italian red wine
450g/1lb waxy new potatoes, scrubbed
225g/8oz French (green) beans, trimmed and cut into short lengths
2–3 sun-dried tomatoes in oil, drained and thinly sliced lengthways
60ml/4 tbsp extra virgin olive oil
15ml/1 tbsp red wine vinegar
salt and ground black pepper

1 Preheat the oven to 180°C/350°F/Gas 4. Put the squid rings in an earthenware dish with half the garlic, the wine and pepper to taste. Cover and cook for 45 minutes, or until the squid is tender.

2 Put the potatoes in a pan, cover with cold water and add a good pinch of salt. Bring to the boil, cover and simmer for about 15 minutes, until tender. Using a slotted spoon, lift out the potatoes and set aside. Add the beans to the boiling water and cook for 3 minutes. Drain.

3 When the potatoes are cool enough to handle, slice them thickly on the diagonal and place them in a bowl with the warm beans and sun-dried tomatoes. Whisk the oil, vinegar and the remaining garlic in a jug (pitcher) and add salt and pepper to taste. Pour over the potato mixture.

4 Drain the squid and discard the liquid. Add the squid to the potato mixture and mix very gently. Arrange on individual plates and season liberally with pepper.

COOK'S TIP

The French potato called Charlotte is perfect for this salad because it retains its shape when boiled. Prepared squid can be bought from supermarkets with fresh fish counters, and from fishmongers.

Energy 198kcal/2380kJ; Protein 13g; Carbohydrate 7g, of which sugars 1g; Fat 13g, of which saturates 2g; Cholesterol 169mg; Calcium 28mg; Fibre 1.5g; Sodium 234mg.

Tuna Carpaccio

Fillet of beef is most often used for carpaccio, but meaty fish, such as tuna and swordfish, make an unusual change. The secret is to slice the fish wafer-thin, made possible by freezing it first, a technique used by the Japanese for making sashimi.

INGREDIENTS

Serves 4

2 fresh tuna steaks, about 450g/1lb total weight
60ml/4 tbsp extra virgin olive oil
15ml/1 tbsp balsamic vinegar
5ml/1 tsp caster (superfine) sugar
30ml/2 tbsp bottled green peppercorns or capers, drained
salt and ground black pepper
lemon wedges and green salad, to serve

1 Remove the skin from each tuna steak and place each steak between two sheets of clear film (plastic wrap) or non-stick baking parchment. Pound with a rolling pin until the steak is flattened slightly.

2 Roll up the tuna steaks as tightly as possible, then wrap tightly in clear film. Place the tuna steaks in the freezer for 4 hours, or until firm.

3 Unwrap the tuna and cut crossways into the thinnest possible slices. Arrange the slices on individual serving plates.

4 Whisk together the oil, vinegar, sugar and peppercorns or capers, season and pour over the tuna. Cover and allow to come to room temperature for 30 minutes before serving with lemon wedges and green salad.

COOK'S TIP

Raw fish is safe to eat as long as it is very fresh, so check with your fishmonger before purchase and make and serve the carpaccio the same day. Do not buy fish that has been frozen and thawed.

Energy 294kcal/1223kJ; Protein 27g; Carbohydrate 1g, of which sugars 1g; Fat 20g, of which saturates 3g; Cholesterol 32mg; Calcium 18mg; Fibre 0g; Sodium 151mg.

Salade Mouclade

Mouclade is a long-established dish from La Rochelle in south-west France. The dish consists of mussels in a light curry cream sauce, and is usually served hot. Here the flavours appear in a salad of warm lentils and lightly cooked spinach. Serve at room temperature during the summer months.

INGREDIENTS

Serves 4

45ml/3 tbsp olive oil
1 medium onion, finely chopped
350g/12oz/1½ cups Puy or green lentils, soaked for 2 hours and drained
900ml/1½ pints/3¾ cups vegetable stock
2 kg/4½lb fresh mussels in their shells
75ml/5 tbsp white wine
2.5ml/½ tsp curry paste
a pinch of saffron
30ml/2 tbsp double (heavy) cream
2 large carrots, peeled
4 celery sticks
900g/2lb young spinach, stems removed
15ml/1 tbsp garlic oil
salt and cayenne pepper

1 Heat the oil in a heavy pan and soften the onion for 6–8 minutes. Add the lentils and vegetable stock, bring to the boil and simmer for 45 minutes. Remove from the heat and cool.

2 Clean the mussels thoroughly, discarding any that are damaged. Any that are open should close if given a sharp tap; if they fail to do so, discard these too.

3 Place the mussels in a large pan, add the wine, cover and steam over a high heat for 12 minutes. Strain the mussels in a colander, collecting the cooking liquor in a bowl, and discard any that have not opened during the cooking. Take all but four of the mussels out of their shells.

4 Pass the mussel liquor through a fine sieve (strainer) or muslin (cheesecloth) into a wide pan to remove any grit or sand.

5 Add the curry paste and saffron, then reduce over a high heat until almost dry. Remove from the heat, stir in the cream, season to taste and combine with the mussels.

6 Cut the carrot and celery into 5cm/2in matchsticks and cook in salted boiling water for 3 minutes. Drain, cool and moisten with olive oil.

7 Wash the spinach, put the wet leaves into a large pan, cover and steam for 30 seconds. Immerse in cold water then press the leaves dry in a colander. Moisten with garlic oil and season.

8 Spoon the lentils into the centre of four plates. Place heaps of spinach around the edge, with some carrot and celery on top. Spoon over the mussels and garnish with the reserved mussels in their shells.

Energy 628kcal/2646kJ; Protein 50.8g; Carbohydrate 63.7g, of which sugars 11.2g; Fat 19.1g, of which saturates 4.6g; Cholesterol 90mg; Calcium 560mg; Fibre 11.5g; Sodium 902mg.

Hot Coconut, Prawn and Papaya Salad

Transport yourself to the Far East with this wonderful dish that combines juicy papaya and succulent prawn tails in a spicy coconut dressing.

INGREDIENTS

Serves 4–6

225g/8oz raw or cooked prawn (shrimp) tails, peeled and deveined
2 ripe papayas
225g/8oz cos or iceberg lettuce leaves, Chinese leaves (Chinese cabbage) and young spinach leaves
1 firm tomato, peeled, seeded and roughly chopped
3 spring onions (scallions), shredded
1 small bunch fresh coriander (cilantro), shredded, and 1 large chilli, sliced, to garnish

For the dressing
15ml/1 tbsp creamed coconut
90ml/6 tbsp vegetable oil
juice of 1 lime
2.5ml/½ tsp hot chilli sauce
10ml/2 tsp Thai fish sauce (optional)
5ml/1 tsp sugar

2 If using raw prawn tails, cover with cold water in a pan, bring to the boil and simmer for no longer than 2 minutes. Drain and set aside.

3 Cut the papayas in half from top to bottom and remove the black seeds. Peel away the skin and cut the flesh into equal pieces.

4 Place the salad leaves in a bowl. Add the prawn tails, papayas, tomato and spring onions. Pour over the dressing, garnish with the coriander and chilli, and serve.

1 To make the dressing, place the creamed coconut in a screw-top jar and add 30ml/2 tbsp boiling water to soften it. Add the oil, lime juice, chilli sauce, fish sauce, if using, and sugar. Shake well and set aside. Do not chill.

Energy 220kcal/913kJ; Protein 9g; Carbohydrate 7g, of which sugars 7g; Fat 17g, of which saturates 3g; Cholesterol 105mg; Calcium 73mg; Fibre 2g; Sodium 632mg.

Roasted Chicken and Walnut Salad

The chickens may be cooked the day before eating and the salad finished on the day itself. Serve with warm garlic bread.

INGREDIENTS

Serves 8

4 fresh tarragon or rosemary sprigs
2 x 1.75kg/4–4½lb chickens
65g/2½oz/5 tbsp softened butter
150ml/¼ pint/⅔ cup chicken stock
150ml/¼ pint/⅔ cup white wine
115g/4oz/1 cup walnut pieces
1 small cantaloupe melon
lettuce leaves
450g/1lb seedless grapes or stoned (pitted) cherries
salt and ground black pepper

For the dressing
30ml/2 tbsp tarragon vinegar
120ml/4fl oz/½ cup light olive oil
30ml/2 tbsp chopped fresh mixed herbs such as parsley, mint, tarragon

1 Preheat the oven to 200°C/400°F/Gas 6. Put the sprigs of tarragon or rosemary inside the chickens and season with salt and pepper.

2 Spread the chickens with 50g/2oz/4 tbsp of the softened butter, place in a roasting pan and pour the stock around. Cover loosely with foil and roast for about 1½ hours, basting twice, until browned and the juices run clear. Remove from the roasting pan and leave to cool.

3 Add the wine to the roasting pan. Bring to the boil on the stove and cook until syrupy. Strain and leave to cool. Heat the remaining butter in a frying pan and gently fry the walnuts until lightly browned. Scoop the melon flesh into balls or cut into cubes. Joint the chickens.

4 To make the dressing, whisk the vinegar and olive oil together with a little salt and pepper. Remove the fat from the chicken juices and add the juices to the dressing with the herbs. Adjust the seasoning to taste.

5 Arrange the chicken pieces on a bed of lettuce leaves, scatter over the grapes or cherries and the melon balls or cubes, and spoon over the dressing. Sprinkle with the toasted walnuts and serve immediately.

Energy 251kcal/1045kJ; Protein 21.6g; Carbohydrate 3g, of which sugars 2.7g; fat 17g, of which saturates 3.2g; Cholesterol 56mg; Calcium 47mg; fibre 2g; Sodium 382mg.

Chicken Liver Salad

This delicious salad may be served as a main course for a summer lunch party, or as a tasty first course served on individual plates. The richness of the chicken livers is complemented perfectly by the sweet tangy wholegrain mustard dressing. Serve with warm crusty bread to mop up the dressing.

INGREDIENTS

Serves 4

mixed salad leaves such as frisée, oakleaf lettuce, radicchio
1 avocado, diced
30ml/2 tbsp lemon juice
2 pink grapefruit
350g/12oz chicken livers
30ml/2 tbsp olive oil
1 garlic clove, crushed
salt and ground black pepper
whole fresh chives, to garnish

For the dressing
30ml/2 tbsp lemon juice
60ml/4 tbsp olive oil
2.5ml/½ tsp wholegrain mustard
2.5ml/½ tsp clear honey
15ml/1 tbsp snipped fresh chives
salt and ground black pepper

1 To make the dressing, put the lemon juice, olive oil, mustard, honey and fresh chives into a screw-top jar, and shake vigorously. Season to taste with salt and freshly ground black pepper.

2 Arrange the previously washed and well drained mixed salad leaves attractively on a large serving plate.

3 Peel and dice the avocado and mix with the lemon juice to prevent browning. Add to the plate of mixed leaves.

4 Peel the grapefruit, removing as much of the white pith as possible. Split into segments and arrange with the leaves and avocado on the serving plate.

5 Dry the chicken livers on kitchen paper and remove any unwanted pieces.

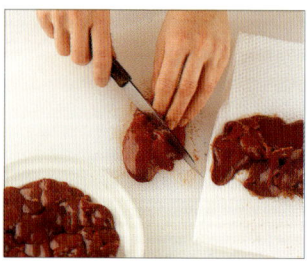

6 Using a sharp knife, cut the larger chicken livers in half. Leave the smaller ones whole.

7 Heat the oil in a large frying pan. Stir-fry the chicken livers and garlic briskly until the livers are brown all over (they should be slightly pink inside).

8 Season the chicken livers to taste with salt and black pepper, remove from the pan and drain on kitchen paper.

9 Place the chicken livers, while still warm, onto the salad leaves and spoon over the dressing. Garnish with the whole chives and serve immediately.

Energy 325kcal/1346kJ; Protein 16g; Carbohydrate 1g, of which sugars 1g; Fat 28g, of which saturates 8g; Cholesterol 236mg; Calcium 197mg; Fibre 1g; Sodium 206mg.

Chicken Salad with Lavender

Lavender may seem an odd salad ingredient, but its delightful scent has a natural affinity with garlic, orange and other herbs. A serving of polenta makes this salad both sustaining and delicious.

INGREDIENTS

Serves 4

4 chicken breast fillets
900ml/1½ pints/3¾ cups light chicken stock
175g/6oz/1 cup fine polenta or corn meal
50g/2oz/4 tbsp butter
450g/1lb young spinach leaves
175g/6oz lamb's lettuce leaves
8 small tomatoes, halved
salt and ground black pepper
8 fresh lavender sprigs, to garnish

For the lavender marinade
6 fresh lavender flowers
10ml/2 tsp finely grated orange rind
2 garlic cloves, crushed
10ml/2 tsp clear honey
30ml/2 tbsp olive oil
10ml/2 tsp chopped fresh thyme
10ml/2 tsp chopped fresh marjoram
salt

2 To make the polenta, bring the chicken stock to the boil in a heavy pan. Add the fine polenta or corn meal in a steady stream, stirring all the time until thick: this will take 2–3 minutes. Turn the cooked polenta out on to a 2.5cm/1in deep buttered tray and allow to cool.

3 Heat the grill (broiler) to a moderate temperature. (If using a barbecue, let the embers settle to a steady glow.) Grill (broil) the chicken breasts for about 15 minutes, turning them once.

4 Cut the cooled polenta into 2.5cm/1in cubes with a wet knife. Heat the remaining butter in a large frying-pan and fry the polenta cubes until golden brown.

5 Divide the salad leaves and tomatoes between four large serving plates. Slice each chicken breast and lay over the salad. Place the polenta cubes among the salad and season to taste. Garnish with the sprigs of lavender and serve.

1 To make the marinade, strip the lavender flowers from their stems and combine with the orange rind, garlic, honey and a pinch of salt. Add the olive oil, thyme and marjoram. Slash the chicken, spread over the mixture and leave to marinate in a cool place for at least 20 minutes.

COOK'S TIP

This lavender marinade is a delicious flavouring for salt-water fish as well as chicken. Try it spread over grilled (broiled) cod, haddock, halibut, sea bass or bream.

Energy 268kcal/1121kJ; Protein 22.2g; Carbohydrate 29.5g, of which sugars 6.5g; Fat 6.6g, of which saturates 0.9g; Cholesterol 47mg; Calcium 187mg; Fibre 4.6g; Sodium 66mg.

Dijon Chicken Salad

This attractive and classical dish is ideal to serve for a simple but tasty and elegant lunch. Serve with extra salad leaves and some warm herb and garlic bread.

INGREDIENTS

Serves 4

4 skinless chicken breast fillets
mixed salad leaves such as frisée, oakleaf lettuce, radicchio

For the marinade
30ml/2 tbsp tarragon wine vinegar
5ml/1 tsp Dijon mustard
5ml/1 tsp clear honey
90ml/6 tbsp olive oil
salt and ground black pepper

For the mustard dressing
30ml/2 tbsp Dijon mustard
3 garlic cloves, crushed
15ml/1 tbsp grated onion
60ml/4 tbsp white wine

1 To make the marinade mix the vinegar, mustard, honey, olive oil, salt and pepper together in a shallow glass or earthenware dish that is large enough to hold the chicken fillets in a single layer.

2 Add the chicken breasts to the dish, making sure they do not overlap each other.

3 Turn the chicken over in the marinade to coat completely, cover with clear film (plastic wrap) and chill overnight.

4 Preheat the oven to 190°C/375°F/Gas 5. Transfer the chicken and the marinade into an ovenproof dish, cover with kitchen foil and bake for about 35 minutes, or until tender. Leave the chicken to cool in the liquid.

5 To make the mustard dressing, put all the ingredients into a screw-top jar and shake vigorously.

6 Thinly slice the chicken, and fan out the slices.

7 Arrange the chicken slices on a serving dish with the salad leaves. Spoon over some of the mustard dressing and serve. Serve the rest of the dressing separately in a bowl or jug (pitcher).

COOK'S TIP

The dressing can be made several days in advance and stored in the refrigerator.

Energy 344kcal/1437kJ; Protein 37g; Carbohydrate 4.7g, of which sugars 4.3g; Fat 18.8g, of which saturates 2.9g; Cholesterol 105mg; Calcium 36mg; Fibre 0.9g; Sodium 167mg.

Duck Breast and Pasta Salad

The acidity of fruit is a very good accompaniment to a rich meat such as duck as it adds a tartness which makes the meat more digestible. This luxurious salad includes apple, orange and, in the dressing, dried cherries. The pasta adds a welcome element of carbohydrate and makes the dish a complete meal.

INGREDIENTS

Serves 6

2 duck breast fillets
salt and ground black pepper
5ml/1 tsp coriander seeds, crushed
350g/12oz rigatoni
1 eating apple, diced
2 oranges, segmented
extra fresh chopped coriander (cilantro)
   and mint, to garnish

For the dressing
150ml/¼ pint/⅔ cup orange juice
15ml/1 tbsp lemon juice
10ml/2 tsp clear honey
1 shallot, finely chopped
1 garlic clove, crushed
1 celery stick, chopped
75g/3oz dried cherries
45ml/3 tbsp port
15ml/1 tbsp chopped fresh mint
30ml/2 tbsp chopped fresh
   coriander (cilantro)

1 Preheat the grill. Remove the skin and fat from the duck breast fillets, season with salt and pepper and rub with the crushed coriander seeds.

2 Grill the duck breast fillets for 7–10 minutes (depending on the size). Wrap the duck breasts in foil and leave for 20 minutes.

3 Cook the pasta in a large pan of salted, boiling water, until al dente. Drain thoroughly and rinse under cold running water. Leave the pasta to cool.

4 To make the dressing, put the orange juice, lemon juice, honey, shallot, garlic, celery, cherries, port, mint and fresh coriander into a small bowl. Whisk together and leave to marinate for 30 minutes.

5 Unwrap the breasts from the foil and, using a very sharp carving knife, slice the duck very thinly. (It should still be slightly pink in the centre.)

6 Put the pasta into a large mixing bowl, add the dressing, diced apple and segments of orange. Toss well to coat the pasta.

7 Transfer the salad to a serving plate with the duck slices and garnish with the extra coriander and mint.

Duck Salad with Orange Sauce

The rich, gamey flavour of duck provides the foundation for this delicious salad. Serve it in late summer or autumn and enjoy the warm flavours of orange and coriander. Garlic croûtons add extra crunchy texture.

INGREDIENTS

Serves 4

1 small orange
2 duck breast fillets
150ml/¼ pint/⅔ cup dry white wine
5ml/1 tsp ground coriander seeds
2.5ml/½ tsp ground cumin or fennel seeds
30ml/2 tbsp caster (superfine) sugar
juice of ½ small lime or lemon
75g/3oz day-old bread, thickly sliced
45ml/3 tbsp garlic oil
½ escarole lettuce
½ frisée lettuce
30ml/2 tbsp sunflower oil
salt and cayenne pepper
4 sprigs fresh coriander (cilantro), to garnish

1 Halve the orange and slice thickly. Discard any pips and place the slices in a small pan. Cover with water, bring to the boil and simmer for 5 minutes to remove the bitterness. Drain the orange slices and set aside.

2 Pierce the skin of the duck breast fillets diagonally with a small knife (this will help release the fat). Rub the skin with salt.

3 Place a steel or cast-iron frying pan over a steady heat and cook the breasts for 20 minutes, turning once, until they are medium-rare. Transfer to a warm plate, cover and keep warm.

4 Heat the sediment in the frying pan until it begins to darken and caramelize. Add the wine and stir to loosen the sediment. Add the ground coriander, cumin or fennel seeds, sugar and orange slices.

5 Boil quickly and reduce to a coating consistency. Sharpen with the lime or lemon juice and season to taste with salt and cayenne pepper. Transfer the orange sauce to a bowl, cover and keep warm.

6 Remove the crusts from the bread and cut the bread into short fingers. Heat the garlic oil in a heavy frying pan and brown the croûtons. Season with salt, then turn out on to kitchen paper.

7 Moisten the salad leaves with a little sunflower oil and distribute between four large serving plates.

8 Slice the duck breast fillets diagonally with a carving knife. Divide the meat into four and lift on to each salad plate. Spoon on the orange sauce, scatter with croûtons, decorate with a sprig of fresh coriander and serve warm.

Energy 231kcal/971kJ; Protein 17.3g; Carbohydrate 13.3g, of which sugars 4.5g; Fat 11.1g, of which saturates 1.7g; Cholesterol 83mg; Calcium 68mg; Fibre 1.5g; Sodium 185mg.

Sesame Duck and Noodle Salad

This salad is complete in itself and makes a lovely summer lunch. The marinade is a marvellous blend of oriental flavours.

INGREDIENTS

Serves 4

2 duck breast fillets
15ml/1 tbsp oil
150g/5oz sugar snap peas
2 carrots, cut into 7.5cm/3in sticks
225g/8oz medium egg noodles
6 spring onions (scallions), sliced
salt
30ml/2 tbsp fresh coriander (cilantro) leaves, to garnish

For the marinade
15ml/1 tbsp sesame oil
5ml/1 tsp ground coriander
5ml/1 tsp five-spice powder

For the dressing
15ml/1 tbsp vinegar
5ml/1 tsp soft light brown sugar
5ml/1 tsp soy sauce
1 garlic clove, crushed
15ml/1 tbsp sesame seeds, toasted
45ml/3 tbsp sunflower oil
30ml/2 tbsp sesame oil
ground black pepper

1 Slice the duck breasts thinly across and place in a shallow dish. Mix together the ingredients for the marinade, pour over the duck and turn well to coat thoroughly. Cover with clear film (plastic wrap) and leave in a cool place for 30 minutes.

2 Heat the oil in a frying pan, add the slices of duck breast and stir-fry for 3–4 minutes, until cooked. Set aside.

3 Bring a pan of lightly salted water to the boil. Place the sugar snap peas and carrots in a steamer that will fit on top of the pan. When the water boils, add the noodles. Place the steamer on top and steam the vegetables while cooking the noodles.

4 Set the steamed vegetables aside. Drain the noodles, refresh under cold running water and drain again. Place them in a large serving bowl.

5 To make the dressing, mix the vinegar, sugar, soy sauce, garlic and sesame seeds in a bowl. Add a generous grinding of pepper, then whisk in the oils.

6 Pour the dressing over the noodles and mix well. Add the peas, carrots, spring onions and duck slices and toss to mix. Sprinkle the coriander leaves over the top and serve immediately.

Prosciutto Salad with an Avocado Fan

Avocados are amazingly versatile – they can serve as edible containers, be sliced or diced in a salad, or form the foundation of a delicious soup or sauce. However, they are at their most elegant when sliced thinly and fanned on a plate.

INGREDIENTS

Serves 4

3 avocados
150g/5oz prosciutto
75–115g/3–4oz rocket (arugula) leaves
24 marinated black olives, drained

For the dressing
15ml/1 tbsp balsamic vinegar
5ml/1 tsp lemon juice
5ml/1 tsp prepared English mustard
5ml/1 tsp sugar
75ml/5 tbsp olive oil
salt and ground black pepper

1 To make the dressing, combine the balsamic vinegar, lemon juice, mustard and sugar in a bowl. Whisk in the oil, season to taste and set aside.

2 Cut two of the avocados in half. Remove the stones (pits) and skins, and cut the flesh into 1cm/½in thick slices. Toss with half the dressing. Place the prosciutto, avocado slices and rocket on four serving plates. Sprinkle the olives and the remaining dressing over the top.

3 Halve, stone and peel the remaining avocado. Slice each half lengthways into eighths. Gently draw a cannelle knife across the quarters at 1cm/½in intervals to create regular stripes.

4 Make four cuts lengthways down each avocado eighth, leaving 1cm/½in intact at the end. Carefully fan out the slices and arrange on the side of each plate.

Energy 341kcal/1407kJ; Protein 9.1g; Carbohydrate 3.2g, of which sugars 2.1g; Fat 32.4g, of which saturates 5.9g; Cholesterol 22mg; Calcium 59mg; Fibre 3.7g; Sodium 1043mg.

Melon and Prosciutto Salad

Sections of cool, fragrant melon covered with slices of prosciutto make this a delicious appetizer. When fresh strawberries are in season, serve it with a savoury-sweet strawberry salsa.

INGREDIENTS

Serves 4

1 large melon (cantaloupe, Galia or Charentais)
175g/6oz prosciutto, thinly sliced

For the salsa
225g/8oz strawberries
5ml/1 tsp caster (superfine) sugar
30ml/2 tbsp sunflower oil
15ml/1 tbsp orange juice
2.5ml/½ tsp finely grated orange rind
2.5ml/½ tsp grated fresh root ginger
salt and ground black pepper

1 Halve the melon and take the seeds out with a spoon. Cut the rind away with a paring knife, then slice the melon flesh thickly. Chill until ready to serve.

2 To make the salsa, hull the strawberries and cut them into large dice. Place in a small mixing bowl with the sugar and crush lightly to release the juices. Add the oil, orange juice and rind and ginger. Season with salt and a generous twist of black pepper.

3 Arrange the melon slices on a serving plate and lay the prosciutto over the top. Serve the salsa separately in a small bowl.

Energy 147kcal/614kJ; Protein 9.2g; Carbohydrate 12.2g, of which sugars 12.2g; Fat 7.1g, of which saturates 1.2g; Cholesterol 25mg; Calcium 29mg; Fibre 1.1g; Sodium 568mg.

Wild Mushroom Salad with Prosciutto

Autumn provides a wealth of ingredients for the salad maker. Most treasured of all are wild mushrooms, found mainly in deciduous woodland. If you are not familiar with edible species, larger supermarkets and specialist delicatessens often sell a wide range.

INGREDIENTS

Serves 4

175g/6oz prosciutto, thickly sliced
45ml/3 tbsp butter
450g/1lb wild or cultivated mushrooms such as chanterelles, field blewits, oyster mushrooms, champignons de Paris, sliced
60ml/4 tbsp brandy
½ oakleaf lettuce
½ frisée lettuce
15ml/1 tbsp walnut oil
salt and ground black pepper

For the herb pancake
45ml/3 tbsp plain (all-purpose) flour
75ml/5 tbsp milk
1 egg, plus 1 egg yolk
60ml/4 tbsp grated Parmesan cheese
45ml/3 tbsp chopped fresh mixed herbs such as parsley, thyme, tarragon, marjoram, chives
salt and ground black pepper

1 To make the pancakes, combine the flour with the milk in a measuring jug (cup). Beat in the egg and egg yolk with the Parmesan cheese, herbs and seasoning. Place a non-stick frying pan over a steady heat. Pour in enough mixture to coat the bottom of the pan.

2 When the batter has set, turn the pancake over and cook briefly on the other side. Turn the pancake out and leave to cool. Continue until you have used all the batter.

3 Roll the pancakes together and cut into 1cm/½in ribbons. Cut the prosciutto into similar-sized ribbons and toss together with the pancake ribbons.

4 Heat the butter in a pan until it foams. Add the mushrooms and cook for 6–8 minutes.

5 Add the brandy and ignite with a match. The flames will subside when the alcohol has burnt off. Moisten the salad leaves with walnut oil and distribute among four serving plates. Place the ham and pancake ribbons in the centre, spoon on the mushrooms, season and serve warm.

Energy 350kcal/1460kJ; Protein 19.4g; Carbohydrate 13g, of which sugars 4.2g; Fat 21.3g, of which saturates 9.9g; Cholesterol 158mg; Calcium 241mg; Fibre 3.3g; Sodium 744mg.

Beef and Herby Pasta Salad

Lean, tender beef is marinated with ginger and garlic, then lightly grilled (broiled) and served warm with a herby pasta salad.

INGREDIENTS

Serves 6

450g/1lb beef fillet
450g/1lb fresh tagliatelle with sun-dried tomatoes and herbs
115g/4oz cherry tomatoes
½ cucumber

For the marinade
15ml/1 tbsp soy sauce
15ml/1 tbsp sherry
5ml/1 tsp grated fresh root ginger
1 garlic clove, crushed

For the herb dressing
30–45ml/2–3 tbsp horseradish sauce
150ml/¼ pint/⅔ cup natural (plain) yogurt
1 garlic clove, crushed
30–45ml/2–3 tbsp chopped fresh mixed herbs such as chives, parsley, thyme
salt and ground black pepper

1 To make the marinade, mix all the ingredients together in a shallow dish. Add the beef fillet and turn to coat well. Cover with clear film (plastic wrap) and leave for 30 minutes to allow the flavours to penetrate the meat.

2 Preheat the grill (broiler). Lift the fillet out of the marinade and pat it dry with kitchen paper. Place the fillet on a grill rack and grill (broil) for 8 minutes on each side, basting with the marinade during cooking.

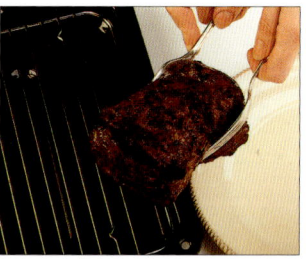

3 Transfer the fillet to a plate, cover with foil and leave to stand for 20 minutes.

4 To make the herb dressing, put all the ingredients into a bowl and mix thoroughly. Cook the pasta until it is al dente, drain thoroughly, rinse under cold water and leave to dry.

5 Cut the cherry tomatoes in half. Cut the cucumber in half lengthways, scoop out the seeds with a teaspoon and slice the flesh thinly into crescents.

6 Put the pasta, tomatoes, cucumber and dressing into a mixing bowl and toss to coat. Slice the beef and arrange on individual serving plates with the pasta salad. Serve warm.

Rockburger Salad with Sesame Croûtons

This salad plays on the ingredients that make up the all-American beefburger in a sesame seed bun. Inside the burger is a layer of Roquefort, the blue ewe's-milk cheese from France.

INGREDIENTS

Serves 4

900g/2lb lean minced (ground) beef
1 egg
1 medium onion, finely chopped
10ml/2 tsp Dijon mustard
2.5ml/½ tsp celery salt
115g/4oz Roquefort or other blue cheese
1 large sesame seed loaf
45ml/3 tbsp olive oil
1 small iceberg lettuce
50g/2oz rocket (arugula) or watercress leaves
120ml/4fl oz/½ cup French Dressing
4 ripe tomatoes, quartered
4 large spring onions (scallions), sliced
ground black pepper

1 Place the minced beef, egg, onion, mustard, celery salt and pepper in a mixing bowl. Combine thoroughly. Divide the mixture into 16 equal portions.

2 Flatten the pieces between two sheets of plastic or waxed paper to form 13cm/5in rounds.

3 Place 15g/½oz of the blue cheese on eight of the burgers. Sandwich with the remaining burgers and press the edges firmly. Store between sheets of plastic or waxed paper and chill until ready to cook.

4 To make the sesame croûtons, preheat the grill (broiler) to a moderate temperature. Remove the sesame seed crust from the loaf, then cut the crust into short fingers. Moisten with olive oil and toast evenly for 10–15 minutes.

5 Grill (broil) the burgers at the same temperature for 10 minutes, turning once.

6 Toss the salad leaves with the French Dressing, then distribute between four large serving plates. Place two rockburgers in the centre of each plate and arrange the tomatoes, spring onions and sesame croûtons around the edge.

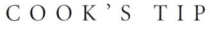

COOK'S TIP

If you can't find a sesame seed loaf use a French stick. Cut the stick into slices of around 1cm/½in, brush with olive oil and place on a baking tray. Bake in the oven on a low heat for around 15 minutes until the bread rounds are crisp and golden.

Energy 1259kcal/5247kJ; Protein 66.1g; Carbohydrate 69.8g, of which sugars 8.3g; Fat 74.6g, of which saturates 26.5g; Cholesterol 204mg; Calcium 359mg; Fibre 4.5g; Sodium 1528mg.

FRUIT SALADS

Fresh Fruit Salad

This basic fruit salad is always welcome, especially after a rich main course. It is endlessly adaptable – when peaches and strawberries are out of season, use bananas and grapes, or any other fruit.

INGREDIENTS

Serves 6

2 apples
2 oranges
2 peaches
16–20 strawberries
30ml/2 tbsp lemon juice
15–30ml/1–2 tbsp orange flower water
icing (confectioners') sugar (optional)
a few fresh mint leaves, to decorate

1 Peel and core the apples and cut into thin slices. Peel the oranges with a sharp knife, removing all the pith, and segment them, catching the juice in a bowl.

2 Plunge the peaches in boiling water for 1 minute, peel away the skin and cut the flesh into thick slices, discarding the stone (pit).

3 Hull the strawberries and halve or quarter if larger. Place all the fruit in a large serving bowl.

4 Blend together the lemon juice, orange flower water and orange juice. Taste and add a little icing sugar to sweeten, if liked. Pour the fruit juice mixture over the salad and serve decorated with mint leaves.

Dried Fruit Salad

This wonderful combination of fresh and dried fruit makes an excellent dessert throughout the year. Use frozen raspberries and blackberries during the winter months.

INGREDIENTS

Serves 4

115g/4oz/½ cup dried apricots
115g/4oz/½ cup dried peaches
1 pear
1 apple
1 orange
115g/4oz/⅔ cup mixed raspberries and blackberries
1 cinnamon stick
50g/2oz/¼ cup caster (superfine) sugar
15ml/1 tbsp clear honey
15ml/1 tbsp lemon juice

1 Soak the dried apricots and peaches in water for 1–2 hours, until plump, then drain and halve or quarter. Peel and core the pear and apple and cut into cubes.

2 Peel the orange with a sharp knife, removing all the pith, and cut into wedges. Place all the fruit in a large pan with the raspberries and blackberries.

3 Add 600ml/1 pint/2½ cups water, the cinnamon stick, sugar and honey and bring to the boil. Cover and simmer very gently for 10–12 minutes, then remove the pan from the heat.

4 Stir in the lemon juice. Allow to cool, then transfer to a bowl and chill in the refrigerator for 1–2 hours before serving.

Fresh: Energy 29Kcal/163kJ; Protein 0.8g; Carbohydrate 9.3g, of which sugars 9.3g; Fat 0.1g, of which saturates 0g; Cholesterol 0g; Fibre 1.6g; Calcium 10mg; Sodium 0mg .
Dried: Energy 169kcal/721kJ; Protein 2.9g; Carbohydrate 41.1g, of which sugars 41.1g; Fat 0.4g, of which saturates 0g; Cholesterol 0mg; Calcium 57mg; Fibre 4.2g; Sodium 18mg.

Cool Green Fruit Salad

A sophisticated, simple fruit salad for any time of the year.

INGREDIENTS

Serves 6

3 Ogen or Galia melons
115g/4oz seedless green grapes
2 kiwi fruit
1 star fruit (carambola)
1 green-skinned apple
1 lime
175ml/6fl oz/¾ cup sparkling grape juice

1 Cut the melons in half and remove the seeds. Keeping the shells intact, scoop out the flesh with a melon baller, or scoop it out with a spoon and cut into cubes. Reserve the melon shells.

2 Remove any stems from the grapes and, if they are large, cut them in half. Peel and chop the kiwi fruit. Thinly slice the star fruit. Core and thinly slice the apple and place in a mixing bowl with the melon, grapes, kiwi fruit and star fruit.

3 Thinly pare the rind from the lime and cut it in fine strips. Blanch the lime strips in boiling water for 30 seconds, drain and rinse in cold water. Squeeze the juice from the lime and toss the juice into the bowl of fruit.

4 Spoon the prepared fruit into the reserved melon shells and chill the shells in the refrigerator until required. Just before serving, spoon the sparkling grape juice over the fruit and scatter with the strips of lime rind.

COOK'S TIP

On a hot summer's day, serve the filled melon shells nestling on a platter of crushed ice to keep them beautifully cool.

Energy 102kcal/436kJ; Protein 1.7g; Carbohydrate 24.4g, of which sugars 24.4g; Fat 0.4g, of which saturates 0g; Cholesterol 0mg; Calcium 46mg; Fibre 1.9g; Sodium 81mg.

Winter Fruit Salad

This is a colourful, refreshing and nutritious fruit salad, which is ideal served with yogurt or cream.

INGREDIENTS

Serves 6

225g/8oz can pineapple cubes in fruit juice
200ml/7fl oz/scant 1 cup freshly squeezed orange juice
200ml/7fl oz/scant 1 cup unsweetened apple juice
30ml/2 tbsp orange or apple liqueur
30ml/2 tbsp clear honey (optional)
2 oranges, peeled
2 green-skinned apples, chopped
2 pears, chopped
4 plums, stoned (pitted) and chopped
12 fresh dates, stoned (pitted) and chopped
115g/4oz/½ cup ready-to-eat dried apricots
fresh mint sprigs, to decorate

1 Drain the pineapple, reserving the juice. Put the pineapple juice, orange juice, apple juice, liqueur and honey, if using, in a large serving bowl and stir.

COOK'S TIP

Use other unsweetened fruit juices such as pink grapefruit and pineapple juice in place of the orange and apple juice.

2 Segment the oranges, catching any juice in the bowl. Put the orange segments and pineapple in the fruit juice mixture.

3 Add the chopped apples and pears to the bowl.

4 Stir in the plums, dates and dried apricots, cover and chill for several hours. Decorate with fresh mint sprigs to serve.

Energy 141kcal/603kJ; Protein 1.9g; Carbohydrate 32g, of which sugars 32g; Fat 0.4g, of which saturates 0g; Cholesterol 0mg; Calcium 60mg; Fibre 4.2g; Sodium 12mg.

Italian Fruit Salad and Ice Cream

If you visit Italy in the summer, you will find little pavement fruit shops selling small dishes of macerated soft fruits, which are delectable on their own, but also make a wonderful ice cream.

INGREDIENTS

Serves 6

900g/2lb mixed summer fruits such as strawberries, raspberries, loganberries, redcurrants, blueberries, peaches, apricots, plums, melons
juice of 3–4 oranges
juice of 1 lemon
15ml/1 tbsp liquid pear and apple concentrate
60ml/4 tbsp whipping cream
30ml/2 tbsp orange liqueur (optional)
fresh mint sprigs, to decorate

1 Prepare the fruit according to type. Cut it into reasonably small pieces.

2 Put the fruit into a serving bowl and pour over enough orange juice to cover. Add the lemon juice and chill for 2 hours.

3 Set half the macerated fruit aside to serve as it is. Purée the remainder in a blender or food processor.

4 Gently warm the pear and apple concentrate and stir into the fruit purée. Whip the cream and fold it in, then add the liqueur, if using.

5 Churn the mixture in an ice-cream maker. Alternatively, place it in a suitable container for freezing. Freeze until ice crystals form around the edge, then beat the mixture until smooth.

6 Repeat the process once or twice, then freeze until firm.

7 Allow to soften slightly in the refrigerator before serving with the fruit, decorated with sprigs of mint.

COOK'S TIP

The macerated fruit also makes a delicious drink. Purée in a blender or food processor, then press through a sieve (strainer).

Energy 69kcal/289kJ; Protein 2.2g; Carbohydrate 15.2g, of which sugars 15.2g; Fat 0.2g, of which saturates 0g; Cholesterol 0mg; Calcium 38mg; Fibre 1.7g; Sodium 18mg.

Watermelon, Ginger and Grapefruit Salad

This pretty, pink combination is very light and refreshing for any summer meal.

INGREDIENTS

Serves 4

450g/1lb/2 cups watermelon flesh
2 ruby or pink grapefruit
2 pieces stem ginger and 30ml/2 tbsp of the syrup

1 Remove any seeds from the watermelon and cut the flesh into bitesize chunks.

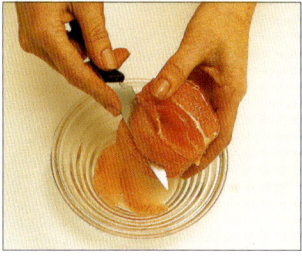

2 Using a small, sharp knife, cut away all the peel and white pith from the grapefruit and carefully lift out the segments, catching any juice in a bowl.

COOK'S TIP

Toss the fruits gently – grapefruit segments will break up easily and the appearance of the dish will be spoiled.

3 Finely chop the stem ginger and place in a serving bowl with the melon cubes and grapefruit segments, adding the reserved grapefruit juice.

4 Spoon over the ginger syrup and toss the fruits lightly to mix (see Cook's Tip). Chill in the refrigerator for about 1 hour before serving.

Energy 96kcal/407kJ; Protein 2g; Carbohydrate 22g, of which sugars 22g; Fat 1g, of which saturates 0g; Cholesterol 0mg; Calcium 44mg; Fibre 3g; Sodium 21mg.

Fresh Fruit with Mango Coulis

Fruit sauce, or coulis, became very fashionable in the 1970s with nouvelle cuisine. This bright, flavourful sauce is easy to prepare and ideal for making a simple fruit salad seem special.

INGREDIENTS

Serves 6

1 large ripe mango, peeled, stoned (pitted) and chopped
rind of 1 unwaxed orange
juice of 3 oranges
caster (superfine) sugar, to taste
2 peaches
2 nectarines
1 small mango, peeled
2 plums
1 pear or ½ small melon
juice of 1 lemon
25–50g/1–2oz heaped tbsp wild strawberries (optional)
25–50g/1–2oz heaped tbsp raspberries
25–50g/1–2oz heaped tbsp blueberries
small fresh mint sprigs, to decorate

1 In a food processor fitted with a metal blade, blend the large mango until smooth. Add the orange rind and juice and sugar to taste and process again until very smooth. Press through a sieve (strainer) into a bowl and chill.

2 Slice and stone (pit) the peaches, nectarines, small mango and plums. Quarter the pear and remove the core or, if using, slice the melon thinly and remove the skin.

3 Place the sliced fruits on a large serving plate, sprinkle with the lemon juice and chill, covered with clear film (plastic wrap), for up to 3 hours before serving. (Some fruits discolour if cut too far ahead of time.)

4 To serve, arrange the sliced fruits on serving plates, spoon the berries on top, drizzle with a little mango coulis and decorate with mint sprigs. Serve the remaining coulis separately in a jug (pitcher).

Energy 82kcal/351kJ; Protein 2g; Carbohydrate 19g, of which sugars 18g; Fat 0g, of which saturates 0g; Cholesterol 0mg; Calcium 23mg; Fibre 4g; Sodium 12mg.

Fruits-of-the-Tropics Salad

This is a creamy, exotic fruit salad flavoured with coconut and spices.

INGREDIENTS

Serves 4–6

1 medium pineapple
400g/14oz can guava halves in syrup
2 medium bananas, sliced
1 large mango, peeled, stoned (pitted) and diced
115g/4oz stem ginger and 30ml/2 tbsp of the syrup
60ml/4 tbsp thick coconut milk
10ml/2 tsp sugar
2.5ml/½ tsp grated nutmeg
2.5ml/½ tsp ground cinnamon
strips of coconut, to decorate

1 Peel, core and cube the pineapple, and place in a serving bowl. Drain the guavas, reserving the syrup, and chop. Add the guavas to the bowl with one of the bananas and the mango.

2 Chop the stem ginger and add to the pineapple mixture.

3 Pour the 30ml/2 tbsp of the ginger syrup and the reserved guava syrup into a blender or food processor and add the remaining banana, the coconut milk and the sugar. Blend to make a smooth, creamy purée.

4 Pour the banana and coconut purée over the fruit and add a little grated nutmeg and a sprinkling of cinnamon on top.

5 Serve chilled, decorated with strips of coconut.

Energy 165kcal/706kJ; Protein 1.5g; Carbohydrate 41.4g, of which sugars 40.5g; Fat 0.5g, of which saturates 0.1g; Cholesterol 0mg; Calcium 46mg; Fibre 4.8g; Sodium 41mg.

Exotic Fruit Salad

A variety of fruits can be used for this salad depending on what is available. Look out for fresh mandarin oranges, star fruit, papaya, physalis and passion fruit.

INGREDIENTS

Serves 4

75g/3oz/scant ½ cup sugar
30ml/2 tbsp stem ginger syrup
2 pieces star anise
2.5cm/1 in cinnamon stick
1 clove
juice of ½ lemon
2 fresh mint sprigs
1 mango
2 bananas
8 lychees, fresh or canned
225g/8oz/2 cups strawberries
2 pieces stem ginger, cut into sticks
1 medium pineapple

1 Place the sugar in a pan and add 300ml/½ pint/1¼ cups water, the ginger syrup, spices, lemon juice and mint. Bring to the boil and simmer for 3 minutes. Strain into a large bowl.

2 Remove both the top and bottom from the mango and remove the outer skin. Stand the mango on one end and remove the flesh in two pieces either side of the flat stone (pit). Slice the flesh evenly and add to the syrup. Add the bananas, lychees, strawberries and ginger. Chill until ready to serve.

3 Cut the pineapple in half down the centre. Loosen the flesh with a small, serrated knife and remove to form two boat shapes. Cut the pineapple flesh into large chunks and place in the cooled syrup.

4 Spoon the fruit salad carefully into the pineapple halves and bring to the table on a large serving dish or board. There will be enough fruit salad left over to refill the pineapple halves for a second serving.

Energy 66kcal/278kJ; Protein 1g; Carbohydrate 14.6g, of which sugars 14.5g; Fat 0.8g, of which saturates 0.1g; Cholesterol 0mg; Calcium 26mg; Fibre 2.9g; Sodium 7mg.

Melon and Strawberry Salad

A beautiful and colourful fruit salad, this is equally suitable to serve as a refreshing appetizer or to round off a meal.

INGREDIENTS

Serves 4
1 Galia melon
1 honeydew melon
½ watermelon
225g/8oz/2 cups strawberries
15ml/1 tbsp lemon juice
15ml/1 tbsp clear honey
15ml/1 tbsp chopped fresh mint
1 fresh mint sprig (optional)

1 Prepare the melons by cutting them in half and discarding the seeds. Use a melon baller to scoop out the flesh into balls or alternatively a knife to cut it into cubes. Place these in a fruit bowl.

2 Rinse and hull the strawberries, cut in half and add to the melon balls or cubes.

COOK'S TIP

Use whichever melons are available: replace Galia with cantaloupe or watermelon with Charentais, for example. Try to choose three melons with a variation in colour for an attractive effect.

3 Mix together the lemon juice and honey and add 15ml/1 tbsp water to make it easier to spoon over the fruit. Mix into the fruit gently.

4 Sprinkle the chopped mint over the top of the fruit. Serve the fruit salad decorated with the mint sprig, if wished.

Energy 46kcal/197kJ; Protein 1g; Carbohydrate 10.9g, of which sugars 10.9g; Fat 0.2g, of which saturates 0g; Cholesterol 0mg; Calcium 32mg; Fibre 1.6g; Sodium 12mg.

Blueberry, Orange and Lavender Salad

Delicate blueberries feature here in a simple salad of sharp oranges and sweet little meringues flavoured with fresh lavender.

INGREDIENTS

Serves 4

6 oranges

350g/12oz/3 cups blueberries

8 fresh lavender sprigs, to decorate

For the meringue

2 egg whites

115g/4oz/generous ½ cup caster (superfine) sugar

5ml/1 tsp fresh lavender flowers

1 Preheat the oven to 140°C/275°F/Gas 1. Line a baking sheet with six layers of newspaper and cover with non-stick baking parchment. To make the meringue, whisk the egg whites in a large mixing bowl until they hold their weight on the whisk. Add the sugar a little at a time, whisking thoroughly before each addition. Fold in the lavender flowers.

2 Spoon the lavender meringue into a piping bag fitted with a 5mm/¼in plain nozzle. Pipe as many small buttons of meringue on to the prepared baking sheet as you can.

3 Dry the meringues near the bottom of the oven for 1½–2 hours.

4 To segment the oranges, remove the peel from the top, bottom and sides with a serrated knife. Loosen the segments by cutting with a paring knife between the flesh and the membranes, holding the fruit over a bowl to catch the juices.

5 Arrange the orange segments on four plates.

6 Combine the blueberries with the lavender meringues and pile in the centre of each plate. Decorate with sprigs of lavender and serve.

Energy 253kcal/1076kJ; Protein 5g; Carbohydrate 62g, of which sugars 49g; Fat 1g, of which saturates 0g; Cholesterol 0mg; Calcium 116mg; Fibre 4g; Sodium 47mg.

Fresh Fig, Apple and Date Salad

Sweet Mediterranean figs and dates combine especially well with crisp dessert apples. A hint of almond serves to unite the flavours.

INGREDIENTS

Serves 4

6 large apples
juice of ½ lemon
175g/6oz/generous 1 cup fresh dates
25g/1oz white marzipan
5ml/1 tsp orange flower water
60ml/4 tbsp natural (plain) yogurt
4 ripe green or purple figs
4 almonds, toasted

1. Core the apples. Slice thinly, then cut into fine matchsticks. Moisten with lemon juice to keep them white.

2. Remove the stones (pits) from the dates and cut the flesh into fine strips, then combine them with the apple slices.

3. Soften the marzipan with the orange flower water and combine with the yogurt. Mix well.

4. Pile the apples and dates in the centre of four serving plates. Remove the stem from each of the figs and divide the fruit into quarters without cutting right through the base. Squeeze the base with the thumb and forefinger of each hand to open up the fig.

5. Place a fig in the centre of each fruit salad, spoon in the yogurt filling and decorate with a toasted almond.

Energy 223kcal/943kJ; Protein 4.5g; Carbohydrate 43.8g, of which sugars 43.7g; Fat 4.5g, of which saturates 0.4g; Cholesterol 0mg; Calcium 170mg; Fibre 4.8g; Sodium 46mg.

Blackberry Salad with Rose Granita

The blackberry is a member of the rose family and combines especially well with rose water. Here a rose syrup is frozen into a granita and served over strips of white meringue.

INGREDIENTS

Serves 4

150g/5oz/⅔ cup caster (superfine) sugar
1 fresh red rose, petals finely chopped
5ml/1 tsp rose water
10ml/2 tsp lemon juice
450g/1lb/2⅔ cups blackberries
icing (confectioners') sugar, for dusting
fresh rose petals, to decorate

For the meringue
2 egg whites
115g/4oz/generous ½ cup caster (superfine) sugar

1 To make the granita, bring 150ml/¼ pint/⅔ cup water to the boil in a stainless-steel or enamel pan. Add the sugar and rose petals, then simmer for 5 minutes.

2 Strain the syrup into a deep metal tray, add a further 450ml/¾ pint/scant 2 cups water, the rose water and lemon juice and leave to cool. Freeze the mixture for 3 hours, or until solid.

3 Meanwhile preheat the oven to 140°C/275°F/Gas 1. Line a baking sheet with six layers of newspaper and cover with non-stick baking parchment.

4 To make the meringue, whisk the egg whites until they hold their weight on the whisk. Add the caster sugar a little at a time, and whisk until firm.

COOK'S TIP

Blackberries are widely cultivated from late spring to autumn and are usually large, plump and sweet. The finest wild blackberries have a bitter edge and a strong depth of flavour – best appreciated with a sprinkling of sugar.

5 Spoon the meringue into a piping bag fitted with a 1cm/½in plain nozzle. Pipe the meringue in lengths across the paper-lined baking sheet. Dry the meringue near the bottom of the oven for 1½–2 hours.

6 Break the meringue into 5cm/2in lengths and place three or four pieces on each of four large serving plates. Pile the blackberries next to the meringue.

7 With a tablespoon, scrape the granita finely. Shape into ovals and place over the meringue. Dust with icing sugar, decorate with rose petals, and serve.

Energy 295kcal/1255kJ; Protein 2g; Carbohydrate 75g, of which sugars 75g; Fat 0g, of which saturates 0g; Cholesterol 0mg; Calcium 54mg; Fibre 7g; Sodium 36mg.

Raspberries with Mango Custard

This remarkable salad unites the sharp quality of fresh raspberries with a special custard made from rich, fragrant mangoes.

INGREDIENTS

Serves 4

1 large mango
3 egg yolks
30ml/2 tbsp caster (superfine) sugar
10ml/2 tsp cornflour (cornstarch)
200ml/7fl oz/scant 1 cup milk
8 fresh mint sprigs, to decorate

For the raspberry sauce
450g/1lb/2⅔ cups raspberries
45ml/3 tbsp caster (superfine) sugar

1 To prepare the mango, remove the top and bottom with a serrated knife. Cut away the outer skin, then remove the flesh by cutting either side of the flat central stone (pit). Save half of the mango flesh for decoration and roughly chop the remainder.

2 For the custard, combine the egg yolks, sugar, cornflour and 30ml/2 tbsp of the milk smoothly in a small bowl.

3 Rinse a small pan with cold water to prevent the milk from catching. Bring the rest of the milk to the boil in the pan, pour it over the ingredients in the bowl and stir evenly.

4 Strain the mixture through a sieve (strainer) back into the pan, stir to simmering point and allow the mixture to thicken.

5 Pour the custard into a food processor, add the chopped mango and blend until smooth. Allow the custard to cool.

6 To make the raspberry sauce, place 350g/12oz/2 cups of the raspberries in a stain-resistant pan. Add the sugar, soften over a gentle heat and simmer for 5 minutes. Rub the fruit through a fine nylon sieve (strainer) to remove the seeds. Allow to cool.

7 Spoon the raspberry sauce and mango custard into two pools on four serving plates. Slice the reserved mango and fan out or arrange in a pattern over the raspberry sauce. Scatter the remaining raspberries over the mango custard. Decorate each plate with two sprigs of mint and serve.

COOK'S TIP

Mangoes are ripe when they yield to gentle pressure. Some varieties show a red-gold or yellow flush when they are ready to eat.

Energy 202kcal/856kJ; Protein 6g; Carbohydrate 32g, of which sugars 32g; Fat 6g, of which saturates 3g; Cholesterol 158mg; Calcium 111mg; Fibre 9g; Sodium 33mg.

Pineapple Crush with Strawberries and Lychees

The sweet, tropical flavours of pineapple and lychees combine well with richly scented strawberries to make this a most refreshing salad.

INGREDIENTS

Serves 4
2 small pineapples
450g/1lb/4 cups strawberries
400g/14oz can lychees
45ml/3 tbsp Kirsch or white rum
30ml/2 tbsp icing (confectioners') sugar

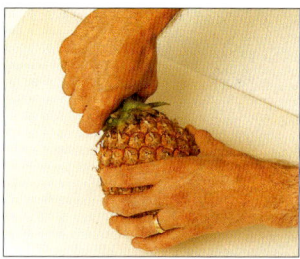

1 Remove the crowns from both pineapples by twisting sharply. Reserve the leaves for decoration.

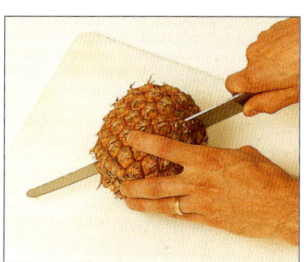

2 Cut both pineapples in half diagonally using a large, serrated knife.

3 Cut around the flesh inside the skin of both pineapples with a small, serrated knife, keeping the skin intact. Remove the core from the pineapple and discard. Chop the flesh. Reserve the skins.

4 Hull the strawberries and gently combine with the pineapple and lychees, taking care not to damage the fruit.

5 Mix the Kirsch or rum with the icing sugar, pour over the fruit and freeze for 45 minutes.

6 Turn out the fruit into the pineapple skins, decorate with the reserved pineapple leaves and serve.

COOK'S TIP

A ripe pineapple will resist pressure when squeezed and will have a sweet, fragrant smell. In winter freezing conditions can cause the flesh to blacken.

Energy 326kcal/1364kJ; Protein 2.1g; Carbohydrate 35.3g, of which sugars 35.3g; Fat 20.7g, of which saturates 12.6g; Cholesterol 53mg; Calcium 79mg; Fibre 3g; Sodium 18mg.

Muscat Grape Frappé

The flavour and perfume of the Muscat grape is rarely more enticing than when captured in this sophisticated, icy-cool salad. Because of its alcohol content this dish is not suitable for young children.

INGREDIENTS

Serves 4

½ bottle Muscat wine, Beaumes de Venise, Frontignan or Rivesaltes
450g/1lb Muscat grapes

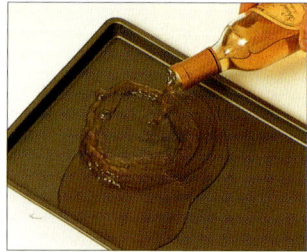

1 Pour the wine into a stainless-steel or enamel tray, add 150ml/¼ pint/⅔ cup water and freeze for 3 hours, or until the wine is completely solid.

2 Remove the seeds from the grapes with a pair of tweezers. If you have time, you can also peel the grapes. Scrape across the frozen wine with a tablespoon to make a fine ice. Combine the grapes with the ice, spoon into four shallow glasses and serve.

Energy 156kcal/659kJ; Protein 1g; Carbohydrate 23g, of which sugars 23g; Fat 0g, of which saturates 0g; Cholesterol 0mg; Calcium 28mg; Fibre 1g; Sodium 14mg.

Grapefruit Salad with Campari and Orange

The bitter-sweet flavour of Campari combines especially well with citrus fruit such as grapefruit and oranges. Because of its alcohol content, this dish is not suitable for young children.

INGREDIENTS

Serves 4

45ml/3 tbsp caster (superfine) sugar
60ml/4 tbsp Campari
30ml/2 tbsp lemon juice
4 grapefruit
5 oranges
4 fresh mint sprigs, to decorate

1. Bring 150ml/¼ pint/⅔ cup water to the boil in a small pan, add the sugar and simmer until dissolved. Transfer to a bowl, allow to cool, then add the Campari and lemon juice. Chill until ready to serve.

2. Cut the peel from the top, bottom and sides of the grapefruit and oranges with a serrated knife. Segment the fruit into a bowl by slipping a small paring knife between the flesh and the membranes. Combine the fruit with the Campari syrup and chill.

3. Spoon the salad into four dishes, decorate with a sprig of fresh mint and serve.

COOK'S TIP

When buying citrus fruit, choose brightly-coloured varieties that feel heavy for their size.

Energy 247kcal/1047kJ; Protein 5g; Carbohydrate 54g, of which sugars 54g; Fat 1g, of which saturates 0g; Cholesterol 0mg; Calcium 189mg; Fibre 9g; Sodium 24mg.

Dressed Strawberries

Fragrant strawberries release their finest flavour when moistened with a sauce of fresh raspberries and scented passion fruit.

INGREDIENTS

Serves 4

350g/12oz/2 cups raspberries, fresh or frozen
45ml/3 tbsp caster (superfine) sugar
1 passion fruit
675g/1½lb/6 cups small strawberries
8 plain finger biscuits (cookies), to serve

4 Push the blended fruit sauce through a fine nylon sieve (strainer) using the back of a spoon, to remove the seeds.

5 Fold the strawberries into the sauce, then spoon into four stemmed glasses. Serve with plain finger biscuits.

1 Place the raspberries and sugar in a stain-resistant pan and soften over a gentle heat to release the juices. Simmer for 5 minutes. Allow to cool.

2 Halve the passion fruit and scoop out the seeds and juice.

3 Turn the raspberries into a food processor or blender, add the passion fruit and blend until smooth.

Energy 151kcal/640kJ; Protein 4g; Carbohydrate 33g, of which sugars 30g; Fat 1g, of which saturates 20g; Cholesterol 25mg; Calcium 60mg; Fibre 9g; Sodium 25mg.

Mixed Melon Salad with Wild Strawberries

Ice-cold melon is a delicious way to end a meal. Here several varieties are combined with strongly flavoured wild or woodland strawberries. If wild berries are not available, use ordinary strawberries or raspberries.

INGREDIENTS

Serves 4

1 cantaloupe or Charentais melon
1 Galia melon
900g/2lb watermelon
175g/6oz/1½ cups wild strawberries
4 fresh mint sprigs, to decorate

1 Halve all the melons using a large knife.

2 Remove the seeds from the cantaloupe and Galia melons with a spoon.

3 With a melon scoop, take out as many balls as you can from all three melons. Combine in a large bowl and refrigerate.

4 Add the wild strawberries and turn out into four stemmed glass dishes.

5 Decorate the melon balls with sprigs of fresh mint and serve immediately.

Energy 101kcal/429kJ; Protein 2g; Carbohydrate 23g, of which sugars 23g; Fat 1g, of which saturates 0g; Cholesterol 0mg; Calcium 53mg; Fibre 3g; Sodium 49mg.

Fruit Kebabs with Mango and Yogurt Sauce

To enjoy these mixed fruit kebabs, dip them into the refreshingly minty mango and yogurt sauce.

INGREDIENTS

Serves 4

½ pineapple, peeled, cored and cubed
2 kiwi fruit, peeled and cubed
150g/5oz/scant 1 cup strawberries, hulled and cut in half lengthways if large
½ mango, peeled, stoned (pitted) and cubed

For the sauce
120ml/4fl oz/½ cup fresh mango purée, made from 1–1½ peeled and stoned (pitted) mangoes
120ml/4fl oz/½ cup natural (plain) yogurt
5ml/1 tsp sugar
a few drops of vanilla extract
15ml/1 tbsp finely shredded fresh mint leaves
1 fresh mint sprig, to decorate

1 To make the sauce, beat together the mango purée, yogurt, sugar and vanilla with an electric hand mixer.

2 Stir in the shredded mint. Cover the sauce and chill until required.

3 Thread the fruit on to twelve 15cm/6in wooden skewers, alternating the pineapple, kiwi fruit, strawberries and mango.

4 Transfer the mango and yogurt sauce to an attractive bowl, decorate with a mint sprig and place in the centre of a large serving platter. Surround with the kebabs and serve.

Tropical Fruits in Cinnamon Syrup

These glistening fruits are best prepared a day in advance to allow the flavours to develop and mingle.

INGREDIENTS

Serves 6

450g/1lb/2¼ cups caster (superfine) sugar
1 cinnamon stick
1 large or 2 medium papayas (about 675g/1½lb) peeled, seeded and cut lengthways into thin pieces
1 large or 2 medium mangoes (about 675g/1½lb) peeled, stoned (pitted) and cut lengthways into thin pieces
1 large or 2 small star fruit (carambola) (about 225g/8oz) thinly sliced

1 Sprinkle one third of the sugar over the bottom of a large pan. Add the cinnamon stick and half of the papaya, mango and star fruit pieces.

2 Sprinkle half of the remaining sugar over the fruit pieces in the pan. Add the remaining fruit and sprinkle with the remaining sugar.

3 Cover the pan and cook the fruit over medium heat for 35–45 minutes, until the sugar dissolves completely. Shake the pan occasionally, but do not stir or the fruit will collapse.

4 Uncover the pan and simmer for about 10 minutes, until the fruit begins to appear translucent. Remove the pan from the heat and allow to cool. Discard the cinnamon stick.

5 Transfer the fruit and syrup to a bowl, cover and refrigerate overnight before serving.

Kebabs: Energy 107kcal/456kJ; Protein 3g; Carbohydrate 22g, of which sugars 22g; Fat 1g, of which saturates 1g; Cholesterol 3mg; Calcium 93mg; Fibre 3g; Sodium 30mg.
Tropical: Energy 359kcal/1530kJ; Protein 1g; Carbohydrate 94g, of which sugars 94g; Fat 0g, of which saturates 0g; Cholesterol 0mg; Calcium 31mg; Fibre 4g; Sodium 8mg.

Banana and Mascarpone

If you are a fan of cold banana custard, you'll love this recipe. It is a grown-up version of an old favourite. No one will guess that the secret is ready-made custard sauce.

INGREDIENTS

Serves 4-6

250g/9oz/generous 1 cup mascarpone

300ml/½ pint/1¼ cups fresh ready-made custard sauce

150ml/¼ pint/⅔ cup Greek (US strained plain) yogurt

4 bananas

juice of 1 lime

50g/2oz/½ cup pecan nuts, coarsely chopped

120ml/4fl oz/½ cup maple syrup

1 Combine the mascarpone, custard sauce and yogurt in a large bowl and beat together until smooth. Make this mixture up to several hours ahead, if you like. Cover and chill, then stir before using.

2 Slice the bananas diagonally and place in a separate bowl. Pour over the lime juice and toss together until the bananas are coated in the juice.

3 Divide half the custard mixture among four to six dessert glasses and top each portion with a generous spoonful of the banana mixture.

4 Spoon the remaining custard mixture into the glasses and top with the rest of the bananas. Scatter the nuts over the top. Drizzle maple syrup over each dessert and chill for 30 minutes before serving.

Bananas with Lime and Cardamom

Cardamom and bananas go together perfectly, and this luxurious dessert makes an original treat.

INGREDIENTS

Serves 4

6 small bananas

50g/2oz/¼ cup butter

seeds from 4 cardamom pods, crushed

50g/2oz/½ cup flaked (sliced) almonds

thinly pared rind and juice of 2 limes

50g/2oz/⅓ cup light muscovado (brown) sugar

30ml/2 tbsp dark rum

vanilla ice cream, to serve

1 Peel the bananas and cut them in half lengthways. Heat half the butter in a large frying pan. Add half the bananas, and cook until the undersides are golden. Turn carefully, using a fish slice or metal spatula. Cook until golden all over.

2 Once cooked, transfer the bananas to a heatproof serving dish. Cook the remaining bananas in the same way.

3 Melt the remaining butter, then add the cardamom seeds and almonds. Cook, stirring until the almonds are golden.

4 Stir in the lime rind and juice, then the sugar. Cook, stirring, until the mixture is smooth, bubbling and slightly reduced. Stir in the rum. Pour the sauce over the bananas and serve immediately, with vanilla ice cream.

Mascarpone: Energy 433kcal/1798kJ; Protein 7g; Carbohydrate 40g, of which sugars 35g; Fat 20g, of which saturates 15g; Cholesterol 48mg; Calcium 170mg; Fibre 2g; Sodium 262mg.
Lime: Energy 347kcal1452kJ; Protein 4g; Carbohydrate 42g, of which sugars 39g; Fat 10g, of which saturates 7g; Cholesterol 27mg; Calcium48mg; Fibre 5g; Sodium 83mg.

Melon Trio with Ginger Biscuits

The eye-catching colours of these three different melons really make this dessert, while the crisp biscuits (cookies) provide a perfect contrast in terms of texture.

INGREDIENTS

Serves 4

¼ watermelon
½ honeydew melon
½ charentais melon
60ml/4 tbsp stem ginger syrup

For the biscuits (cookies)
25g/1oz/2 tbsp unsalted butter
25g/1oz/2 tbsp caster (superfine) sugar
5ml/1 tsp clear honey
25g/1oz/¼ cup plain (all-purpose) flour
25g/1oz/¼ cup luxury glacé (candied) mixed fruit, finely chopped
1 piece of stem ginger in syrup, drained and finely chopped
30ml/2 tbsp flaked (sliced) almonds

1 Remove the seeds from the melons, cut them into wedges, then slice off the rind. Cut all the flesh into chunks and mix in a bowl. Stir in the ginger syrup, cover with clear film (plastic wrap) and chill until ready to serve.

2 Meanwhile, make the biscuits. Preheat the oven to 180°C/350°F/Gas 4. Heat the butter, sugar and honey in a pan until melted. Remove the pan from the heat and stir in the remaining biscuit ingredients to combine.

3 Line a baking sheet with non-stick baking parchment. Space four spoonfuls of the mixture on the paper at regular intervals, leaving plenty of room for spreading.

4 Flatten the mixture into rounds and bake for 15 minutes or until the tops are golden.

5 Let the biscuits cool on the baking sheet for 1 minute, then lift each one in turn, using a metal spatula, and drape over a rolling pin to cool and harden. Repeat with the remaining ginger mixture to make eight biscuits.

6 Serve the melon chunks with some of the syrup and the ginger biscuits.

COOK'S TIP

For an even prettier effect, scoop the melon flesh into balls with the large end of a melon baller.

Energy 243kcal/ 1024kJ; Protein 3g; Carbohydrate 38g, of which sugars 32g; Fat 10g, of which saturates 4g; Cholesterol 14mg; Calcium 53mg; Fibre 3g; Sodium 68mg.

Jamaican Fruit Trifle

This trifle is actually based on a Caribbean fool that consists of fruit stirred into thick vanilla-flavoured cream. This version is much less rich, redressing the balance with plenty of fruit and crème fraîche.

INGREDIENTS

Serves 8

1 large sweet pineapple, peeled and cored, about 350g/12oz
300ml/½ pint/1¼ cups double (heavy) cream
200ml/7fl oz/scant 1 cup crème fraîche
60ml/4 tbsp icing (confectioners') sugar, sifted
10ml/2 tsp pure vanilla extract
30ml/2 tbsp white or coconut rum
3 papayas, peeled, seeded and chopped
3 mangoes, peeled, stoned (pitted) and chopped
thinly pared rind and juice of 1 lime
25g/1oz/⅓ cup coarsely shredded or flaked coconut, toasted

1 Cut the pineapple into large chunks, place in a food processor or blender and process briefly until chopped. Tip into a sieve placed over a bowl and leave for 5 minutes so that most of the juice drains from the fruit.

2 Whip the double cream to very soft peaks, then lightly but thoroughly fold in the crème fraîche, sifted icing sugar, vanilla extract and rum.

3 Fold the drained, chopped pineapple into the cream mixture. Place the chopped papayas and mangoes in a large bowl and pour over the lime juice. Gently stir the fruit mixture to combine, without breaking up the fruit. Shred the pared lime rind and add to the bowl.

4 Divide the fruit mixture and the pineapple cream among eight dessert plates. Decorate with the lime shreds, toasted coconut and a few small pineapple leaves, if you like, and serve immediately.

COOK'S TIP

It is important to let the pineapple purée drain thoroughly, otherwise the pineapple cream will be watery. Don't throw away the drained pineapple juice – mix it with sparkling mineral water for a refreshing drink.

Energy 479kcal/1995kJ; Protein 2.3g; Carbohydrate 41g, of which sugars 40.7g; Fat 34.2g, of which saturates 22.7g; Cholesterol 80mg; Calcium 79mg; Fibre 3.6g; Sodium 27mg.

Tropical Fruit Gratin

This out-of-the-ordinary gratin is strictly for grown-ups. A colourful combination of fruit is topped with a simple sabayon before being flashed under the grill (broiler).

INGREDIENTS

Serves 4
2 tamarillos
½ sweet pineapple
1 ripe mango
175g/6oz/1½ cups blackberries
120ml/4fl oz/½ cup sparkling white wine
115g/4oz/½ cup caster (superfine) sugar
6 egg yolks

1 Cut each tamarillo in half lengthways and then into thick slices. Cut the rind and core from the pineapple and take spiral slices off the outside to remove the eyes. Cut the flesh into chunks.

2 Peel the mango, cut it in half and cut the flesh from the stone (pit) in slices.

3 Divide all the fruit, including the blackberries, among four 14cm/5½in gratin dishes set on a baking sheet and set aside. Heat the wine and sugar in a pan until the sugar has dissolved. Bring to the boil and cook for 5 minutes.

4 Put the egg yolks in a large heatproof bowl. Place over a pan of simmering water and whisk until pale. Slowly pour on the hot sugar syrup, whisking all the time, until the mixture thickens. Preheat the grill (broiler).

5 Spoon the mixture over the fruit. Place the baking sheet on a low shelf under the hot grill until the topping is golden. Serve hot.

Grilled Pineapple with Papaya sauce

Pineapple cooked this way takes on a superb flavour and is sensational when served with the papaya sauce.

INGREDIENTS

Serves 6
1 sweet pineapple
melted butter, for greasing and brushing
2 pieces drained stem ginger in syrup, cut into fine matchsticks, plus 30ml/2 tbsp of the syrup from the jar
30ml/2 tbsp demerara (raw) sugar
a pinch of ground cinnamon
fresh mint sprigs, to decorate

For the sauce
1 ripe papaya, peeled and seeded
175ml/6floz/¾ cup apple juice

1 Peel the pineapple and take spiral slices off the outside to remove the eyes. Cut it crossways into six slices, each 2.5cm/1in thick. Line a baking sheet with a sheet of foil, rolling up the sides to make a rim. Grease the foil with melted butter. Preheat the grill (broiler).

2 Arrange the pineapple slices on the lined baking sheet. Brush with butter, then top with the ginger matchsticks, sugar and cinnamon. Drizzle over the stem ginger syrup. Grill (broil) for 5–7 minutes or until the slices are golden and lightly charred on top.

3 Meanwhile, make the sauce. Cut a few slices from the papaya and set aside, then purée the rest with the apple juice in a blender or food processor.

4 Press the purée through a sieve (strainer) placed over a bowl, then stir in any juices from cooking the pineapple.

5 Serve the pineapple slices with a little sauce drizzled around each plate. Decorate with the reserved papaya slices and the mint sprigs.

Tropical: Energy 294kcal/1241kJ; Protein 6g; Carbohydrate 47g, of which sugars 47g; Fat 9g, of which saturates 2g; Cholesterol 382mg; Calcium 77mg; Fibre 5g; Sodium 20mg.
Pineapple: Energy 90kcal/382kJ; Protein 1g; Carbohydrate 20g, of which sugars 20g; Fat 2g, of which saturates 1g; Cholesterol 4mg; Calcium 23mg; Fibre 2g; Sodium 14mg.

Citrus Fruit Flambé

A fruit flambé makes a dramatic finale for a dinner party. Topping this refreshing citrus fruit dessert with crunchy pistachio praline makes it extra special.

INGREDIENTS

Serves 4

4 oranges
2 ruby grapefruit
2 limes
50g/2oz/¼ cup butter
50g/2oz/⅓ cup light muscovado (brown) sugar
45ml/3 tbsp Cointreau
fresh mint sprigs, to decorate

For the praline
oil, for greasing
115g/4oz/½ cup caster (superfine) sugar
50g/2oz/½ cup pistachio nuts

1 First, make the pistachio praline. Brush a baking sheet lightly with oil. Place the caster sugar and nuts in a small, heavy pan and cook gently, swirling the pan occasionally until the sugar has melted.

2 Continue to cook over a fairly low heat until the nuts start to pop and the sugar has turned a dark golden colour. Pour on to the oiled baking sheet and set aside to cool. Using a sharp knife, chop the praline into rough chunks.

3 Cut all the rind and pith from the citrus fruits. Holding each fruit in turn over a large bowl, cut between the membranes so that the segments fall into the bowl, with any juice.

4 Heat the butter and muscovado sugar together in a heavy frying pan until the sugar has melted and the mixture is golden. Strain the citrus juices into the pan and continue to cook, stirring occasionally, until the juice has reduced and is syrupy.

5 Add the fruit segments and warm through without stirring. Pour over the Cointreau and set it alight. As soon as the flames die down, spoon the fruit flambé into serving dishes. Sprinkle some praline over each portion and decorate with mint.

Energy 446kcal/1872kJ; Protein 4.8g; Carbohydrate 65.2g, of which sugars 64.8g; Fat 17.4g, of which saturates 7.4g; Cholesterol 27mg; Calcium 127mg; Fibre 4.4g; Sodium 155mg.

Exotic Fruit Salad

Passion fruit makes a superb dressing for any fruit, but really brings out the flavour of exotic varieties. You can easily double the recipe, then serve the rest for the next day's breakfast.

INGREDIENTS

Serves 6
1 mango
1 papaya
2 kiwi fruit
coconut or vanilla ice cream, to serve

For the dressing
3 passion fruit
thinly pared rind and juice of 1 lime
5ml/1 tsp hazelnut or walnut oil
15ml/1 tbsp clear honey

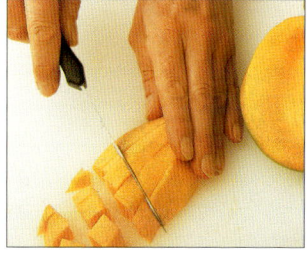

1 Peel the mango, cut it into three slices, then cut the flesh into chunks and place it in a large bowl. Peel the papaya and cut it in half. Scoop out the seeds, then chop the flesh.

2 Cut both ends off each kiwi fruit, then stand them on a board. Using a small sharp knife, cut off the skin from top to bottom. Cut each kiwi fruit in half lengthways, then cut into thick slices. Combine all the fruit in a large bowl.

3 Make the dressing. Cut each passion fruit in half and scoop the seeds out into a sieve (strainer) set over a small bowl. Press the seeds well to extract all their juices. Lightly whisk the remaining dressing ingredients into the passion fruit juice, then pour the dressing over the fruit. Mix gently.

4 Chill for 1 hour before serving with scoops of ice cream.

COOK'S TIP
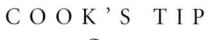
A clear golden honey scented with orange blossom or acacia blossom would be perfect for the dressing.

Energy 66kcal/278kJ; Protein 1g; Carbohydrate 14.6g, of which sugars 14.5g; Fat 0.8g, of which saturates 0.1g; Cholesterol 0mg; Calcium 26mg; Fibre 2.9g; Sodium 7mg.

Index

Apples, 10, 18
  apple and celeriac salad, 48
  apple coleslaw, 54
  chicory, fruit and nut salad, 50
  fresh fig, apple and date salad, 233
  radish, mango and apple salad, 62
  Waldorf ham salad, 161
Apricots, 10, 19
Artichokes: artichoke and egg salad, 99
  prawn and artichoke salad, 136
  sweet-and-sour artichoke salad, 77
Arugula see Rocket
Asparagus: asparagus and orange salad, 97
  pasta, asparagus and potato salad, 177
  warm pasta salad with, 169
Aubergine, lemon and caper salad, 52
Avocados, 8
  avocado and smoked fish salad, 93
  avocado, crab and herb salad, 144
  avocado salad, 68
  avocado, tomato and mozzarella salad, 174
  egg, bacon and avocado salad, 102
  fresh spinach and avocado salad, 61
  guacamole salsa in red leaves, 67
  pasta, olive and avocado salad, 180
  prawn, avocado and citrus salad, 188
  prosciutto salad with an avocado fan, 213

Bacon: chicken liver, bacon and tomato salad, 162
  chicken Maryland salad, 156
  egg, bacon and avocado salad, 102
  frisée salad with, 96
  smoked bacon and green bean pasta salad, 168
Bananas
  banana and mascarpone, 246
  plantain and green banana salad, 105
  with lime and cardamom, 246
Basil, 14
  basil and chilli oil, 23
  basil and lemon dressing, 26
Beans: brown bean salad, 118
  nutty salad, 40
  peppery bean salad, 114
  smoked ham and bean salad, 115
  Tuscan tuna and bean salad, 71
  white bean and celery salad, 116
Beansprouts: tofu and cucumber salad, 104
  beansprout and mooli salad, 57
  Thai fruit and vegetable salad, 68
Beef: beef and herby pasta salad, 216
  "Poor Boy" steak salad, 160
  rockburger salad with sesame croûtons, 218
Beetroot (beet): sweet potato, egg, pork and beetroot salad, 164
Belgian endive see Chicory
Bell peppers see Peppers
Black-eyed beans (peas): smoked ham and bean salad, 115
Blackberries, 10
  blackberry salad with rose granita, 234
Blue cheese and chive dressing, 25
Blueberries, 10
  blueberry, orange and lavender salad, 232
Bread: corn-fed chicken salad with garlic bread, 150

croûtons, 84
  garlic croûtons, 126
  panzanella, 100
  tomato and bread salad, 94
Broad beans: green green salad, 89
  sweet-and-sour artichoke salad, 77
  warm broad bean and feta salad, 80
Brown bean salad, 118
Buckwheat noodles with smoked salmon, 132
Bulgur wheat see Cracked wheat

Cabbage, 16
  apple coleslaw, 54
  carrot, raisin and apricot coleslaw, 55
  coleslaw with pesto mayonnaise, 65
  fennel coleslaw, 56
  lentil and cabbage salad, 117
Caesar salad, 36
Capers, 22
  aubergine, lemon and caper salad, 52
  Spanish salad with capers and olives, 44
Carambola see Star fruit
Carrots, 8
  carrot and orange salad, 46
  carrot and parsley salad, 30
  carrot, raisin and apricot coleslaw, 55
  courgettes, carrots and pecan salad, 178
  sweet potato and carrot salad, 108
Cashew nuts: chicory, fruit and nut salad, 50
  nutty salad, 40
Cauliflower: winter vegetable salad, 92
Celeriac and apple salad, 48
  white bean and celery salad, 116
Ceps salad, 42
Cheese: avocado salad, 68
  avocado, tomato and mozzarella salad, 174

  soft cheese and chive dip, 27
  tomato and feta cheese salad, 73
  tricolour salad, 70
  Turkish salad, 38
  warm broad bean and feta salad, 80
Cherries, 10
Chicken: chicken and pasta salad, 149
  chicken Maryland salad, 156
  chicken salad with lavender, 204
  chicken, tongue and Gruyère cheese salad, 158
  corn-fed chicken salad with garlic bread, 150
  curried chicken salad, 159
  Dijon chicken salad, 206
  egg noodle salad with sesame chicken, 148
  roasted chicken and walnut salad, 201
  spicy chicken salad, 154
  warm chicken salad, 152
  see also Liver
Chicory: chicory, fruit and nut salad, 50
  chicory salad with Roquefort, 188
Chinese leaves (Chinese cabbage), 13
Citrus fruit, 18
Citrus fruit flambé, 252
Clams: mixed shellfish salad, 142

  blue cheese and chive dressing, 25
  chicken, tongue and Gruyère cheese salad, 158
  chicory salad with Roquefort, 188
  classic Greek salad, 43
  goat's cheese and fig salad, 172
  halloumi and grape salad, 80
  rockburger salad with croûtons, 218
  rocket and goat's cheese salad, 82
  rocket, pear and Parmesan salad, 72
  Roquefort and walnut pasta salad, 176

Coleslaw: apple, 54
  carrot, raisin and apricot, 55
  fennel, 56
  with pesto mayonnaise, 65
Composed salads, 188
Coriander, 14
  rocket and coriander salad, 34
Corn, 8
  chicken Maryland salad, 156
  spicy corn salad, 102
Corn-fed chicken salad with garlic bread, 150
Coronation salad, 107
Cos lettuce, 12
Courgettes, 8
  courgettes, carrots and pecan salad, 178
  marinated courgettes, 86
Couscous: couscous salad, 121
  goat's cheese and fig salad, 172
Crab, avocado and herb salad, 144
Cracked wheat: cracked wheat salad, 119
  orange and cracked wheat salad, 122
  with fennel and pomegranate, 122
Cranberries, 10
Crème fraîche dressing with spring onions, 27
Croûtons, 84
  garlic croûtons, 126
Crudités, 30
Cucumber, 8
  tofu and cucumber salad, 104
  marinated cucumber salad, 59
  pepper and cucumber salad, 66
  tomato and cucumber salad, 30
  tzatziki, 58
Curry paste, 15
  coronation salad, 107
  curried chicken salad, 159
  curry fried pork and rice vermicelli salad, 163
  prawn salad with curry dressing, 138
Custard: banana and mascarpone, 246

Dates, 10, 19
  fresh fig, apple and date salad, 233
Devilled ham and pineapple salad, 170
Dijon chicken salad, 206
Dill and lemon oil, 23
Dips, 27
Dressings, 24–7
Dried fruit salad, 222
Duck: duck breast and pasta salad, 208
  duck salad with orange sauce, 210
  sesame duck and noodle salad, 212

Egg noodle salad with sesame chicken, 148
Eggplants see Aubergines
Eggs: artichoke and egg salad, 99
  coronation salad, 107
  egg, bacon and avocado salad, 102
  hard-boiled eggs with tuna sauce, 98
  leek and egg salad, 90
  poached egg salad with croûtons, 84
  potato salad with egg and lemon dressing, 111
  sweet potato, egg, pork and beetroot

Index • 255

salad, 164
Escarole, 12
Exotic fruit salad, 230, 253

Fava beans *see* Broad beans
Fennel, 8
  fennel coleslaw, 56
  fennel, orange and rocket salad, 52
  mixed shellfish salad, 142
Figs, 10
  fresh fig, apple and date salad, 233
  goat's cheese and fig salad, 172
Flavourings, 22
Flower garden salad, 60
Frankfurter salad with mustard dressing, 166
French (green) beans: French bean salad, 106
  Moroccan tuna salad, 128
  salade Niçoise, 126
  tomato, savory and French bean salad, 78
French dressing, 24
French herb dressing, 24
Frisée salad with bacon, 96
Fruit, 10–11, 18–19
  chicory, fruit and nut salad, 50
  citrus fruit flambé, 252
  cool green fruit salad, 224
  dried fruit salad, 222
  exotic fruit salad, 230, 253
  fresh fruit with mango coulis, 228
  fresh fruit salad, 222
  fruit kebabs with mango and yogurt sauce, 244
  fruits-of-the-tropics salad, 229
  Italian fruit salad and ice cream, 226
  Jamaican fruit trifle, 249
  Thai fruit and vegetable salad, 68
  tropical fruit gratin, 250
  tropical fruits in cinnamon syrup, 244
  winter fruit salad, 225
Fruity brown rice salad, 120

Gado gado, 186
Garlic, 8, 16
  corn-fed chicken salad with garlic bread, 150
  garlic croûtons, 126
  spinach and roast garlic salad, 47
Genoese squid salad, 196
Ghanaian prawn salad, 137
Goat's cheese: goat's cheese and fig salad, 172
  rocket and goat's cheese salad, 82
Granita, rose, 234
Grapefruit, 10
  grapefruit salad with Campari and orange, 241
  minted melon and grapefruit cocktail, 33
  watermelon, ginger and grapefruit salad, 227
Grapes, 10
  halloumi and grape salad, 80
  Muscat grape frappé, 240
Greek salad, 43
Greek-style yogurt and mustard dip, 27
Green beans, 8
  green bean and sweet red pepper salad, 88

smoked bacon and green bean pasta salad, 168
Green green salad, 89
Green salad, mixed, 48
Guacamole salsa in red leaves, 67
Halloumi and grape salad, 80
Ham: devilled ham and pineapple salad, 170
  melon and prosciutto salad, 214
  smoked ham and bean salad, 115
  Waldorf ham salad, 161
  warm pasta salad with asparagus, 169
  wild mushroom salad with prosciutto, 215

Herbs, 14
  chopping, 17
  herb mayonnaise, 27
  oils and vinegars, 23
Horseradish: smoked trout and horseradish salad, 135

Ice cream, Italian fruit salad and, 226
Italian fruit salad and ice cream, 226

Jamaican fruit trifle, 249
Jerusalem artichokes: radicchio, artichoke and walnut salad, 100
Julienne strips, 17

Kiwi fruit, 10, 19
Kumquats, 10

Lamb's lettuce, 13
Langoustines: San Francisco salad, 192
Lavender, 14
  blueberry, orange and lavender salad, 232
  chicken salad with, 204
Leeks: leek and egg salad, 90
  winter vegetable salad, 92
Lemon, 10, 22
  aubergine, lemon and caper salad, 52

potato salad with egg and lemon dressing, 111
Lentils: lentil and cabbage salad, 117
  salade mouclade, 198
Lettuce, 12–13
  lettuce and herb salad, 32
Lime, 10, 22
  bananas with cardamom and, 246
Little Gem (Bibb) lettuce, 13
Liver: chicken liver, bacon and tomato salad, 162
  chicken liver salad, 202
Lobster salad, millionaire's, 194
Lollo rosso, 12

Lychees, 10
  pineapple crush with strawberries and, 238

Mangoes, 10, 19
  fresh fruit with mango coulis, 228
  fruit kebabs with mango and yogurt sauce, 244
  mango, tomato and red onion salad, 63
  radish, mango and apple salad, 62
  raspberries with mango custard, 236
  warm fish salad with mango dressing, 129
Maryland salad, chicken, 156
Mayonnaise, 25
  aïoli, 30
  coleslaw with pesto mayonnaise, 65
Mediterranean herb oil, 23
Mediterranean pasta salad, 182
Melon, 10, 19
  melon and prosciutto salad, 214
  melon and strawberry salad, 231
  melon trio with ginger biscuits, 248
  minted melon and grapefruit cocktail, 33
  mixed melon salad with wild strawberries, 243
Meringues: blackberry salad with rose granita, 234

blueberry, orange and lavender salad, 232
Millionaire's lobster salad, 194
Mint, 14
  minted melon and grapefruit cocktail, 33
  prawn and mint salad, 140
Mixed green salad, 48
Mooli and beansprout salad, 57
Moroccan tuna salad, 128
Muscat grape frappé, 240
Mushrooms, 8
  fresh ceps salad, 42
  roast pepper and mushroom pasta salad, 181
  spinach and mushroom salad, 40
  wild mushroom salad with prosciutto, 215
Mussels: mixed shellfish salad, 142
  salade mouclade, 198
Mustard, 22

Nectarines, 10, 19
Noodles: buckwheat noodles with smoked salmon, 132
  curry fried pork and rice vermicelli salad, 163
  egg noodle salad with sesame chicken, 148
  prawn noodle salad with fragrant herbs, 147
  sesame duck and noodle salad, 212
  smoked trout and noodle salad, 134
  Thai noodle salad, 146
  with pineapple, ginger and chillies, 132
Nut oils, 22
Nutty salad, 40

Oak leaf lettuce, 12
Oils, 22, 23
Olive oil, 22
Olives, 22
  black and orange salad, 34
  creamy black olive dip, 27
  pasta, olive and avocado salad, 180
  Spanish salad with capers and olives, 44
  tapenade, 30
Onions, 8, 16
  mango, tomato and red onion salad, 63
  orange and red onion salad with cumin, 44
Oranges, 10
  asparagus and orange salad, 97
  black and orange salad, 34
  blueberry, orange and lavender salad, 232
  carrot and orange salad, 46
  citrus fruit flambé, 252
  duck salad with orange sauce, 210
  fennel, orange and rocket salad, 52
  grapefruit salad with Campari and orange, 241
  orange and cracked wheat salad, 122
  orange and red onion salad with cumin, 44
  orange and water chestnut salad, 64

Panzanella, 100
Papaya, 10, 19
  grilled pineapple with papaya sauce, 250
  hot coconut, prawn and papaya salad, 200
Parsley, 14
  carrot and parsley salad, 30

Passata and horseradish dip, 27
Pasta shapes: Mediterranean pasta salad, 182
  pasta, asparagus and potato salad, 177
  Roquefort and walnut pasta salad, 176
Pasta shells: roast pepper and mushroom pasta salad, 181
Pasta twists: chicken and pasta salad, 149
  pasta, olive and avocado salad, 180
  smoked bacon and green bean pasta salad, 168
Peaches, 10, 19
Peanuts: gado gado, 186
Pears, 10, 18
  pear and pecan nut salad, 171
  rocket, pear and Parmesan salad, 72
Peas: sweet-and-sour artichoke salad, 77
Pecan nuts: courgettes, carrots and pecan salad, 178
  pear and pecan nut salad, 171
Penne: curried chicken salad, 159
  devilled ham and pineapple salad, 170
Pepper, 15
Peppers: green bean and sweet red pepper salad, 88
  grilled pepper salad, 94
  panzanella, 100
  pepper and cucumber salad, 66
  roast pepper and mushroom pasta salad, 181
  roasted pepper and tomato salad, 86
Peppery bean salad, 114
Persian salad, 38
Pesto: coleslaw with pesto mayonnaise, 65
  pesto dip, 27
Pineapple, 10, 19
  devilled ham and pineapple salad, 170
  fruity brown rice salad, 120
  grilled pineapple with papaya sauce, 250
  noodles with ginger, chillies and, 132
  pineapple crush with strawberries and lychees, 238
  Thai fruit and vegetable salad, 68
Plantains: Ghanaian prawn salad, 137
  plantain and green banana salad, 105
Pomegranate, cracked wheat with fennel and, 122
"Poor Boy" steak salad, 160
Pork: curry fried pork and rice vermicelli salad, 163
  sweet potato, egg, pork and beetroot salad, 164
Potatoes, 8
  avocado, crab and herb salad, 144
  coronation salad, 107
  frankfurter salad with mustard dressing, 166
  Genoese squid salad, 196
  pasta, asparagus and potato salad, 177
  potato salad with egg and lemon dressing, 111
  potato salad with garlic sausage, 113
  potato salads, 110
  salade Niçoise, 126
  smoked trout and horseradish salad, 135
  spicy potato salad, 112
Prawns: Ghanaian prawn salad, 137
  hot coconut, prawn and papaya salad, 200
  prawn and artichoke salad, 136

prawn and mint salad, 140
prawn, avocado and citrus salad, 188
prawn noodle salad with fragrant herbs, 147
prawn salad with curry dressing, 138
Prosciutto salad with an avocado fan, 213

Radicchio, 13
  radicchio, artichoke and walnut salad, 100
Radish, mango and apple salad, 62
Raspberries, 10
  dressed strawberries, 242
  with mango custard, 236
Raw vegetable platter, 30

Red kidney beans: nutty salad, 40
  peppery bean salad, 114
Red mullet: Thai scented fish salad, 190
Redfish: warm fish salad with mango dressing, 129
Rhubarb, 10
Rice: fruity brown rice salad, 120
Rigatoni: duck breast and pasta salad, 208
Rockburger salad with sesame croûtons, 218
Rocket, 13
  fennel, orange and rocket salad, 52
  rocket and coriander salad, 34
  rocket and goat's cheese salad, 82
  rocket, pear and Parmesan salad, 72
  tricolour salad, 70
  Roquefort and walnut pasta salad, 176
Rosemary and red wine vinegar, 23
Roses, 14
  blackberry salad with rose granita, 234
Russian salad, 83

Saffron, 15
Salade mouclade, 198
Salade Niçoise, 126
Salmon: grilled salmon and spring vegetable salad, 130

Salsa, guacamole, 67
San Francisco salad, 192
Sausages: frankfurter salad with mustard dressing, 166
  potato salad with garlic sausage, 113
Scallions see Spring onions
Shellfish salad, 142
Sesame duck and noodle salad, 212
Shrimp see Prawns
Simple cooked salad, 76
Smoked bacon and green bean salad, 168
Smoked ham and bean salad, 115
Smoked mackerel: avocado and smoked fish salad, 93

Smoked salmon: buckwheat noodles with, 132
  smoked salmon salad with dill, 188
Smoked trout: smoked trout and horseradish salad, 135
  smoked trout and noodle salad, 134
Spanish salad with capers and olives, 44
Spices, 15
Spinach: fresh spinach and avocado salad, 61
  spinach and mushroom salad, 40
  spinach and roast garlic salad, 47
Spring onions, 8, 17
Squash à la Grecque, 79
Squid salad, Genoese, 196
Starfruit, 10, 19
Strawberries, 10
  dressed strawberries, 242
  melon and strawberry salad, 231
  mixed melon salad with wild strawberries, 243
  pineapple crush with lychees and, 238
Sweet-and-sour artichoke salad, 77
Sweet potatoes: sweet potato and carrot salad, 108
  sweet potato, egg, pork and beetroot salad, 164

Tagliatelle: beef and herby pasta salad, 216
  warm pasta salad with asparagus, 169
Tapenade, 30
Tarragon vinegar, 23
Techniques, 16–19
Thai fruit and vegetable salad, 68
Thai noodle salad, 146
Thai scented fish salad, 190
Thousand Islands dressing, 24
Thyme, 14
Thyme oil, 23
Tofu: tofu and cucumber salad, 104
  fresh spinach and avocado salad, 61
  gado gado, 186
Tomatoes, 8, 17
  avocado, tomato and mozzarella salad, 174
  chicken liver, bacon and tomato salad, 162
  mango, tomato and red onion salad, 63
  panzanella, 100
  passata and horseradish dip, 27
  Persian salad, 38
  roasted pepper and tomato salad, 86
  Spanish salad with capers and olives, 44
  sun-dried tomato dip, 27
  tomato and bread salad, 94
  tomato and cucumber salad, 30
  tomato and feta cheese salad, 73
  tomato, savory and French bean salad, 78
  tricolour salad, 70
Tongue, chicken and Gruyère cheese salad, 158
Tricolour salad, 70
Trifle, Jamaican fruit, 249
Tropical fruit gratin, 250
Tropical fruits in cinnamon syrup, 244
Tuna: hard-boiled eggs with tuna sauce, 98
  Mediterranean pasta salad, 182
  Moroccan tuna salad, 128
  salade Niçoise, 126
  tuna carpaccio, 197
  Tuscan tuna and bean salad, 71
Turkish salad, 38
Tuscan tuna and bean salad, 71
Tzatziki, 58

Vegetables, 8–9
Vermicelli: curry fried pork and rice vermicelli salad, 163
Vinegars, 22–3
Waldorf ham salad, 161
Walnuts: radicchio, artichoke and walnut salad, 100
  roasted chicken and walnut salad, 201
  Roquefort and walnut pasta salad, 176
Water chestnut and orange salad, 64
Watercress, 13
Watermelon, ginger and grapefruit salad, 227
White bean and celery salad, 116
White currants, 18
Winter fruit salad, 225
Winter vegetable salad, 92

Yogurt: Greek-style yogurt and mustard dip, 27
  spiced yogurt dressing, 27
  tzatziki, 58
  yogurt dressing, 25

Zucchini see Courgettes

Notes

NOTES

NOTES

NOTES

Notes

Notes

Notes

NOTES